THANK GOD

INFANTRY

From D-Day to VE-Day with the 1st Battalion
The Royal Norfolk Regiment

John Lincoln

SUTTON PUBLISHING

First published in the United Kingdom in 1994 by
Alan Sutton Publishing Limited, an imprint of Sutton Publishing Limited
Phoenix Mill · Thrupp · Stroud · Gloucestershire GL5 2BU

Paperback edition first published in 1999

British Library Cataloguing in Publication Data

A catalogue record for this book is available from the British Library.

ISBN 0 7509 2051 1

Cover illustration: 26 November 1944. Men of the 1st Battalion The Royal
Norfolk Regiment halt for a rest on their way to an advanced postion.
(Photograph: Crown Copyright, Imperial War Museum, B 12156)

The author and publisher gratefully acknowledge the generous grant
from the Norwich Union.

Typeset in Plantin Light 10/12 pt.
Typesetting and origination by
Sutton Publishing Limited.
Printed in Great Britain by
Redwood Books Limited, Trowbridge, Wiltshire.

An officer, weary-eyed, shook hands just as I left. 'We won,' he said. 'We always do.'

To which I would like to say: 'Amen. Thank God and the Infantry.'

'Diary of a Battle, Kervenheim' from *Men Under Fire*,
R.W. Thompson (Macdonald & Co. Ltd, 1947)

This book is dedicated to the Poor Bloody Infantry, the men who, in spite of all the machinery of war, knew that they alone must ultimately go forward on foot to occupy the ground being fought over, must live and fight and die under the roughest conditions, without acclaim or accolade.

Officers of the battalion, Christmas 1943. *Back row*: Lt. J.F.J. Williams, Lt. R.M.C. Toft, Lt. J.F. Campbell, Lt. M.R. Fearon, Lt. T.J. Harrison, Lt. J.C. Squire, Lt. D.F. Bell. *Second row*: Lt. O.A. Ward, Lt. L.G.E. Pyshorn, Lt. R.F. Hodd, Lt. (QM) R.F. Howard, Lt. H.J. Beeson, Lt. C.R. Parfitt, Lt. E.A. Woodhouse, Lt. E.G.G. Williams. *Third row*: Revd E. Suffrin (CF), Lt. W.F. Groom, Lt. V.A. Howe, Capt. R.C. Wilson. *Front row*: Capt. A.J. Robertson, Capt. F. Fitch MC, Major W.H. Brinkley, Major F.P. Barclay MC, Lt.-Col. R.H. Bellamy, Capt. W.E.G. Bagwell, Major E.A. Cooper-Key, Capt. P.G. Baker, Capt. D.W. Smith.

Officers of the battalion, June 1945. *Back row*: Lt. R.J. Lincoln, Lt. W.H.R. Pease, Lt. C. Barnby, Lt. J.V. Mattinson, Lt. R. Wikely, Lt. J.C. Donald, Lt. A.R. Gill. *Second row*: Lt. E.K.A. Hastings, Lt. J.R. Percival, Capt. (QM) R.A. Howard MBE, Capt. H.J. Beeson, Capt. W.J. Smart, Capt. P.C. Swindells, Lt. D.B. Balsom, Lt. E.H. Olley, Lt. E.H. Harrison. *Front row*: Capt. R.W. Hodd, Major J.P. Searight, Major F.C. Atkinson, Major H.M. Wilson, Lt.-Col. F.P. Barclay DSO, MC, Capt. R.C. Wilson MC, Major J.D. Millar, Major V. Evans MC, Capt. C.W. Morgan.

CONTENTS

LIST OF MAPS

Note: map X is reproduced from the *History of The Royal Norfolk Regiment, 1919–1951, Volume III* by Lieutenant-Commander P.K. Kemp RN, by kind permission of the Regimental Association of the Royal Norfolk Regiment.

PREFACE

A history of the 1st Battalion The Royal Norfolk Regiment for the period 1939 to 1945 was published in 1947; the foreword by the Commanding Officer at the time, Lieutenant-Colonel F.P. Barclay DSO, MC reads as follows:

> Lest we or those who follow us forget, this Record – for Record in more senses than one it is – has been made.
>
> From D-Day to VE-Day it shows the activities and achievements of the 1st Battalion The Royal Norfolk Regiment. It is a straight, ungarnished narrative of an infantry battalion which has been referred to by Field-Marshal 'Monty' as 'second to none' in all his battalions of the 21st Army Group. . . .
>
> The ever-grateful prayers and remembrances of all are due to those who have laid down their lives or been permanently crippled during this great conflict. For their families we always have a special thought. Their sense of duty and their spirit of sacrifice to conquer have not been in vain. Had it not been for these and the magnificent team-work and cheerfulness displayed throughout by the whole battalion, then the reputation built up and maintained from D-Day to VE-Day could not have read thus: 'Not once has the battalion failed to capture its objective, nor ever has it yielded an inch of ground.'

The late Brigadier F.P. Barclay DSO, MC, DL prepared another foreword in anticipation of this book:

> Conspicuous among the features that set the 1st Battalion of The Royal Norfolk Regiment on the highest military pedestal in the Second World War were its magnificent morale and superb spirit. These all-important factors resulted in every battle being won, no matter what the cost. The initial bond between all ranks was further cemented by the successful confrontation of challenges, the mutual and collective overcoming of severe hardships, plus the overall demanding conditions of war. . . .

This book also is a 'straight ungarnished narrative' – the reminiscences in it are recorded as written or spoken by each individual contributor so that the reader may better understand and appreciate the humour and the horror of those days and recognize the attitudes, the outlook on life which binds together soldiers who have fought side by side under the constant threat of instant death or mutilation. Each account is prefaced by the name of the contributor; ranks quoted are those held at the time.

Through each individual memory runs one main theme, the friendship, the comradeship of infantrymen in war, the sense of close fraternity between one man and another in circumstances where each implicitly trusts his life to his companion and knows that his companion has similar faith and trust in him. The word 'companion' literally means 'sharer of bread' and derives from battle – the man with whom you shared your bread was the man alongside whom you fought, in whom you placed your confidence, upon whom you relied; to him you gave your loyalty and trust as he gave his, without question, to you – the strongest bond of all.

This is the Infantrymen's story, told in their own words by those who were there, in the fighting line, in direct contact with the enemy.

R.J. Lincoln MC
January 1994

ACKNOWLEDGEMENTS AND PICTURE CREDITS

Sincere thanks are due to the many members of the 1st Battalion The Royal Norfolk Regiment who served during the campaign, and others associated with the battalion, with whom I have talked or corresponded, for their help and interest. Their memories have made this book possible and I acknowledge with gratitude the help of many old and new friends and comrades. In particular I am very much indebted to those listed below for specific help as indicated:

The late Brigadier F.P. Barclay DSO, MC, DL for his leadership of and encouragement to the D-V Club over a period of forty-five years which has been the prime inspiration for this book and for his permission to include extracts from his memoirs entitled 'Features of Fun, Fact and Follies in a Full Life'.

Lieutenant-Colonel H.M. Wilson MC, President of the D-V Club, for his major contribution to the original 1st Battalion History, for allowing me to quote at length from his memoirs, for his keen support, his constant interest and very much appreciated help in checking the original draft.

Paul Buckerfield for his recollections and for proof-reading the final copy.

Mevrouw Carla Coenen-van Hoof and 'Michel' for their friendliness, their hospitality and their memories.

George D.H. Dicks MC (B Company) for extracts from a personal account written in May 1945, for his friendship, great interest, keen memory and for his appraisal of the draft.

Erik A. Gray (S Company) for his account of action in early August 1944 and his help and hospitality when researching the *Battalion War Diary*.

Bill Holden (S Company) for his memories of Normandy and Holland, for allowing me to use the records produced from his own considerable research to publish the amended Roll of Honour, for papers relating to Helmond and for the immense amount of work he has put in for the Regiment and to foster the fine links which exist with friends in Holland and Normandy.

Major J.P.C. Searight (OC S and D Company) not only for the extracts reprinted from an article entitled 'Twenty Four Hours – Or A Lifetime' written under the pen-name 'Yeoman' and published in the *British Army Journal*, vol. 7, January 1952, but also for his valued friendship and the use of photographs and material from his records of the campaign.

The officers and members of the 'Vrienden Royal Norfolk Regiment' and the many friends in Helmond for their unfailing help and good comradeship.

Major W.H. Reeve, Regimental Secretary, and his predecessors, for keeping the regimental spirit alive and preserving regimental records after the regiment ceased to exist.

Eastern Counties Newspapers Ltd, publishers of the *Eastern Daily Press* and *Eastern Evening News*, for permission to include extracts from contemporary newspaper reports and to the *Listener* for the article reporting the broadcast by Howard Marshall in 1945.

M. Jean Brisset, author of *La Charge du Taureau*, translated by Thomas J. Bates, for his permission to quote extracts.

The authors of the *History of the 1st Battalion The Royal Norfolk Regiment* and *Assault Division* and the publishers of *Men under Fire* for their approval to quote excerpts from those publications and the *British Army Review*, Ministry of Defence, for consent to reprint part of the article by Philip Searight, which is Crown Copyright.

Extracts from the Battalion War Diary (quoted from documents ref. W0171/1350 and W0171/5247) are also Crown Copyright and are reproduced with the permission of the Controller of Her Majesty's Stationery Office.

Finally, Michael G. Falcon CBE, DL and the Directors of Norwich Union for their financial help towards the publication of this book.

Most of all my thanks to the members of the D-V Club and the 1st Battalion The Royal Norfolk Regiment D-Day Veterans, indeed all who served in the battalion between D-Day and VE-Day – I am proud to have served with you and I hold the memories of those days in high esteem.

PICTURE CREDITS

Photographs on pp. 20, 111, 133, 134, 144, 147, 150, 160, 164, 191 are reproduced by permission of the Imperial War Museum. All others were provided by members of the battalion and friends or have been taken from the *Battalion History*.

The photograph on p. 124 was very kindly provided by the Curator of Stichting Nederlands Nationaal Oorlogs-en Verzetsmuseum, Overloon.

CHAPTER ONE

Destiny of Empires

As preparations for the greatest military operation in history mounted to a climax in June 1944 the British Empire had been at war for almost five years. Those years had been hard – for some of that time Great Britain and the Commonwealth stood alone and suffered many reversals.

At dawn on 1 September 1939 German troops crossed the Polish border. The British Government issued an ultimatum to Hitler to withdraw by 11 a.m. on Sunday 3 September; the ultimatum expired unanswered and the Prime Minister, Neville Chamberlain, spoke to the nation on radio that morning to declare that the country was at war.

France announced war on Germany that same afternoon followed closely by Australia and New Zealand – South Africa affirmed its involvement three days later and Canada within the week. The British Expeditionary Force crossed to France but there was little immediate activity.

Spring of 1940 brought dramatic changes – Winston Churchill became Prime Minister on 10 May, the day that German forces began to advance west to the Channel coast. Very soon the Allies were facing disaster in Europe yet the evacuation of more than three hundred thousand troops from Dunkirk was treated almost as a victory. That the advance of German panzers west across Belgium and France was halted, allowing those troops to escape, was little short of a miracle.

The planned invasion of the British Isles by the Germans, codenamed Sealion, caused intense preparation on both sides of the Channel and the subsequent Battle of Britain in August and September, a most noble effort by the 'Few', was a close-run combat and so nearly lost. Germany switched its attention to bombing London and in the first three months of the 'Blitz' over twelve and a half thousand Londoners were killed. In early October Sealion was postponed and in January cancelled.

Dunkirk and the Battle of Britain created in the nation a unique feeling of apprehension mixed with excitement and generated a national resolution, 'We may be down but we are certainly not out'. As men joined the Forces the manpower situation slowly worsened, women became involved in many jobs and in skills previously denied them and worked long, hard hours alongside men. Eventually conscription required that all men and all single women between the ages of eighteen and fifty-one register for war service. The departure of husbands to the services placed strain on many wives – the pay of a private soldier was often less than 17½p a day, £1.22 per week; if he was married, with two children, his wife would receive 90p for herself and 90p for the children, just £1.80 per week plus whatever allowance her husband made to her – many wives therefore had to find work.

Italy declared war on 10 June 1940 following hard on the Allied defeat at Dunkirk; Germany invaded Russia on 22 June 1941, America entered the war following the Japanese bombing of Pearl Harbor on 7 December 1941.

In 1942 Great Britain and the Commonwealth, now with the full and considerable support of America and in alliance with Russia, began to move slowly forward in North Africa. Winston Churchill, convinced of ultimate success, promised only 'blood, toil, tears and sweat' – the nation's attitude was 'Britain can take it'.

The tide of war was turning in favour of the Allies in 1943 – the Axis defeat at El Alamein, described by Winston Churchill as 'Not the beginning of the end, rather the end of the beginning', the landings of Operation Torch in November 1942 led to the enemy surrender in North Africa the following May and in July 1943 the Allies invaded Sicily, clearing the island by mid-August. The first landing in Italy was made on 3 September 1943, immediately followed by the Italian surrender and a further Allied landing at Salerno.

The problems of supply affecting all Allied forces and, of course, the British nation itself since the onset of war in 1939 had been considerably worsened by the constant attacks on merchant shipping and March 1943 was, for the Allies, the worst month of the war at sea – forty-three ships were sunk in three weeks. This marked the peak of Allied shipping losses, totalling some three thousand five hundred ships to that date, which thereafter declined significantly.

Throughout 1943 RAF and American Air Force bombers made increasingly heavy raids on Germany and selected targets in occupied Europe. In May the RAF bombed the Ruhr dams in an operation which is now part of history while the Americans developed massive daylight bomber raids over Germany with Flying Fortresses, an increasingly familiar sight over eastern England. The pace and weight of bombing increased in 1944 – on 18 March RAF bombers dropped 3,000 tons of high explosive on Hamburg alone.

In March also the second Chindit expedition, following the success of this newly conceived guerilla force in February of the previous year, was launched against the Japanese in Burma and within four weeks nine thousand men from British, Indian and Ghurka forces, transported by glider, were operating more than one hundred miles inside enemy lines beyond the River Chindwin, to be joined, subsequently, by other land forces marching in from Assam and Northern Burma. At the end of March the Japanese surrounded Imphal, near the India/Burma border, on 4 April Kohima, to the north, was attacked and there a desperate battle raged, almost continuously, until the end of May.

Over Germany air raids continued, but not without loss – on 24 March over 800 bombers attacked Berlin, 72 aircraft were lost and almost 400 crew members killed. The first 4,000 lb bomb was dropped during this month and attacks from the air on rail centres in France started in preparation for Overlord, codename for the invasion of the Continent. On the night of 30 March 800 British bombers struck Nuremburg; 95 planes were lost and 545 airmen were killed, the largest loss of aircrew of any single Allied raid on Germany.

In Italy the enemy had initially retreated then turned to defend the narrow leg of Italy; in January 1944 8th Army forces commenced the attack at Cassino, ten days later the Allies landed behind the German line at Anzio. In March attempts were still being made to capture Monte Cassino which was holding up the Allied advance north to Rome. On the Eastern Front, Russian forces had crossed the border into Poland – Hitler, to secure his supplies of oil and raw materials, ordered his troops to occupy Hungary.

On 1 April 1944 movement into a 10 mile belt of coastline from the Wash to Land's End was banned in preparation for D-Day. During the first half of that month shore batteries on the French Channel coast were bombed, care being taken, by attacking installations all along the coast, to ensure that the enemy would not be able to identify the location of the coming assault. On the 11th six RAF Mosquitoes made a successful pin-point bombing attack on the building housing Gestapo records in The Hague destroying files containing details of members of the Dutch Resistance.

Towards the end of April further bombing attacks were carried out on railway yards in France causing many civilian casualties and one of many practice Allied assault landings on the south coast, at Slapton Sands, Dartmouth, was attacked by German torpedo boats with the loss of more than six hundred American troops.

The fourth battle for Monte Cassino started on 11 May and in spite of overwhelming numerical superiority Allied troops took a full week to overcome the German defence. In the battles for Monte Cassino many thousands of Allied soldiers had been killed or were missing. Its capture allowed the troops driving up the leg of Italy to link with those who had landed at Anzio some four months previously and together move on to Rome, the centre of which was reached by American troops on the evening of 4 June.

Many launch sites of the V1 'flying bomb' on the Channel coast, although well protected by anti-aircraft guns, were relentlessly attacked by American and British aircraft, destroying more than half the sites but at the high cost of 771 aircrew dead or missing. In mid-June the first V1 bombs fell on the south-east. During the whole period of war some 80,000 tons of high explosive was dropped on the British Isles killing over sixty thousand civilians and destroying or damaging five million homes.

The Royal Norfolk Regiment, like many county regiments, was very proud of its traditions. It was raised in 1685 under Colonel Henry Cornwall and from 1747 was called the 9th Regiment of Foot; in 1782 it became known as the 9th or East Norfolk Regiment, in 1799 was awarded the distinction and privilege of bearing the figure of Britannia as its badge and in 1881 became known as the Norfolk Regiment. The Colours, used as a rallying point in battle, always resolutely guarded, were first awarded in 1751 – the King's Colour, a Union Flag, bore the Roman numeral IX in the centre and the Regimental Colour carried the figure of Britannia on a yellow ground.

The regiment served with distinction in many parts of the world; in the First World War battalions of the regiment fought in France, the Dardanelles, Palestine and Mesopotamia at the high cost, as with all foot regiments, of extensive casualties, more than five thousand dead and twenty-five thousand wounded.

In 1935, on the 250th anniversary of the raising of the regiment, to mark the birthday of King George V and in commemoration of his Silver Jubilee it was designated The Royal Norfolk Regiment.

The regiment bore the nickname 'The Holy Boys', derived from the Peninsular War when the local population considered the figure of Britannia was that of the Virgin Mary. Its Battle Honours are many and include campaigns in the West Indies 1794, the Peninsular War 1808–14, Afghanistan 1842 and 1879–80, the Boer War 1900–2; it earned 53 battle honours in the First World War fighting in all major battles on the Western Front and many in the Middle East.

The 2nd Battalion was sent to France in September 1939 and in January 1940 gained the first decorations for gallantry awarded to the British Expeditionary Force, Captain F.P. Barclay received the Military Cross, Lance-Corporal Davis the Military Medal – during the fighting retreat to the coast the first of five Victoria Crosses awarded to members of the regiment (the highest number of any regiment in the Second World War) was won by CSM George Gristock during a fierce rearguard action on 21 May in which he received fatal wounds. During the withdrawal ninety members of the battalion were massacred at le Paradis and fewer than 140 reached England via Dunkirk. The 7th Battalion embarked for France in January 1940 and in early June were part of 51st Highland Division fighting near Abbeville – escape via le Havre was out of the question and the division concentrated on the small port of St Valéry-en-Caux hoping to be evacuated; this was not to be and on 12 June the Divisional Commander ordered surrender. Only thirty-one men of this battalion returned to England.

The 4th, 5th and 6th Battalions, Territorials from Norwich and Norfolk, landing in Singapore in January 1942, were immediately caught up in brief but bitter fighting and ordered to surrender in mid-February. Many men of the Norfolks died there, many more as prisoners of the Japanese during three and a half years of degrading imprisonment.

The 2nd Battalion was re-formed after Dunkirk and in June 1942 arrived in Bombay to commence jungle training. In March 1944 the Japanese launched an offensive in Burma, striking for India. The 2nd Battalion was ordered to relieve Kohima and from mid-April to the end of May fought a bitter battle during which Captain J. Randle was awarded the Victoria Cross for bravery and self-sacrifice.

The 1st Battalion The Royal Norfolk Regiment was serving in India at the outbreak of war and did not return to Great Britain until the summer of 1940 when it became part of the 24th Guards Independent Brigade Group based in south-east England. In spring 1942 it joined with the 2nd Battalion The Royal Warwickshire Regiment and the 2nd Battalion The King's Shropshire Light Infantry to form 185 Infantry Brigade which became the motorized infantry brigade within 79th Armoured Division and moved to the Harrogate area where, apart from an introduction to combined operations, it remained until spring 1943 when 185 Brigade was transferred to 3rd British Infantry Division.

In 1940, under Major-General B.L. Montgomery DSO, the 3rd Division had been among the last to leave Dunkirk and it led the way back in June 1944, still under his leadership but now as Commander of all Allied land forces. The divisional sign, worn by all ranks, painted on all vehicles and marking all routes followed, was a geometric design of three black triangles surrounding a red triangle. This sign was at the forefront on D-Day when the division landed on Sword Beach at the left of the British assault.

Preparation for D-Day is described in the *Battalion History* thus:

Briefing was a serious business. Imagine a series of large store tents each with special lighting and flooring and a twenty-foot map. The master-plan was unfolded to every man, but security was such that bogus place-names were used throughout, and even now any reference to any part of the immediate bridgehead is still referred to as 'Hillman', 'Rover', etc.

During and after this period of intensive study of air photographs, maps and models, the battalion was 'sealed'. That meant that no one was allowed in or out of the perimeter within which we lived. We knew that the hour was at hand and that soon we should go through the marshalling camps to our embarkation hards.

On 3rd June, 'Green Camp' in Camp J2 was reached for the last time. As in our practices, so in the final stage was everything 'laid on' in the finest order. The smallest detail of equipment or the replacement of a trained signaller were at instant call. Without wishing to ape the journalists, an air of grim determination had settled on the battalion. Typical of our Norfolk men, nothing much was said at the time. We all longed to get on with it, and our innermost thoughts are still secret. All eyes were on the weather, as upon this depended the sailing of this great armada, and so the destiny of empires.

On 13 May General Eisenhower visited the division at Petworth and on 22 May HM King George VI came to meet the assault troops. The second-in-command of the battalion throughout the campaign, Major (subsequently Lieutenant-Colonel) H.M. Wilson MC comments on the king's visit:

> . . . a visit to 3rd Division by His Majesty the King, and COs and Seconds in command were lucky enough to meet and talk to him in a tea tent. The King had enormous charm and an obvious sense of humour. One felt you were talking to a real friend and not a Monarch miles removed from the common plebs.
>
> On 2 June 1944 we moved out of Haywards Heath and into 'Green Camp'. This was a tented camp near Lewes and here we met complete security and were sealed in. However, everything had been thought of even down to entertainment and on Sunday evening we had Vic Oliver to tell us stories and try and sing. The troops enjoyed it and that was important.
>
> Our evenings were quiet and I suppose we were all wondering how we should react under fire intended to kill us. We never talked about this but everyone had his private thoughts on the subject.

Captain T.J. Harrison, Intelligence Officer on D-Day, appointed Adjutant in August, recalls a lighter side of the preparations for D-Day, incidents in 1943–4 when the battalion started 'wet-shod' training in Loch Fyne practising boarding and disembarking from assault craft, not quite 'by numbers' but nearly so:

> It was decided to get to know our craft commanders and listen to their problems at a cocktail party in the HQ Officers' Mess. After all, much of the D-Day landings must be at the mercy of the Royal Navy.
>
> The party was a success until it became clear that the guests had spliced not only the mainbrace but the spinnaker, jib and anything else within reach!
>
> This was too much for our younger element. The noisiest Naval ringleader was put in the back of a 3-tonner, driven to the nearest railway station and shoved into the next train to stop, irrespective of destination, intended or otherwise.

Lieutenant D.F. Bell, second-in-command of the Carrier Platoon, recalls an occasion just prior to D-Day, when the skippers of the landing craft were to be entertained at Camp J9:

> I was told that there was some equipment (two three-tonner loads, in fact) that was urgently required to be added to certain units of the Battalion transport locked up in warehouses at the East London docks. I was to set off early the next morning, (J9 had already been sealed for some days) distribute the equipment amongst the various vehicles and, whatever else, be back in time for the 'party'.

We eventually found the locked warehouses, had a great deal of difficulty in gaining access – the London dockers were in the throes of some industrial action, working to rule or whatever, and were not happy about letting us in. After much arguing and threats of armed force, we were eventually able to off-load the equipment and set off for the South Coast again only to have one of the trucks break down in Bow. I finished up being towed by the second truck at the end of a very short tow rope, at break-neck speed, some fifty odd miles back to J9 in time to get changed and get to the party – to congratulations from the CO for a job well done.

Few of the countless thousands who were involved directly or indirectly in the greatest seaborne invasion of all time can have known or imagined the complexity of the operation known as Overlord. Preparation for the return to north-west Europe started immediately following the evacuation of the BEF from Dunkirk in the early summer of 1940. Army and naval units began training for offensive operations against the enemy coast. During the latter part of 1941 Winston Churchill ordered that preparations should be made to turn from the defensive to the offensive, to plan for the return of Allied forces to Europe. Operation Overlord came into being and first plans estimated that fifteen armoured and twenty infantry divisions would be required.

Preparations had to be kept secret, resources developed and refined, new ideas produced and researched, the men and women who would take part trained and equipped. It was an immense undertaking which Britain and the Commonwealth alone, under pressure from Russia to provide a second front as soon as possible to relieve the strain on Red Army forces, would find extremely difficult to initiate with such force of men and arms as to guarantee success.

The entry of the United States of America into the conflict at the end of 1941 changed the situation dramatically and the following year America proposed a plan requiring forty-eight divisions to invade France by April 1943. The attack by Canadian troops at Dieppe in August 1942, during which more than half the assault force was lost, and the shortage of appropriate assault craft, influenced the decision to transfer the Allies' major effort to French North Africa. Operation Torch in November 1942 was the largest operation the Allies had yet attempted and comprised three simultaneous landings at Algiers, Oran and Casablanca involving 70,000 troops, over 500 ships and 1,000 aircraft, almost half the force sailing direct from the United States. The enemy was taken by surprise, the assault was successful.

In mid-1943 it was decided that three seaborne divisions (subsequently increased to five) and two airborne divisions would be required for the initial Overlord assault with two further seaborne divisions landing within twelve hours which, with other divisions following behind, would produce a total of eighteen divisions in the beach-head in the first two weeks.

The build-up of facilities and supplies would not allow an invasion of the Continent in 1943 but a date was set for May 1944. This was subsequently postponed for one month and a tentative date fixed for Monday 5 June. This date depended on three major factors: first, that the assault must be carried out in daylight to allow observation and neutralization of enemy positions; secondly, that the landings by assault craft should be made after low water, on a rising tide; thirdly, that there should be moonlight during the latter part of the night to facilitate airborne landings before dawn – after 5 June conditions would not be suitable for another fortnight. At the end of May the weather was perfect but on 1 June conditions began to deteriorate, bringing high winds and low cloud.

The day before the planned invasion Force 5 winds and 10/10ths low cloud in the Channel compelled a postponement for twenty-four hours leaving the assault troops aboard ship to face an extra night of waiting, some in squally, uncomfortable conditions. On the basis that a break in the bad weather was forecast, if only of short duration, and that further postponement must be for two weeks or more, the Supreme Commander, General Dwight D. Eisenhower, appointed to that post in December 1943, ordered that D-Day would be 6 June.

The enormous size and scope of the undertaking is difficult to imagine – the landings were preceded by intense bombing of rail networks and communication centres, the Allied Air Forces flew two hundred thousand sorties during April and May 1944 and in the five weeks before D-Day almost two thousand aircraft were lost and twelve thousand airmen killed.

The greatest armada of ships and aircraft ever known was assembled for the D-Day assault, more than 4,000 medium and heavy bombers launched the attack from the air, almost 4,000 fighters maintained mastery of the skies, 1,360 transport aircraft and 3,500 gliders carried the airborne troops while a further 1,500 reconnaissance and Coastal Command aircraft kept constant watch.

Over 4,000 vessels carried the assault troops and supporting arms, more than 1,000 naval ships protected the invading forces and provided fire power against enemy strongpoints while a further 1,500 ancillary and supply ships reinforced the initial assault, a total of some 7,000 ships, the majority of them British.

High in priority in the planning for D-Day was the development of weapons to bridge the period between the preliminary softening-up of enemy positions by bombers and naval shelling and the deployment of troops on the ground after landing. This was the time of greatest danger to the assaulting troops. The enemy-held coast was guarded by artillery strongpoints, fortified infantry positions, extensive minefields and a wide variety of lethal obstacles on the beaches. The British 79th Armoured Division had been made responsible for support weapons, known as 'Funnies', based primarily on Churchill and Sherman tanks – the DD (Duplex Drive) swimming tank was a standard Sherman fitted with twin propellers and a high canvas screen which was raised above the tracks and provided enough buoyancy to enable each tank to proceed in deep water under its own power. On landing the screen was lowered and the tank operated normally – launched from larger craft at some distance from the beaches these DD tanks landed with the first wave of troops giving them essential armoured close support.

Other specialist armoured vehicles were created to fill specific roles in the assault; the Crab, a flail tank, cleared the ground ahead of all mines, the Crocodile, a flame-throwing tank towing a 400 gallon trailer of fuel, other AVREs (Assault Vehicle, Royal Engineers) carried roadways or bridges to traverse difficult ground, yet another type was armed with a heavy mortar for use against fortified positions.

A multitude of specialized assault craft were used, from the standard LCA (Landing Craft Assault) to carry the first troops to shore, other types of LCA to deal with beach obstacles; the LCT (Landing Craft Tank) which was used in a variety of roles including as a platform for batteries of 5 inch rocket shells, each LCT(R) capable of firing over one thousand rockets in half a minute; the LCI (Infantry) carried 240 troops in the second wave of the assault. Larger craft included pre-war passenger vessels carrying the LCAs in their davits, LSTs (Landing Ship Tank) carrying more than sixty vehicles and many, many other vessels to convey, protect and supply the first troops ashore.

The scale of Operation Overlord can be better understood from just one statistic: 170,000,000 maps were printed for that operation alone.

In the weeks preceding D-Day intense effort was made to restrict the enemy's response to invasion by attacks on installations and lines of communication – damage to rail targets reduced traffic to one third, the majority of the bridges over the Seine between Paris and the sea were destroyed, airfields bombed. Resistance forces were alerted and all manner of subterfuge and deception employed to mask the true intent of the invasion forces with the result that on D-Day there was a heavier concentration of enemy troops between Dieppe and Boulogne and a considerable delay before any of those troops were moved south-west towards Normandy.

The Allied assault force, 21st Army Group, under command of General Sir Bernard (later Field Marshal Lord) Montgomery, comprised British 2nd Army and US 1st Army. The US 1st Army (Lieutenant-General Omar Bradley) was formed of US VII Corps (Utah Beach), beyond which the US 82nd and 101st Airborne Divisions landed during the night of 5/6 June 1944, and US V Corps (Omaha Beach). British 2nd Army (Lieutenant-General M.C. Dempsey) also comprised two Corps, XXX Corps (50 Division), landing on Gold Beach, and I Corps (3rd Canadian Infantry Division, Juno Beach, and 3rd British Infantry Division, Sword Beach), with numerous Commando units and many other specialist formations. The British 6th Airborne Division, assigned the task of capturing the bridges over the Caen–Ouistreham Canal and the River Orne, landed troops from the air during the preceding night on the extreme left flank of the seaborne assault.

British 3rd Division, landing on Queen Beach, the third sector of Sword Beach, at the western end of Ouistreham, was ordered to take the high ground north of Caen and, if possible, Caen itself; 8 Brigade leading and inclining towards the River Orne, 185 Brigade to follow-up and advance almost due south towards Caen while behind them 9 Brigade moved right, inland of Lion-sur-Mer. Five enemy infantry divisions faced the assault force in the bridgehead while two more were established in the Cherbourg Peninsula, in addition 21st Panzer Division was located in and around Caen with 12th SS Panzer Division in reserve to the left.

Captain A.M. Kelly commanded A Company of the battalion in the assault on the beaches but was wounded on D-Day. His memories are of the preparations for that day:

> One of the striking features of the operation was the training which preceded it. My strongest recollection is of the combined ops training, starting at Inveraray, continuing in the Western Highlands and culminating in divisional exercises in the Moray Firth and on the South coast. We became used to working with the Navy and to travel by sea in small craft. In these exercises and in the invasion transport and protection were provided by Force 'S', inspired by Captain Bush, RN – a strong personality who never failed to impress on divisional conferences. I think the special value of training with the Navy was the confidence it induced during the operation. The Channel crossing seemed to be an exact repeat of the rehearsals, the main difference being the vastly greater number of ships. The 'exercise' feeling was not lost until we came close to the French coast and met fire from shore batteries.
>
> My late brother, Reggie, was a naval surgeon with Force 'S', with the task of caring for the wounded evacuated on a tank landing ship. At the time I did not realize he was in Force 'S', but he later told me that from the tank landing ship he watched the D-Day fighting and his first patient was my corporal stretcher-bearer.

The weather on 5 June was bad; few German aircraft left the ground, those that did reported no untoward activity and the German High Command, believing that the Allies needed four days of good weather and because such a spell was not forecast, relaxed alertness. The final stages of the deception plan were put into effect, the French Resistance was warned by messages broadcast by the BBC, a thousand British bombers dropped 5,000 tons of bombs on major gun positions and the advance guard, parachute and glider-borne troops, landed in Normandy just before midnight.

The thoughts of the one man charged with the supreme responsibility for this immense operation can be partly judged by the draft statement General

Eisenhower is said to have prepared on 5 June 1944, as the assault forces approached the Normandy coast, against the possibility that those forces would be repulsed:

> Our landings in the Cherbourg – Havre area have failed to gain a satisfactory foothold and I have withdrawn the troops. (The troops have been withdrawn.)
>
> My decision to attack at this time and place was based on the best information available.
>
> If any blame or fault attaches to this attempt, it is mine alone.

The heavy burden of duty and trust which he carried at that moment must have been almost unbearable.

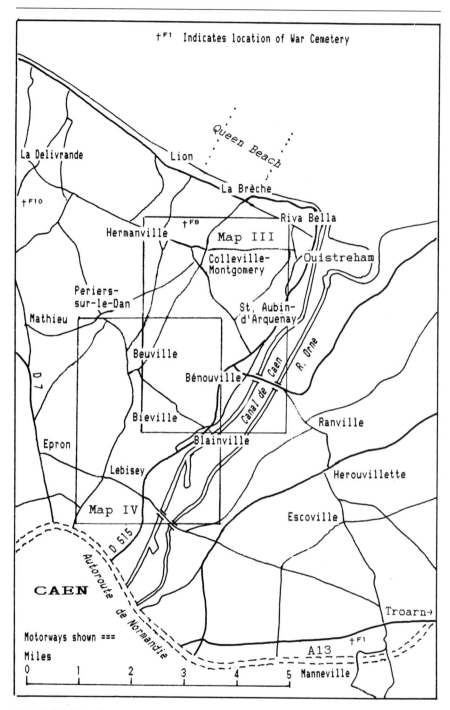

Map II: The Caen Sector.

CHAPTER TWO

The Most Historic Day: 6 June 1944

Three airborne divisions landed in Normandy in the early hours of D-Day, on the flanks of the assault. The American 82nd Airborne Division landed to the west of Utah Beach, the US 101st Airborne to the south, short of Carentan. The British 6th Airborne Division was charged with securing the bridges over the Caen Canal and the River Orne, north-east of Caen, and holding the ground east of those waterways to prevent elements of the German XVth Army, known to be in that area, from threatening the landings on that flank.

Naval warships commenced shelling shortly after 0500 hours and at 06.30 the first American troops were ashore at Utah Beach, the most westerly of the landings. Towards the centre of the assault area the American force landing on 'Omaha' beach, north-west of Bayeux, experienced rough seas and greater resistance from the enemy.

The British and Canadian landings were scheduled for 07.25 hours; on the right, British XXX Corps comprising, initially, 50th Division with 8th Armoured Brigade on Gold Beach, east of Arromanches and on the left, British I Corps formed of 3rd Canadian Division with 2nd Canadian Armoured Brigade on Juno Beach, in the region of Bernières-sur-Mer, and British 3rd Division with 27th Armoured Brigade on Sword Beach, at la Brèche d'Hermanville. A stretch of some 4 miles of coast between the Canadian beach-head and the British 3rd Division landings on Sword Beach was considered unsuitable for assault craft so 4th SS (Commando) Brigade was ordered to land at its extremities and secure the gap between.

The 1st Battalion The Royal Norfolk Regiment embarked at 22.15 hours on 3 June to be told the following morning that the operation had been postponed. History seldom records the small details, the minutiae of major events which are long remembered by those who were there – fifty years after the event many who took part can recall incidents with crystal clarity. Lance-Corporal N. Griffin, regimental signaller with D Company, relates:

The first clear recollection is of being on board a Landing Craft Infantry and setting sail from Newhaven. Some four hours later when we were allowed up on deck I was absolutely staggered by the vast armada which had gathered together! Wherever you looked there were ships of all shapes and sizes! The sky was full of black storm clouds and the wind was uncomfort ibly strong. The sun, however, was still penetrating the clouds in places and throwing brilliant shafts of sunlight across the water. Against this silvery background the ships looked sinisterly black!

At about 8 pm we were sent below to be told that the landing might have to be delayed because of the bad weather but that it would take place when the weather improved. We spent a wretched night I recall!! Not many of us were good enough sailors to withstand the heavy sea we encountered and sick bags soon became inadequate! By morning the deck on which colleagues and I were battened down was about an inch deep in vomit and speaking personally I wished I were dead!

At daybreak we were allowed up on deck and never has fresh salty sea air smelt so good!! The opportunity was taken to swill down and to try and clear the foul smelling decks below and in fact quite a good job was made of this. However, some of the smell lingered because, for example, the leather soles of our boots had become impregnated – but it was now bearable.

The *Battalion History* records more detail:

It was rough outside the shelter of the harbour, and soon the troops were feeling it pretty badly. It was not until we were well at sea that the signal came over the naval wireless that the landing was 'on' and that we could now open up our proper maps and for the first time know where we were going to land. The final briefing took place in the minute cabin of the LCI, with each member of the group every now and then rushing out, to come back not quite so green as when he left. And so darkness fell before the most historic day of our generation.

Lance-Corporal Griffin describes final preparations; how weapons, ammunition and other equipment were again checked; the issue of waterproof leggings. The night passed with little sleep:

Suddenly we were told 'This is it, up on deck and prepare for landing!' Up we went and took up positions on the port side of the bow superstructure. Lying on the deck on our left was the ramp down which we would go ashore. This was not really the time for sightseeing but of course we all had a good look round and truly it was a staggering sight to see so many ships so close together – literally hundreds! One or two were on fire but most were busy putting people or equipment ashore while others, having performed their task, were reversing out to sea ready to take on whatever task was next required.

Our ship's Captain was truly a 'Captain Birdseye' character with a full set of ginger whiskers. He did us proud in landing, in fact he went so far on to the beach that we got what is technically called a 'Dry' landing. He went so far in that when his ratings lowered the ramps for us we stepped off into only about two feet or less of water which from our point of view was marvellous.

Lieutenant E.G.G. Williams, commanding 18 Platoon, D Company, and known to all as 'Egg', remembers:

The last pay parade – when French Francs were issued (£1=200fr.) together with 'non-medical contraceptives', which Johnny Williams was too embarrassed to hand out and which subsequently were blown up and flown from their rifles as we marched down to Newhaven.

The singing from all the craft in Newhaven and the lovely evening anchored off the Nab Tower with all the 'Funnies'.

The smoke-filled wardroom where we were issued with our maps and the leaden stomach thanks to the anti-seasick pills.

A number of extracts included in this book are taken from the account of his military career written by Major H.M. Wilson MC; he remembers that day:

Dawn brought a wonderful sight. The enemy coast was there alright, still some miles away but we were pushing on nicely. During the night I heard planes of the Airborne Division going overhead so we knew the operation was well and truly 'on'. At 6.40 a.m. we could see smoke and shell bursts on the beach in our sector. There were a lot of fighter aircraft about and we were delighted to see they were all ours – the army had enormous faith in the RAF.

Our time for landing was 7.45 a.m. Well before then we were all ready. C Company was equipped with folding bicycles which were to take them inland quickly. Our craft was designed to drop a shallow ladder on each side of the bows down which we were to file off as quickly as possible. As the starboard ladder had just been lowered it was immediately hit by either a shell or a mortar bomb which squarely put it out of action, but, by good fortune, no one was hurt, so down the port side we all had to go.

The invading fleet was in view of the French coast by dawn and a massive bombardment commenced from battleships, destroyers, specialist support craft, which included multiple rocket launchers, and assault artillery. The weather had slightly improved but the waves were sufficiently rough to cause problems with the DD tanks which, although launched closer to shore than planned, still had some three miles to swim in conditions that swamped some. The tide was rising fast and the beaches were cluttered with obstacles – stakes, steel hedgehogs, concrete blocks, many with mines or shells attached which exploded on contact with any craft.

The 'Funnies' got ashore with difficulty and with such support as the DD tanks could give them commenced to clear paths – their presence undoubtedly ensured a successful assault but at a high price; half the specialist vehicles were knocked out.

Major (later Lieutenant-Colonel) W.H. Brinkley, commanding D Company on D-Day, describes the close liaison achieved with the naval forces and the friendship which developed between naval and military personnel. The battalion spent a major part of the winter of 1943/4 practising landing exercises with the Royal Navy at Burghead Bay and other areas on the coast of Scotland. When the time came to move south the battalion travelled by road and was very pleasantly surprised, in June, to find, at Newhaven, that the Channel crossing would be made in the same LCIs and friendships were renewed for the assault.

Forty years later he heard again from the Commander of LCI(L) 126 which carried D Company to Normandy, Lieutenant E.W. Moore RNVR, who wrote:

. . . The last time I saw you was at the head of your lads shouting 'Bash on Bill' as you all ran up the beach from my landing craft.

Your name has crossed my mind thousands of times since then, wondering, hoping that you had survived and I have told many people of the way you and your lads stormed up the beach . . .

. . . My poor old ship caught a packet after we dropped you, when we started to pull off, Jerry hit us with three mortar shells and several 88s apart from machine gunning us, this knocked out our radio shack, cut our telegraphs and wrecked the steering gear.

I had only one casualty among my boys, but two survivors from an LCA were badly wounded in my wardroom when one of the shells burst. I dropped them off on the Arethusa and came back to Newhaven as soon as possible across the minefields as we were on hand steering, but got back before the Bridge Inn [Newhaven] closed for a pint or two.

A relaxing pint was quite a contrast to the situation of the 1st Battalion that first evening. Lieutenant E.G.G. Williams, in that same LCI:

I had left something – I think it was my map case – in the wardroom and as I dived in to recover it there was a big bang and a hole appeared through which I looked at the beaches – with broached LCA and a burning tank.

Our ramp having been damaged by the mortar bomb which struck the gun platform we had to go down the starboard ramp. Getting the driest landing on record and then struggling to get out of all that fancy wet gear behind a sand dune on the beach.

Waving to a bunch of Commandos brewing up in the deep wadi alongside the lateral road – then seeing the torch hanging from the pack

Bofors Gun on its Crusader chassis moving in from the beach on D-Day.

of the man in front of me disappear – leaving the handle swinging – and the Commandos sprawled in the ditch. It must have burst on their tea kettle!

The rockets (two) coming across the swamp and 'removing' my gentleman's gentleman Longden.

'Squash' Lemon, [CSM D Coy] standing back to let the tank pass and putting his heel on a Schumine – my ears are still ringing – and 'Squash' just shook his leg!

That lovely tin of self-heating cocoa at Norfolk House after digging in.

On patrol that night – crawling up to a 'slit trench' which turned out to be a hole dug for the anti-landing posts being erected. The Frenchman contracted to dig them was reputed to have come to the CO asking if he was going to pay him.

Revd J.F.B. Jowitt, then a twenty-year-old sub-lieutenant RNVR commanding LCT 1096, one of the flotilla responsible for carrying 3 Division to the Normandy beaches, in an account of his experiences, relates:

We set sail from Shoreham in weather that was not at all promising, and were very concerned for the men for whom there was inadequate shelter in the open hold. However, D-Day was postponed for 24 hours and we put into Newhaven where all army personnel disembarked and we sailors had a good night's sleep in our bunks! By next morning all were aboard again, and we put to sea, which was still unsettled. We were about to start on the most important voyage of our lives! At this point, as far as I was concerned, the full realisation of what we were about to undertake dawned on me. I was not at that time in any way a committed Christian, but I did feel it was my duty to hold a short service of prayer for my crew and passengers, so the former were mustered on the messdeck and the First Lieutenant and I led a short service which we found in a Naval issue prayer book.

In due course we set off at a mere 6 knots, heading West for Piccadilly Circus and then South for Normandy. At first there was sufficient sea to cause spray to come over the hold, which must have made life miserable for the soldiers. But during the night the wind dropped and the sea became calmer so that by the time we entered the swept channels through the minefields the weather was no problem. When we arrived at the coast we were west of our landing area, so we proceeded eastward in line ahead until we reached our beach, when we did a 90 degree turn to starboard together, enabling us to go in in line abreast.

Some time after the war he found a sheet from a Naval Message Pad, dated 'First Tide 6 June 1944', addressed to CO, LCT 1096, headed 'Thanks for the Buggy Ride' and signed by the six Army officers transported by his craft, which included Captain J.B. Dye and Lieutenant D.F. Bell, together with the signature of his first lieutenant.

It took me right back to about 1000 hrs on 6 June 1944, an hour before we touched down on Sword Beach. Disembarking started straight away, but took longer than we expected, because being the top of high water some of the tracked vehicles, having to make 90 degree turns as soon as they came off the ramp, lost their tracks and had to be towed away. The beach was also under fire, and we had to wait for some casualties to be patched up and put on board for us to take back to England. However, in due course we were free to pull off the beach, which we did as fast as possible as a curtain of fire was falling in the water some 100 yards astern. Looking back on the whole operation I can't help but feel that God was in it and our prayers had been answered.

Company Sergeant-Major T.G. Catlin MM, C Company, tells of the preparations for D-Day:

C Company was cycle borne, not the familiar heavy type of bicycle but a light weight model with wing nuts so they could be folded – I must say not the easiest of machines to ride in full battle order (many a sore backside).

We left Newhaven and when in mid-Channel the maps of the landing were unsealed and distributed. I was responsible for carrying the reserve set, these had to be folded and sealed in the waterproof map case, quite an ordeal whilst being sick. Final briefing took place and we donned our waterproof leggings and jackets.

With daylight came the amazing sight of ships and craft of all shapes and sizes. We were eventually called in and to our amazement a dry landing; a shell hit our LCI causing a ramp to be put out of action. Outwardly everyone seemed calm and ready for the task ahead. On leaving the craft we proceeded to the Battalion assembly area, we left our cycles once clear of the beach-head, later that night a tank ran over them (we were quite pleased).

Major H.M. Wilson MC:

My little party consisted of Company Quartermaster Sergeants of four rifle companies and Battalion HQ. We were armed with signs with which we were to mark the route to our forming-up positions inland. With a jolt and a shudder our LCI rammed the beach and we were off down the Port ladder as the Starboard one had been hit and was out of action. A wave and 'thumbs up' from the bridge saw us all safely on to the beach and I remembered to salute as I left HM's ship. Everyone had a dry landing so we quickly kicked off our overtrousers and looked for a beach exit. There it was, quite handy, being controlled by a Sapper subaltern who was calmly searching for mines. He suggested we nip through his exit quickly as any minute he thought a mine was going up. He needn't have urged us through, our one thought was to get off the beach as quickly as possible as the further inland we got the safer it would be at that stage.

Major (later Lieutenant-Colonel) E.A. Cooper-Key MC, commanding B Company, recollects:

I landed with B Company on Sword Beach and we had just moved off the beaches when I saw Major Humphrey Wilson, the Battalion Second-in-command, surrounded by a group of jabbering Frenchmen.

Humphrey had spent many years in India and Urdu was second nature to him.

He was regaling the French in Urdu and when he saw me he turned round and said, 'Eric, these bloody fools can't even speak their own language!'

Lance-Corporal Griffin's memories throw considerable light on the duties and dangers of a front-line signaller:

Our Company Commander ordered us ashore and down the ramps we went and on to the beach – ashore on the Continent at last! It was my job to see that the No. 18 wireless set was close by the Company Commander at all times. He was first ashore and accordingly I was just a pace or two

Troops marching inland on D-Day (IWM B 5082).

behind. I carried ashore a standard rifle as my weapon, to the barrel of which I had tied two signalling flags in case I should need them to maintain communication!!

We followed the Company Commander across the beach which was full of troops and guns and armoured vehicles of all sorts. Some were burning and there were also a few bodies laying huddled up awaiting stretcher bearers. We hurried up over the sea wall of the little French seaside town which was just as the photographs had said it would be, crossed the road and turned away from the beach up a track alongside some houses, heading in the general direction of Caen.

According to plan, 185 Brigade passed through the assault brigade and by 1100 hours were assembled on the main axis of advance, 1st Battalion The Royal Norfolk Regiment on the left, 2nd Battalion King's Shropshire Light Infantry to the centre and 2nd Battalion Royal Warwickshire Regiment on the right.

The KSLI were to advance with tanks to a ridge ahead to overcome enemy strongpoints but the tanks were delayed and at midday they moved forward on foot without tank support – by 1300 hours one of the two strongpoints ahead, codenamed 'Morris', had been cleared by the remaining battalion of 8 Brigade, 1st Battalion Suffolk Regiment, but the other, codenamed Hillman, could not be suppressed. The *Battalion History* reports that all went well until the area between Hermanville and Colleville was reached:

Here we suffered our first casualties, as we were under direct observation from a dominating feature which was much more strongly held than had been anticipated. This feature later proved to be a very sharp thorn in the flesh, and when eventually overrun it was found to be a proper 'hedgehog' with feet of concrete, mines, Anti-tank guns, and the rest. This was the feature which should have been captured by the assault brigade. It is no discredit that they failed in this task, and it was not until flails, AVREs and tanks could be brought up that the place eventually fell.

The leading elements of VII US Corps, scheduled to assault Utah Beach, landed a mile south of their target due to the loss of the craft responsible for navigation but with few casualties. At Omaha Beach, which was strongly fortified, the American commander decided to launch DD tanks some 4 miles out. The sea, however, was too rough and most of the tanks sank, only five reaching land. A naval force, charged with saturating the beach defences with rocket fire, arrived late. The assaulting troops, in spite of lack of support, forced their way forward with the loss of three thousand casualties.

Private Geoffrey A. Duncan, 10 Platoon, B Company, in an account he prepared for school-children researching D-Day, wrote:

For most of us it was the first time in combat, our baptism of fire – as our sergeant so dryly observed, 'This is what sorts out the men from the boys.' Most of the lads in our platoon including myself were still in their teens but he was a great character and hadn't been given his stripes because he could shout the loudest.

We boarded the Landing Ship Infantry at Newhaven on 5 June and were herded down below to our deck areas. I say herded as each of us was loaded down like a pack mule, we had been issued with assault jerkins, a sort of canvas waistcoat with pouches on the outside and pockets on the inside, into these you packed ammunition, grenades, Bren gun magazines, 2 inch Mortar bombs plus emergency rations and many other items a front line soldier required; we estimated that each of us was carrying at least 80lbs on our backs not including our rifle. . . .

Darkness fell and sleep was out of the question for me, we were all keyed up and I spent the small hours in fitful dozing and pondering what the morning had in store. All sorts of thoughts were running through my mind; especially my family were foremost in my mind . . . my thoughts were suddenly shattered by the shout 'Stand to and get your kit on.' The night had passed and we were making our run in to the beach, I hastily pulled on my waterproof suit. . . .

Struggling down the gangway I blessed the Captain who kept his promise to take us in as close to the beach as was humanly possible. It was ironic that during all our practice landings prior to D-Day we never had any waterproof clothing at all and got soaked wading ashore, now here I was virtually stepping straight on to dry land. Once ashore one had

Moving inland at Lion-sur-Mer on D-Day.

to discard the waterproof suit and this is where I ran into trouble, my suit got hooked up on the entrenching tool on my back, God, I thought, I shall get clobbered before I even get off the beach.

I finally struggled free from my suit and must have aged ten years in as many seconds, then ran up the beach to rejoin my section who were making for the exit leading from the beach to the coast road. I turned and looked back down the beach – the Landing Ship from which we had just disembarked had received a direct hit on the bridge (I often wonder if the skipper who looked after us so well survived) – then scrambled through the gap in the barbed wire defences making doubly sure we kept within the two white marker tapes which told us this track had been cleared of mines. The shells were constantly shrieking overhead, we would hit the deck and get bawled out by our sergeant, 'On your feet, that one landed a mile away,' – there's an old saying you never hear the one that gets you but I must admit it gave me very little comfort at the time.

Major H.M. Wilson MC recalls the first movement forward beyond the beach:

On reaching the coast road I saw our route clearly down a little lane due south past a boggy patch to a little orchard some 1,000 yards inland. Since there was one of our DD tanks of 13/18 Hussars without anything to shoot at standing quite near this little lane I asked the tank commander if he would prove the route for us and run his tank down the lane. This he did and we just filed along walking in his track marks so we were quite safe from mines.

As we walked along dropping off our signs – 68 with a white arrow and 3 Div sign – a certain amount of mortar fire came over our heads but it was meant for the road now behind us and no one was hit.

Quite soon we found ourselves at the RV and we had just finished laying out the area, allotting Company areas and generally reconnoitring the place when along came the battalion.

Except for a small mortar bomb which landed at Robin Wilson's feet and singed his eyebrows, but did no other harm, we were left alone in our FUP. About midday we got our orders to move and inland we trekked through the village which later became Corps HQ and out into the cornfields going due south.

Two companies, A (Captain A.M. Kelly) and B (Major E.A. Cooper-Key) were sent off under Major Wilson to detour round the strongpoint ahead. The enemy spotted this movement and turned two MGs on to the leading company, A. Both companies became engaged in a fire fight which lasted for some two and a half hours. The rest of the battalion moved further round the left flank, and captured the feature which was to become known as Norfolk House. Finally A and B Companies succeeded in disengaging and rejoined the battalion.

Lieutenant Dennis Bell landed some tides ahead of the Carrier Platoon driving a little amphibious vehicle, the CO's run-about, called a 'Weasel'. He recalls:

It was much smaller than a carrier, had rubber tracks, a screw and rudder at the back, was very manoeuvrable and would go like a 'bat out of hell' given the chance. Because I was something of a 'spare file' and because I was driving this Weasel, I became the CO's runner for a day or two.

I left the beach, crossed the dunes and proceeded along the beach road to join up with Battalion HQ in the assembly area outside Hermanville, just as they were instructed to push forward, to the left of and bypassing 'Hillman', eventually arriving at Norfolk House. I was driving nicely through the grain, sussing out the ditches, when some Jerries decided that I looked too much of a *sitting duck* to be left alone and started taking pot-shots at me and dropping the odd mortar bomb around. That's when I discovered how fast the little thing would go. Rather hair-raising though, doing a handbrake turn from something in excess of 50 mph and on the edge of a six foot deep ditch.

The things that stick out most about 'Norfolk House' are, in the early days, dodging the sniper fire when visiting the loos in the wood, visiting Jimmy Green to be sustained by his never ending supply of the 'hard stuff', the massive bomber raid – watching those boys in the Lancasters coming in, in line astern, braving the flak, dropping their bomb loads and, if they didn't get them all away the first time, going round and coming in again and again. 'Bloody fantastic.'

Lieutenant Norman L. Brunning had served for fifteen months in B Company of the 1st Battalion when, two weeks before D-Day, he was transferred to 185 Brigade HQ to be one of two additional liaison officers requested by Brigadier K.P. Smith. His task would be to liaise with 6th Airborne Division at Ranville, for which he modestly comments that his only qualifications were an ability to read a map and to ride a motor cycle. He embarked from Newhaven with Brigade HQ and landed in Normandy about 11.30 hours:

We were too far out to sea to see anything of 8 Bde landing at H-Hour, or 185 Bde some two hours later, and the sound of the ship's engines drowned the noise of firing; but the first sight of all the ships was very impressive – the LSIs of the assault brigades standing off ready to receive casualties; a small fighting-ship, corvette or mine-sweeper, sinking bows first gave us sobering thoughts; and close inshore LCAs smashed by artillery. We lay some distance offshore for about half an hour waiting to disembark, like a sitting duck, during which time only half a dozen shells fell, sending up spurts of water, well clear of any ships.

Bde HQ was set up at Hermanville for about four hours before moving on to an orchard on the far side of Colleville. Prisoners came in a steady stream; a few French were brought in, accused of collaborating with the Germans. Occasionally the odd mortar bomb fell in the vicinity and everyone dived for cover. News filtered in from 8 Bde and from the Battalion – none of it very good – there had been casualties. I managed to visit the Battalion and B Company, who seemed to be in good spirits. Jimmy Campbell and Lew Pyshorn laughed and joked that Jimmy said he was 'too bloody bad to die!' [Lieutenant J.F. Campbell was killed in action the following day.]

Geoffrey Duncan's account continues:

As we cleared the outskirts of Hermanville we lost the cover of buildings and trees on either side of the road and emerged into open country, here we were soon spotted and it wasn't long before the 88s and mortars were giving us a pasting; we didn't hang about there too long but lost several lads on that open stretch of road. As we approached the western outskirts of Biéville we could hear there was stiff opposition on the far side of the village – in the village itself there were knocked out vehicles, German dead sprawled on the road and several lads from the Suffolk Regiment lying dead in various places, one in particular had been shot down in the middle of the road and a tank had run over him. It was a gruesome sight but war is a gruesome business, it was unbelievable how quickly one got hardened to the sight of death and accepted it with very little emotion except when it was one of your own particular friends. Perhaps it's the way it had to be if you wanted to survive in a world gone mad?

Crawling through the corn on one's belly with all the gear we were carrying was a punishing experience, the sweat poured down my face and I thought to myself, what the hell am I doing here, why hadn't I joined the Royal Artillery like my elder brother?, and muttering to myself I crawled on through the corn.

Lying there I was dirty, hungry and tired to the point of exhaustion, it seemed like an eternity before the supporting armour arrived, a fierce battle followed and the enemy position was finally over-run – I was mighty glad to see the last of that field but several brave lads were lying still and silent in that waving sea of corn.

Private W. Evans, serving in 12 Platoon, B Company, remembers vividly his first acquaintance with the symbol of the First World War, the red poppy:

After spending many hours on a landing craft crossing the Channel and being seasick like many others, I was glad to get on the beach. It was more like manoeuvres that we had done so many times before. I could not believe it was the real thing. We had no trouble on the beach. Once off the beach we slowly advanced along narrow dusty roads with Jerry snipers banging away at us. So far we had covered two or three miles and were doing well until we came to a cornfield. Then Jerry machine guns in a small Pill Box opened up. The lads were soon being cut to pieces as the machine guns, with their tremendous rate of fire, scythed through the three foot high golden corn. I remember one of the Company cooks behind me getting a bullet in his neck. That was the day I first saw the red poppies of France in the cornfields, diving to the ground out of the machine gun fire. My nose was stuck right amongst them! They reminded me of the hell and horrors of the 1914 war which my father had talked about so often.

Major H.M. Wilson MC tells of other, unexpected, dangers:

Just before last light we all witnessed the heartening sight of the aerial re-supply of the Parachute Division just across the Orne Canal from where we were. Coloured parachutes of every hue were dropped, each colour representing a commodity of some sort, red for ammunition, green for rations, black for Ordnance spares, batteries etc. It was a most morale-raising spectacle. We also witnessed the arrival of a large number of gliders for whom a Landing Zone had now been prepared but the Halifax bombers which towed them had selected our HQ area into which to drop

Battalion HQ. Left to right: Lt-Col. R.H. Bellamy, Major R.H. Dunn RA, Capt. W.E.G. Bagwell. The identity of the fourth man is not known.

their tow ropes. We spent a lively half hour dodging these great aerial snakes hurtling towards us to land with a proper thump.

That evening 1 Royal Norfolk was firmly established in a wooded area at the top of a gentle rise, codenamed Rover, around a single house which came to be known as Norfolk House.

By midnight on D-Day US forces on Utah had secured the beach-head, and the two American Airborne Divisions were holding pockets to the south and west of the beach. On Omaha there had been a bitter fight, but the troops were ashore and consolidated along a 4 mile stretch of coast and about a mile inland. XXX Corps and the Canadians were ashore on a front of more than 10 miles and had penetrated inland for almost 6 miles to about 3 miles north-west of Caen. A gap still existed between 3rd Canadian Infantry Division and 3rd British Infantry Division, which had linked with 6th Airborne and, moving forward, had been halted some 2½ miles north of Caen.

Hitler was not convinced that these landings were the main thrust, believing them to be no more than a major diversion, and warned his forces to be alert for other assaults.

More than 130,000 men were landed from the sea and over 20,000 men from the air in the first twenty-four hours. The Americans suffered over 6,000 casualties from a total of 73,000 troops, mainly on Omaha Beach where specialized armour had not been used to the same extent as on the

British front – casualties in British 2nd Army amounted to some 4,000 from a force of 82,000.

Eight divisions landed on D-Day, five more the next day rising to a total of twenty-one divisions by D+12 and thirty-nine within three months.

The battalion had suffered its first casualties, twenty men died on D-Day; Lieutenant G.M.C. Toft died of his wounds the following day. Captain A.M. Kelly, Lieutenant O.A. Ward and a number of other ranks were wounded. Captain W.R.C. Lang RAMC, the medical officer, and several stretcher-bearers were also wounded when the RAP was hit by a mortar bomb. Lance-Corporal E. Ballard was mentioned in dispatches for his action in reorganizing the RAP, the first honour to be won by the battalion in the campaign.

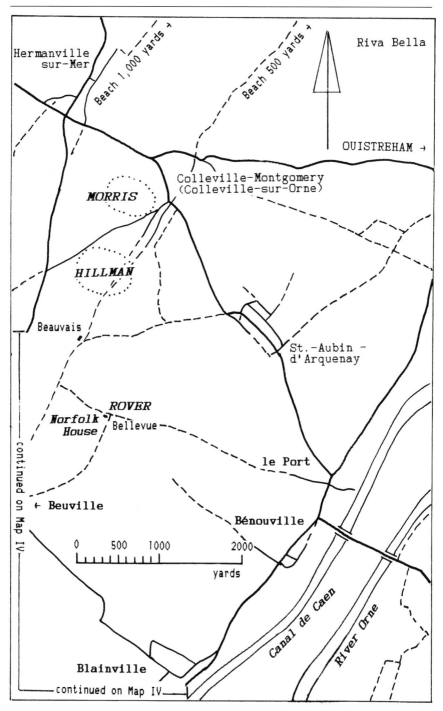

Map III: 'Morris', 'Hillman', 'Rover'.

CHAPTER THREE

Dust Means Death

That first night ashore was filled with mortar and gun fire. Everyone was keyed up ready for counter-attacks, alert yet happy the first day was over and the initial landing accomplished. The following morning 185 Brigade ordered 2 Warwicks to attack the Lebisey ridge overlooking Caen, known to be strongly defended. *Battalion History:*

> Unfortunately plans went astray and the attack went off at half-cock, with the result that the Warwicks found themselves in a very difficult position, being unable to move forward without heavy casualties or backwards without exposing themselves and giving the initiative to the enemy. There was nothing for it, and we had to go and restore the situation. 1600 hours was our H-hour and up we went, through the sniped village, across the anti-tank obstacle and up through the corn to the wood. It was not easy going, but we managed to get our anti-tank guns and mortars to a position from which they could give us some form of support. The forward companies were having a bad time and we suffered quite a number of casualties. Enemy tanks were also reported and altogether it was most unhealthy.
>
> At this point a big decision had to be made, and it was left to the unfortunate CO to make it. Were we to withdraw at last light to the other side of the anti-tank obstacle, or were we to hang on where we were and hope for help at first light? We pulled out, and with us what was left of the Warwicks. The time chosen was just before last light, and this small point undoubtedly made all the difference, as when the last troops left the area the enemy shelled and mortared it severely, fortunately doing us no damage.

Major H.M. Wilson MC fills in the details:

> In the afternoon we moved well away from the road down to the stream facing the Lebisey feature some 1,000 yards ahead. All sorts of rumours were going around of massed tanks and enemy counter attacks but to us everything seemed fairly quiet. At about 4 o'clock we started through the corn, over the stream and through more corn right up to Lebisey and here we halted as we did meet some opposition. Hugh Bellamy sent me back to Brigade HQ to tell the story and get orders. I found the Brigadier who told me that Hugh was the only person who could make any local

decisions and, wishing me goodbye as if I was going to certain death, I went back to Hugh. At 9 o'clock he decided to pull out bringing what there was of the Warwicks, who had lost their CO, with us. This we did without incident and then we just firmed up in the positions we were in on the evening of D-Day with the exception of B company group in the forward position of Blainville.

Lance-Corporal E. Seaman MM, was in charge of the stretcher-bearers of A Company on D-Day. He remembers:

On D-Day we had a hell of a baptism – I was detailed to go with 8 platoon across corn fields where the Brigadier put us in front of our own tanks and we really got slaughtered. We had so many wounded and killed I was the only stretcher-bearer left, of the other stretcher-bearers one, Pte Woolf, was killed and two, 'Fanny' Grimes and 'Tricky' Power, were badly wounded. I and one of the riflemen to help me bandaged and carried them down to an old track across the fields where RAMC ambulances picked them up.

At midnight that night a KOSB padre joined the eight of us left and we buried the dead; then he took us back to his headquarters for a cuppa and we rejoined the Battalion just in time to attack Lebisey Wood for the first time.

I shall never forget that first attack on Lebisey Wood – we had a lot of dead and wounded again. We had one man on the stretcher and another man with a broken leg – when we ran back with the stretcher this man with the broken leg had his arm round my shoulder and was running down the hill.

The second time we went up there I had to clear all our dead up from the first encounter after they had laid there for four or five weeks with booby traps on them.

Private Geoffrey Duncan writes of the second day ashore:

The night passed surprisingly quietly, some spasmodic firing, flares going up and the distant rumble of gunfire out at sea. It didn't seem I had barely shut my eyes when I was rudely awoken by a hefty kick in the butt and it was 'On yer feet for stand to' again. We were all keyed up for the expected dawn counter attack but strangely and thankfully it never materialised, meanwhile the Warwicks were on the move their objective being the high ground Lebisey which not only overlooked Caen but dominated the countryside for miles around. I was to remember Lebisey with great trepidation a few weeks later.

We finally moved off and made reasonably good progress apart from spasmodic sniper fire which claimed some casualties amongst the sections, this sniping was most disconcerting as we were being shot up from the rear! Despite this we kept moving on or near the main road which had a good screen of trees on either side but further along the road our cover of trees ended rather abruptly – as we emerged into the open countryside we could see Lebisey Wood across the sunken fields to our left and sure as hell we had been spotted, it wasn't long before the German mortars and artillery were making life very uncomfortable for us.

We vacated that road in double quick time and sought refuge in the dykes and hedgerows but, knowing we would be cut to pieces if we stayed put, we broke through the hedgerow into a field of standing corn and ran like hell down the sloping field to cries of 'Keep going Lads' accompanied by the crump of shells and as we ran you could hear the small arms fire zipping through the air, probably from German machine guns firing on fixed lines. It had been a long charge across that field and I was absolutely shattered and gasping for breath by the time we reached the edge of the wood.'

Private W. Evans remembers D+1, the second day ashore, and calls to mind a leaflet, signed by General Eisenhower, issued to all troops, which referred to the 'Great Crusade':

First we had to capture the woods called Lebisey and, as we advanced along a sunken road in full view of the Germans, they let us have it. Mortars and shells came raining down. With no cover at all all we could do was bury our heads in the dirt. We lost a lot of lads that day – arms and legs everywhere. Then as we advanced up the fields towards the wood, Jerry snipers were sending up the dirt all around us. We reached the edge of the wood only to find it had been mined by the Jerries, who by now had pinned us down with rifle and machine gun fire. Once again I buried my face in the dirt, lying on my belly trying to dig a hole to crawl into. We were in that position for some time. It was now dark and the order came to withdraw. I thought 'This is it, back to the beaches', but looking back this 'Great Crusade' was in full swing and the Royal Norfolks, doing a little withdrawal, were not going to stop it. Then, in the dark, we had to run from the flat top of the hill to the sunken road half a mile away. I do not know how many of the lads were killed or wounded that night but I am sure I did the four minute mile with machine guns firing into our backs.

Lieutenant E.G.G. Williams' snapshot memories give vivid pictures of events and people:

Up in Lebisey Wood. Giving covering fire while Robin Wilson went out with two stretcher bearers to bring back Warwick wounded. Johnny Williams and I put him in for his MC. I wonder did the stretcher bearers get anything? I and my men had to bury a dozen of the remainder a month later – not a pleasant job. The sergeant's gold fillings brilliant in the sun.

Last out of Lebisey – at full pelt through the corn.

Patrol round Chateau Beau Regard. Corporal Mortimer battering at the door with rifle butt. Suggested he tried the handle – which opened the door. At the same time young Brown was coughing his heart out having been given a drink by a Frenchman. For a moment I thought he had been poisoned and nearly shot the Frenchman – but it was only Calvados! On a later patrol with Sgt. McGrath they brought back some bottles of wine from the cellar. I was surprised that Jerry had left any and told the REs. They investigated and reported that the next bottle in the rack was wired up to 4 Tellermines!

CSM T.G. Catlin MM:

D+1 we received orders for the attack on Lebisey Wood. Soon after leaving the start line we came under heavy shell, mortar and machine gun fire. The Germans held the position in great strength and depth and we received casualties, killed and wounded. My first experience of losing a comrade killed; very disturbing, but something I soon got used to.

Very little progress was made and after dark orders were given to retire back to the area of Norfolk House. I withdrew my company HQ but our company commander was missing, he having gone forward to the leading platoons and got caught in the cross-fire. Later he returned to our HQ – he had climbed a tree, staying put until the firing ceased.

Lance-Corporal Nevil Griffin touches on the subject which is apparent in so many memories, the loss of a friend:

The over-riding memory is of so many of my colleagues who through various causes did not, like me, see the campaign through to the end.

Like for example Pte. Tuffield the first of 10 signals colleagues who were to serve with me during the campaign. We had reached the edge of Lebisey Wood in the late afternoon of Day 2 when eventually the order was given to withdraw for regrouping. As 'Tuff' and I retraced our steps down the sloping field we became the target of a German rifleman firing from the wood. Fortunately the field was very uneven and our withdrawal was thus somewhat erratic which put the rifleman off a bit. We reached a gap in the hedge and made for the other side, in the process poor old 'Tuff' was wounded in the hand but we managed to scramble through to safety on the other side. He was evacuated to Blighty I believe – 'Tuff' was colleague number one to be replaced!

Lieutenant Norman Brunning, on temporary secondment to Brigade HQ, indicates his concern for his many friends in the battalion arising from the lack of news:

At about 6 p.m. reports of the first battle for Lebisey Wood began to come in. The Warwicks were down to about 60–80 men; and very few of them had any weapons. The Norfolks were down to 300 men; the KSLI as fire support battalion had not suffered too badly. It was all very depressing. However, during the night a number of men returned until the Warwicks totalled about 400 and the Norfolks about 500. I felt quite helpless under such circumstances, knowing nothing definite – wondering what had happened to B Company!

On one occasion I visited the Battalion, as I rode along the track towards the farm, a shell landed very close to one of the Anti-tank guns on the far side of the field. The first man on the scene was the Padre, Jimmy Green. On another occasion Sgt. Parker presented me with one of his famous fresh beef steaks, cut from an animal that had strayed on to his minefield.

The attack by the battalion on D+1 to retrieve the situation in front of Lebisey Wood cost nineteen lives including Lieutenants J.F. Campbell and W.M. Sharp. It also marked conspicuous gallantry by Captain R.C. Wilson of D Company who, on reaching the edge of Lebisey Wood, saw a number of men lying wounded in front of the enemy positions in what appeared to be a minefield. With two volunteers he went forward to bring the wounded in; one of the volunteers was wounded but with the other, Sergeant J. Martin, Captain Wilson brought in a number of wounded, under heavy fire, who would otherwise have been left behind when the battalion withdrew.

This account would be incomplete without the reminiscences of the gunners who supported the battalion throughout and upon whom the battalion greatly depended for immediate artillery support. Captain John Talbot MC, RA, Troop Commander D Troop, 16th (OLD ROOKS) Battery, 7th Field Regiment RA, landed on D-Day with his troop of 105 mm SP guns and supported 2nd Warwicks on foot on D+1 in their abortive attempt on Lebisey. He recalls:

We were pinned down all day about 100 yards short of the wood and my Pack RT set was the only link with the Division as all other sets failed to work! After we withdrew back into Biéville at midnight I borrowed my CO's (Nigel Tapp) jeep and drove round to Blainville to recover my Sherman OP tank and its crew who had been alone all day there in no man's land – they were pleased to see me and I decided to make a short cut back in the dusk direct to Beuville along a small road. We could clearly see Lebisey on our left and ultimately ran into a 1 Norfolk outpost on Rover where by shouting 'Seventh Field' I managed to stop their A/Tk gun from opening fire! Perhaps the Norfolks thought 21 Panzer were coming!

On D+2 British troops from Gold Beach linked up with US forces from Omaha at Colleville-sur-Mer. Allied forces met strong ground opposition but experienced little threat from the air – German air forces were restricted by lack of aircraft fuel, a situation known to the Allies and exploited by massive bomber raids on fuel plants in German held territory.

Feldmarschall Rommel, commanding German forces in Normandy, planned to make his main counter-attack on the right of the Allied front, towards the Utah beach-head, but was over-ridden by Hitler who ordered the main attack to be made against British forces approaching Caen. This change of plan by the enemy prevented forward movement of Allied forces to capture Caen and weeks of bitter fighting ensued.

On D+2 the battalion was ordered to send a detachment to the left flank of the brigade, between the villages of Beauregard and Blainville. The detachment, under command of Major H.M. Wilson, comprised B Company, three sections of carriers, two anti-tank sections and pioneers, forming a straight line some 2,000 yards in front of any other Allied troops – which position was known as 'Duffer's Drift'. In the advance to secure this position Sergeant C. Parker of 12 Platoon distinguished himself in capturing a house containing an enemy strongpoint for which action he was subsequently awarded the Military Medal.

The enemy reacted to the invasion and to attacks by Resistance forces with reprisals on French civilians and on Allied prisoners of war. Among the instances on record are the murder of 642 French villagers, including 190 schoolchildren, on 10 June in Oradour-sur-Glane, the killing of 34 Canadian prisoners, most of them wounded, on 7 June between Bayeux and Caen and on 11 June, British prisoners-of-war were forced to stand against a wall to be shot.

Lieutenant C.R. Parfitt, Second-in-Command of the Anti-tank Platoon, recalls another side of war:

Within a day or two of my arrival in Normandy with the rest of the Anti-tank Platoon I noticed a fine pair of hunters wandering free near a demolished barn. I was astonished at the survival of the horses seeing how much shrapnel was embedded in their hides. A little later I bumped into George Seaman (another horse lover) and expressed my deep concern at the deterioration of the animals' wounds. To cut a long story short we jointly decided to have a go at removing the shrapnel; at least that nearest the surface.

At dusk George turned up with one of his 'acquisitions' – a Commando dagger with its well-known sharp point and twin edge. It was quite a game catching and haltering (the halters improvised from thick string) the animals. The risk from their frantic kicks being almost more lethal than the occasional mortar shell falling uncomfortably close. However, once we had removed some of the metal the first hunter stood still, waiting for us to carry on it seemed. More remarkable still to find the other animal calmly standing waiting for his turn.

June 1944. Left to right: Capt. I.A. MacGillivray, Major E.A. Cooper-Key, Capt. J.B. Dye, Lt. C.R. Parfitt.

Later that evening as I was 'resting' in my trench before a late evening recce there was a welcome visit from the same worthy George with a mess-tin containing roast veal and all the trimmings for my supper. (I did not ask any questions.) This seemed to me a good time to uncork my precious VAT 69 (rescued just as my Carrier disappeared under the waves trying to land on French soil). A 'swig' we all enjoyed.

Lieutenant L.G. Edgley-Pyshorn, Platoon Commander in B Company, recalls:

After the first 48 hours of somewhat frenetic activity we eventually dug in, in the area of Blainville. From this point the main activity then was intense patrolling of the area immediately around Lebisey Wood and Caen.

At about D plus 7 or 8 I was leading a small recce patrol in the area from Lebisey Wood towards the Colombelles factory in order to establish certain information. On the return trip back to B Company lines we were suddenly aware of a very heavy engine noise immediately overhead and on looking upwards we could see an object in the sky trailing flames from its rear end. After a short time the object itself dipped quickly and crashed to the ground some two or three hundred yards away enveloped in flames.

We established, some time later, that this was very probably one of the first of the V1 rockets which of course was one of Hitler's answers to the D-Day invasion and his intention was to direct these towards London.

On 13 June some of those first V1s, more commonly known as 'flying bombs', one of Hitler's so-called 'secret weapons', were launched from the Channel coast. Of the first ten dispatched that day only four reached England, one causing the loss of six lives in Bethnal Green.

In mid-June the enemy, although resisting fiercely in Normandy, still looked upon the landings as a major diversionary tactic and anticipated other attacks on the coast of northern France, even in Holland and Norway and south on the Mediterranean coast.

Lieutenant Eric A. Woodhouse first commanded the Assault Pioneer Platoon and subsequently the Carrier Platoon; he remembers:

After the D-Day landing on Sword Beach memories of details are rather vague but the overall impression was of a hell of a lot of noise, explosions, smoke, clutter of bodies and equipment on the beach and our main thoughts centred on objectives to be achieved ashore. I can recall being grateful that we were put ashore on dry land and not up to our necks in water as the Navy was wont to do in training to 'bloody pongoes and brown jobs'.

In one small village we passed through, a young French boy of about 7 or 8 came hareing down the road shouting, 'Tommy – no f——g good here!' We were inclined to agree with him and admire his command of English. Wandering in front of our lines with Bobbie Parfitt and 'Tinkle' Bell we were fired on by an 88 mm gun. I don't think the Jerry gunner liked us much, he kept shooting in front and behind us. Suffice to say three S Coy officers would have done well in the Grand National, we went over or through a six foot hedge and away to our company lines in record time.

There is remembrance of scrounging Calvados and Camembert cheese when possible from liberated farmers. Finding in one small dusty old cinema an ancient piano, time for a quick 'tinkle' on the wobbly but thankfully un-booby trapped keys.

Random thoughts of self-heating soup – the day we got some real bread instead of biscuits – the CO, who shall remain nameless, but always slept on his back with his tin hat covering his essential equipment. Captured German dugouts with the sickly sweet smell of rotting corpses muffled with cologne is not easily erased from the senses. German artillery 'stonks' on our positions usually at meal times.

Captain R.C. Wilson MC considers himself amazingly lucky. He joined the battalion at Weybridge in 1941 and was still serving with it when demobilized in 1946. 'So many, good friends among them,' he writes, 'failed to survive the campaign, and many others bear the scars then acquired. Why was I to be the exception?' Twice wounded, he was able on each occasion to return to the battalion and believes he was the only rifle company officer to have landed on D-Day and to have been serving when the campaign ended. These are his recollections:

The Normandy days stand out with the greatest clarity. Everything was so new, and we were so fit and well-trained – keenly alive to new impressions. Not that there's much evidence of a well-trained individual in the recollections which follow, just a lucky one.

There was, for instance, a fighting patrol I took out, at night, with, I think, Colin Barnby. We were to discover if the enemy was occupying, and if so in what strength, a village – Biéville? – to our front, try to take a prisoner and, generally, to make a nuisance of ourselves. We studied the map and I decided to take the major part of the patrol into the village and send Colin with a smaller party a little further down the road to Caen to try to intercept any stragglers. There was a point at about the right spot where the road crossed a stream, and I told Colin to make that his objective. Our part turned out to be fairly easy. Though there was plenty of evidence that the enemy had been occupying the village, there was nobody around. We collected a few bits and pieces and then made our way to our agreed rendezvous by the time we had arranged. There was no sign of Colin or his party. There'd been no firing, so it didn't seem likely that he'd run into trouble, but where was he? After waiting at least half an hour, we went to find him, and I was relieved, before we'd proceeded far, to meet him. He'd been half way to Caen looking for the stream. It didn't exist. We later discovered, looking more closely at the map, that what we'd assumed to be a stream was a blue 'defence overprint' line.

As we passed the Lebisey crossroad we noticed that a row of Teller mines had been put across the road on our side. I reported this on our return, and suggested that it might be a good idea not to lift them, which could be noticed, but simply to remove their detonators. I'd suggested it, so was given the job, and a few days later went out with a couple of Pioneers and my batman, Taylor – a real poaching type from Bures in Suffolk. We laid up for some time, and then, as all seemed quiet, lifted the mines, removed the detonators as planned and put the mines back. Feeling rather pleased with ourselves we made our way back through the grounds of the Château to Duffers Drift. In the grounds was a lake, and swimming on it was a duck. Taylor remarked with seeming irrelevance: 'I've been carrying this —— rifle ever since we landed and still haven't fired it.' I took the hint and suggested that perhaps he ought to check that it was in working order. It was, but the duck was in the middle of the lake and we had to pull down a lengthy sapling to retrieve the corpse, which Taylor was carrying when we entered our forward position to find that the Brigadier was paying it a visit. Quite undaunted Taylor held up the duck and said, 'Look at this sir, piece of shrapnel right through its neck.'

There was a strip of land between the River Orne and the Orne Canal. Neither the enemy nor ourselves occupied this, but a sort of routine developed in which we would send out a reconnaissance patrol which would observe and report an enemy fighting patrol. We'd then send out one of the latter which hit the air. I took out one of these in an area where the reeds were so high that it was quite easy to lose all sense of direction. I found it quite easy, anyway, and had considerable difficulty in finding the way back to the point where the canal could be crossed. I'd say, 'Here we are back at the canal' and then notice that the water was flowing, so it must be the river. We blundered about for ages (I called it 'making a thorough search') before eventually and luckily getting our bearings and finding our way back.

A summary of the action during the first week of the campaign was issued within the battalion which records that the units opposing the battalion were 12(SS) and 21 Panzer Divisions and that 3 Division was beginning to form the pivot on which the rest of the Expeditionary Force would swing in a gradual left wheel.

Major J.E. Piccaver relates his experiences on joining the battalion in mid-June to command A Company:

I, along with Ronnie Hodd, who I had met up with in my wanderings, joined the 1st Battalion while they were on Norfolk Ridge to be greeted on arrival by Hugh Bellamy, the CO, by my christian name which I must say at this particular stage helped me a lot.

I then was met by Peter Baker, OC Headquarter Company, who took me round the A Company lines at 'Stand To' to meet the Company. (Having been with the 9th Battalion The Royal Norfolk Regiment commanding a company for some time previously, which had as a battalion spent much time supplying reinforcements to other regiments, I was not a little surprised to meet at least six members from my previous company who I had, I must admit, been delighted to transfer – their surprise or horror was greater than mine!)

We were comfortably dug in on Norfolk Ridge until a Platoon Commander of A Company decided to brew up or else light his pipe in his straw lined slit trench which promptly caught fire. The net result of this – smoke signals – followed by a thorough mortaring from Lebisey Wood which incidentally hit Bandy Howard's Anti-tank mines store.

Dennis Bell relates how he temporarily rejoined A Company, in which he had served some years earlier, as a platoon commander after the first attempt to take Lebisey and, until reinforcements arrived, 'went out on several patrols, did my share of scaring and being scared, of chasing and being chased.' He tells of a meeting which led to him living, marrying and spending the rest of his life on the Lincolnshire/Norfolk border:

On arriving back one morning from a platoon strength fighting patrol, which had been unsuccessful in finding any Jerries, although we had disturbed plenty in the same area on previous occasions, before I had time to clean up and make myself presentable, Peter Baker, the acting

Company Commander, introduced me to the new Company Commander, one John Piccaver.

He declined my offered grubby hand but stood back, looked me up and down, and said, 'You're a scruffy looking b——; just because we are fighting a war that's no excuse to go around looking like a tramp,' – my kind of bloke!

I did not know it at the time but that meeting was destined to influence my whole life.

They were happy days, punctuated by the odd incoming stonking every time an RA observer climbed the water tower for a better view, chasing the odd Jerry that ventured too close on the other side of the canal, demolishing the odd house where we had cause to believe they were hiding and capturing a German river gunboat that was endeavouring to escape back up the canal in the direction of Caen. There were a few restless nights, when the Navy was pumping its 16 inch shells into Colombelles – sleep on those occasions was out of the question.

I have often wondered if the Hun ever knew how little there was between him and Ouistreham.

At Norfolk House the battalion became long-stop to any counter-attack and from the forward position, 'Duffer's Drift', the men of the battalion had their patrol inoculation. Private W. Evans continues his reminiscences:

I had a good position on a high bank looking down along a narrow road which stretched for 1,000 yards. To my front, 100 feet or so, was a small stone bridge which had been covered with British mines. I was in my slit trench on this high ground looking over the bridge and up the road, with a Piat (a spring loaded weapon with a punch to dislocate your shoulder) which was probably more dangerous to the operator than it was to the enemy. My mate, Jack Dace, was in a slit trench alongside the bridge, looking up the road. We used to take pot shots at the jerry despatch riders on their motor bikes. Along with ten or twenty of the other lads firing at them they never stood a chance.

One day I was in my slit trench watching the jerries attacking 6th Airborne to my left across the Caen Canal, with their tanks half a mile away. Before I saw it this large jerry truck or staff car was within 100 yards of the bridge. Nobody had fired at it yet. An officer in a brown uniform got out with a lot of papers under his arm and walked towards the mined bridge. Inside the car were three or four officers in silver braid. On seeing my mate this officer ran like hell back to the wagon. He was within twenty feet of Jack who later said his rifle had jammed. By this time 12 Platoon had opened up with everything they had – machine guns, the lot. In my excited state I fired the Piat. The shell headed straight for the car but to my anger it fell short and never even exploded. I cussed. By this time the car was shunting back and forth in the narrow road to get away. I had no time to reload my Piat so I banged away with my rifle. The car must have been built like a tank to withstand all the firing we had banged into it. Some fool fired a two inch mortar smoke bomb to add to the confusion. The car drove away to everyone's surprise and I often wonder whether we did kill any of those high ranking officers.

I remember two re-inforcements that had come up before Lebisey – I never even had time to know their names. A corporal had both his feet blown off. I remember our Company Commander, Cooper-Key, talking to him. The Corporal said, 'I am sorry Sir, I won't be able to go with you to Berlin.' That night my mate and I had been sent back through the woods, which were full of shell-holes, stumbling and falling all over the place, cursing and swearing, to get a large can of tea and rations. On the way back, which was about twenty minutes, the jerries decided to shell and mortar the woods – bombs from multiple barrel mortars. As they fell screaming all around us I could feel the blast tearing at my uniform as I tried to bury my head in the dirt. I remember praying that night 'Oh God, get me out of this hell.' The tea and half of the rations had gone but I had survived another day. We managed to get back to our slit trenches and the next few days were just a blur.

Only about five of the lads of B Company who landed on D-Day were to reach Berlin. My mate Jack was wounded at Perrier Ridge; he was carried away from the stench and hell of war to the quiet green fields of England and I didn't meet him again for forty years. That day we had double rations as we had lost so many of the lads.

Lieutenant J.C. Squire, 7 Platoon, A Company, remembers a great personality in the battalion.

An incident involving Bandy Howard, our beloved Quartermaster. As a grizzled regular he was not too well disposed towards temporary officers particularly Second Lieutenants. I had a very bad habit of dropping off to sleep in 'O' Groups – not for long of course and I usually waited until important matters such as enemy locations had been dealt with.

On one occasion I had catnapped as usual in the section dealing with admin. – I returned to the platoon and gave them an up-to-date report on the situation. Three hours later an irate messenger arrived from HQ. 'Where was I?' he said.

Apparently I had missed the order regarding the rum ration. Bandy Howard had been waiting for 30 minutes at a particular crossroads which was the pick-up point and which the Germans had decided to shell. Although unhurt he was very, very cross and his opinion of temporary officers was reinforced.

I was wounded soon after so I never saw him again and was unable to apologise – which I have always regretted. I also had to explain matters to my platoon and their feelings on being deprived of their rum ration can be imagined.

Not the sort of stuff to stir the soul but then, in those days, the humdrum and the heroic were side by side.

Lieutenant Norman Brunning returned from brigade to join A Company, which was at low ebb having lost all D-Day officers with the sole exception of Lieutenant John Squire. Reflecting on those days, he writes:

For most of us it was our first experience of battle, and possible death; the fear of being blown to pieces – and yet the feeling 'it can't happen to me' – in spite of the briefing beforehand, 75 per cent casualties, 50 per cent dead, which of course did not happen near the beaches. And underlying it all the idea that we could not fail, that success would come in the end. During that period we learned a spirit of comradeship, all of us depending on each other.

On 24 June I returned to the Battalion, John Piccaver and Geoff Probyn had just arrived as reinforcements. I was greeted by Sgt. Cutting who was proud to tell me that he had a full platoon, half of them reinforcements, mainly tradesmen from the Wiltshires, who had to be taught all the infantry weapons; some had never thrown a grenade (after 3 or 4 years' service) or handled anything other than a rifle.

We operated under Double British Summer Time and 'Stood-to' an hour before dark and again an hour before daylight. This meant that we had to be wide awake from 2230 to 2330 hours and from 0430 to 0530 hours, so by the time we had settled down, no-one had more than 4½ hours sleep from 6 June to 9 July when we withdrew to Blainville. We were not allowed to sleep during the daytime unless we had been out on patrol at night.

On the afternoon after a mine hunting expedition I managed to get my head down for a couple of hours and afterwards was greeted by a L/Cpl., 'Nice bout of shelling, Sir!' In explanation of his remark he said a couple of dozen shells had landed in my platoon area, 'shaking up' one or two men, but causing no casualties. The only damage was holes in a steel helmet on top of the slit trench. And I had slept soundly all through it!

Geoffrey Duncan continues the story:

One thing that really got us muttering was the transport hazard, just to our rear ran a road, or more like a dusty track, made by the wear and tear of countless trucks bringing up supplies from the stores stacked up on the beaches. There was very little cover along their route so naturally it was foot down and let's get out of here, but in so doing they threw up clouds of dust which were of course an open invitation to the enemy guns to have a go – which they promptly did and more often than not we got it in the neck from the shells that fell short. Some one must have created a stink and it wasn't long before the Military Police were putting up large signs with the words 'Drive Slowly – Dust Means Death'; we could sympathise with the MPs on traffic control especially those on duty at cross roads – these were favourite targets for the enemy guns.

One bright spot was the news that a mobile bath unit was laid on some distance to our rear, with soap and towel we made our way to the baths a Platoon at a time, I am certain it was the most enjoyable bath I ever had and the first one since before D-Day.

It was some considerable time since we had had a normal diet – it was mainly hard biscuits, a bar of plain chocolate, a few boiled sweets and five cigarettes plus Compo rations if the trucks could get up to our positions, the cooks did a good job under the worst conditions, but with no bread or fruit (fresh or otherwise) it wasn't long before we were suffering severe constipation!

The constant patrols were not without incident and caused a number of casualties, thirteen fatal between 8 June and 7 July including Lieutenant J.F.J. (John) Williams on 11 June, Major F. Fitch MC on the 19th and Captain M.R. Fearon on the 24th.

Nevil Griffin mentions an aspect of war which the fighting soldier can never forget:

I remember the awful carnage among the animals during the first two or three months of our assault. I don't think I shall ever forget the sight of horses and cows bloated and putrifying but having to be left because of enemy pressure. I also remember the awful stench which developed in the heat of that summer as a result of the carnage.

Lieutenant S.A. Kemsley was one of four Canadian officers seconded to the 1st Battalion The Royal Norfolk Regiment under a scheme known as CANLOAN – he had joined the battalion in April 1944 and landed in Normandy early on 8 June with those men held in reserve from the initial assault, nominated as first reinforcements to offset casualties sustained during the landings, joining the battalion on the 9th.

All of the time (1 month) that I was with 15 platoon, C Coy under Major Smith we were taken up with recce patrols, usually three men, always at night of course and mainly in a factory area to the east of our positions towards Colombelles. There was a very tall brick smoke stack and Jerry was using it as an OP so we had to check on them. Three of these 3-man recce patrols I'll never forget.

The first was when we were over in the factory area – the three of us had soft-soled shoes because of debris and fallen wires etc. so if we touched them we would not make too much noise. We heard a metallic

CSM J. Brown and Pte. Le Pelley.

sound of metal to metal so we hit the ground in the shadow of a building and a fighting patrol of twelve or fifteen Jerry marched by all carrying their famous fast firing automatic rifles – well we let them go past as we were supposed to report back and I don't think we would have made it if we had started anything with our little Stens. The IO was glad to get the report anyway.

The second patrol was to another area in front of our positions and the three of us were going along in a shallow ditch beside a hedgerow when all of a sudden a Jerry stick grenade landed beside me and I reacted instantly, picked it up and threw it back over the hedge where it exploded – there were cries and curses which we couldn't understand but we didn't hang around to find out either.

The third patrol, we were working our way across an open space with full moon when suddenly MGs cut loose so we hit the ground and the only shelter in the field were dead bloated cattle – I well remember the bullets thudding into the dead cow and the stench that came out. The MGs must have been on a tripod firing on fixed lines as they sprayed the area then moved away so we crawled into the shadow of a hedgerow. That smell I'll never forget. In a month of patrols 15 platoon never had a casualty on recce patrol which I for one was thankful for.

One day a message came around telling us to stay in our slits at a certain time that night as HMS *Rodney* in the English Channel was going to have a go at knocking down the tall smokestack in the Colombelles factory. When those 16 inch shells went overhead it sounded like being in London Underground when a train went through without stopping. In the morning the chimney was still there – HMS *Rodney* had missed its target and the stack was still standing on 8 July when we started the push on Caen.

I only made it halfway through Lebisey Wood when I had shrapnel through my helmet into my skull bone and another chunk through my neck missing my jugular vein by ¼ inch and knocking me out. The next thing I remember was a doctor working on me in a tent telling me how lucky I was.

Sydney Kemsley describes himself as a Canadian with an English heart as his mother was born and raised in Wateringbury near Maidstone, Kent, while his father came from Swanley, nearer London. He says, 'I really enjoyed serving in the British Army and made some good friends.'

On the night of 23/4 June 1944 a recce was carried out by Captain M.R. Fearon and Colour Sergeant N.A. Thorne of the forward slopes of Lebisey Wood. After completing their task both were wounded and Captain Fearon, hit in the side and unable to move, ordered Colour Sergeant Thorne, wounded in the arm and foot, to return with the information required. Colour Sergeant Thorne, unable to carry Captain Fearon, moved some distance away but waited until he could see that Captain Fearon had been taken care of by the enemy. Only then, in considerable pain, did he return with the information. Captain Fearon unfortunately died of his wounds while a prisoner-of-war later that same day.

On 25 June American troops reached the outskirts of Cherbourg which Hitler had ordered to be held and although the German commander sought approval from his superior for surrender it was not allowed. By the 29th, however, all resistance in the Cherbourg area had ceased.

V1 attacks on south-east England continued – the Prime Minister told the House of Commons on 6 July that, to date, 2,754 people had been killed by flying bombs. On 7 July British bombers dropped 2,500 tons of bombs on Caen, two days later German forces began to withdraw into Caen.

In the early hours of 8 July the battalion formed up for a dawn attack on Lebisey. The previous evening a force of 450 bombers had attacked Caen, literally darkening the sky with smoke and dust and this softening up was followed by a considerable artillery barrage under which the advance was made. The route party, led by the Intelligence Officer, Captain T.J. Harrison, left at 00.01 hours, responsible for reconnaissance and marking the path to be taken, the FUP and start line. The battalion commenced to move at 02.30 hours – H-Hour was 04.30.

Major John Piccaver remembers advancing through the clouds of dust and smoke which drifted from the city:

For the second attack on Lebisey Wood on July 8th A Company was to establish a safe area for Advance Battalion Headquarters in the 'GAP', this being a stage in the second battle for Caen. Having reached our

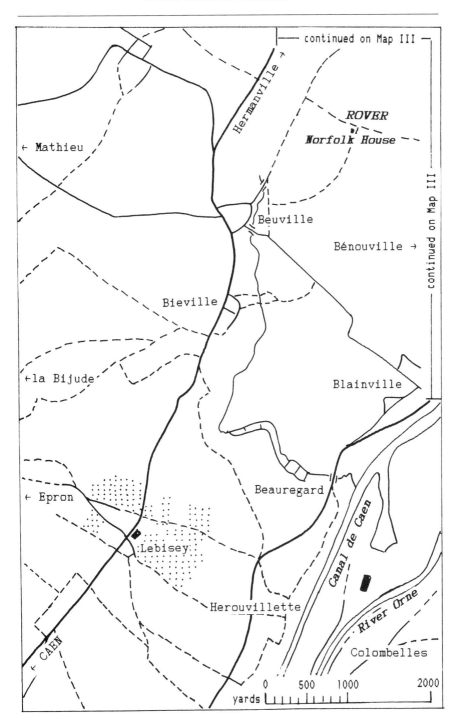

Map IV: Beuville to Lebisey.

starting point the Company was instructed to lie very low in the longish grass until the appointed time for the advance. The CO called me to go forward with him on a recce with a small party to our forward position – however to my horror we seemed to be getting ever closer to the German position and mortar bombs started to come down. The CO was anything but pleased and kept asking me where A Company was?

He had just about decided to call Hubert Holden's D Company forward (who were in reserve) when I tripped over a body lying in the grass. 'Who are you?' I asked, 'A Company, Sir,' was the prompt reply. I think I said 'Bless you' and told the CO we were in A Company lines. We then retired to our appointed places – Phew! (You could always rely on a Norfolk Soldier to do what he was told and in this case it was to lie low and they did.)

Norman Brunning gives some idea of the weight of artillery fire in this attack:

July 8th brought the second attack on Lebisey Wood. Having been leading company in the march from D-Day, A Company brought up the rear. I was horrified to see shells from our own artillery landing well short of the target, and although I tried frantically to do something about it over the radio, I failed, and I am certain that the gun firing short caused a number of casualties in the Battalion, some in my platoon, and also Geoff Probyn.

The 'stonk' on Lebisey Wood is worth a mention; 10 minutes 'normal' each hour from Corps Artillery, cruisers and destroyers, beginning at 2230 hrs. At 0430 hrs until 0520 hrs the guns fired 'rapid', but at 0520 hrs until 0530 they fired as fast as possible, and then lifted to help B Company through the wood and the rest of us to our allotted positions.

The battle did not last long. All resistance was knocked out of the Germans by the heavy bombardment that preceded the attack. We dug in straight away, and at about 9.30 a.m. the order came through to clear the area of all dead. One German did not revive until 10 a.m.! 'Bang! Bang! too much!' was his statement as he was escorted away.

The heavy reek of death lingered everywhere; and not only of cattle. I identified several men of C Company, including Jimmy Campbell, and also of the Warwicks who had been killed in the first attack. The bodies had been left in front of the German slit trenches to battle harden the Germans. In spite of the heavy bombardment by the Navy (Warspite and Arethusa), cruisers and destroyers and Corps Artillery from time to time, I counted less than 20 graves at the eastern end of the wood.

Lieutenant 'Egg' Williams:

Night of 7/8 July. 18 Pln standing patrol on stream crossing for Bn. Dennis Bell to come up track from East. Sound of motorbike engine –

fingers on triggers – Anglo-Saxon Norfolk expletives. Dennis had hit trip-wires.

Final advance through Lebisey – never expected! 18 Pln sent out miles towards Caen. 2 MG42 teams came in with hands up. Captured a dug-in tank – looted the tins of Jerry stew, but (mea culpa) never thought of destroying tank – thank heaven there was no counter attack! Shot up Jerry patrol and killed officer with grenade. Poor old bugger, some wounded. Only casualty young Brown.

We then retired to an open arable field to dig in and were shelled all evening losing several men. A shell landed on my parapet and L/Sgt. Driscoll and I were knocked out. When I came to my legs were wet and warm and I thought that I had lost them – but it was only the hot tea we had been brewing!

'Egg' Williams' commented after writing his memories: 'To date this has cost me ½ bottle Mr Jamieson's very fine Whiskey and the smell of the horse that I dug my trench over at Manneville Wood puts me off writing any more!'

Dennis Bell gives more detail of the motor-bike mishap described in the previous account:

The night of July 7/8 found the Battalion following the 'white tapes' to the forming up area for the push against Lebisey. Once again DFB was sticking his neck out. I was to join up with Battalion HQ on a motor bike, would you believe? I could not follow the tapes – some difficulty about getting the bike over the stream – so I was to proceed from Blainville towards Beauregard, on my own, in the dark and through areas where Jerry was known to have been active.

I turned off the road, up the track, through the farmyard, chugging merrily along and was just passing the end of the barn, going out into the field where I was expecting to be met by one of the companies when all at once the bike stopped dead, a single strand of fencing wire had been run across the track from the end of the barn to a stake in the hedge opposite. Thank God it was low and slack otherwise it would have decapitated me; it struck just above the wheel and below the headlamp. I flew over the handlebars landing in a bed of nettles and giving vent to my feelings in no uncertain manner – there was no way anyone could have mistaken me for a Jerry, but never-the-less, I was pleased to hear someone call out, 'For —— sake don't shoot, I forgot to tell you that "Dingy" would be joining us from that direction.'

Later in the morning I was approaching Lebisey, by the track leading up from the Beauregard road to the left hand front corner of the wood, when I experienced a little friendly bombing by two of our own planes – they had obviously mistaken me for the Hun. On reaching the wood, looking for an elusive carrier section, I heard a noise and looking round I saw a Spandau, sticking out from under an overhanging bush, which was closely following my every movement – I was beginning to feel in need of another pair of pants when I heard Bill Brown's (then Sgt., later RSM) chuckle. His section had overrun this position and were taking an interest in the enemy's weapons when they saw me coming and thought it too good an opportunity to miss in which to right some old wrongs.

Geoffrey Duncan:

. . . the barrage was lifted to enable us to enter the wood and root out the defenders, we had only gone a few yards when we found ourselves on the wrong end of a German counter barrage of mortars and field artillery which was firing air burst shells, the red hot shrapnel sprayed down on us – there was no way of escaping this type of shelling even if you were in a trench, all you could do was hug the ground and wait for the barrage to lift – if there is such a place as Hell we were there. Lying face down in a depression I was whispering my prayers when I received a terrific blow on the back of my legs which went completely dead – my first reaction was; my legs had gone! Sliding my hands down the back of my thighs I felt my knees and a little below and, Praise be to God, my legs were still intact, can you imagine my intense relief to know I was still in one piece? The barrage still continued in all its fury; the overriding thought in my mind at that time was, I had been wounded but I was still there – if the barrage continued and I got hit again would my luck run out?

After what seemed a lifetime the shelling lifted and I crawled back past several lads who would not see family and friends again to the edge of the wood. Managing to crawl to one of the enemy trenches I dropped in, thankful they didn't dig theirs as deep as I did and what a fright I got when I realised I was sharing my refuge with a dead German, he had a small wound at the side of his temple but otherwise he was unmarked. Looking at him I saw he was just a young lad, but what did that make me, an old man of nineteen, I guessed it was a case of 'There but for the grace of God go I'.

Shortly afterwards and to my relief I spotted a team of stretcher bearers coming up the hill – were they a sight for sore eyes! After some yelling they spotted me and ran over, lifted me out of the trench and proceeded to cut my trouser legs off from thigh to gaiter, what a way to get a new pair of trousers! Dressing my wounds they bandaged me with field dressings then it was on the stretcher and back down the hill to the Regimental Aid Post – although there was still plenty of gunfire going on their only concern was getting the wounded back safely for treatment.

Geoffrey Duncan's account voices his admiration and thanks to all medical staff and his gratitude for their care and attention. Eventually he was loaded aboard a Dakota for evacuation to England and, after hospitalization and a spell of convalescence he was back with the battalion and rejoined 10 Platoon, B Company:

What a shock it was to find only one of the original platoon had survived, the others were either wounded or killed in action, it was a most traumatic experience – I can picture them now, young lads full of fun, on the threshold of life, we had shared the good times and the bad, passed round the last cigarettes, borrowed each others' kit for guard duty; to name but a few. I salute them all and consider myself privileged to have served with them, for that kind of comradeship you never find again in civilian life.

In this action the battalion suffered 116 casualties including 25 killed. POWs totalled around 75, enemy casualties were estimated at 40 to 50. Major D.W. Smith, in command of C Company, the left forward company, was wounded but continued to lead his company for which action he was later awarded the Military Cross.

Lieutenant 'Bobbie' Parfitt, Anti-tank Platoon, so badly wounded that he was thought dead, recalls what, for him, was almost the final journey:

After severe wounds and a brave rescue by Sgt. Savage my evacuation from Lebisey Wood began. Firstly to the Battalion First Aid point, then onwards strapped to the roof of a jeep. My companion was a young German lieutenant (in civilian life a music student from Heidelberg) who had lost both feet through stepping on a mine.

Finally the Base Field Hospital near an airfield was reached. By this time I was drifting into unconsciousness: up to this point I had remained just awake, despite a massive loss of blood and pain-killing injections.

At the Field Hospital I remember very little of what was happening. However, at dawn the next morning I recollect being surrounded by what seemed to be a 'white haze'; trying to twitch the stiff fingers of my left hand (my right being strapped across my chest because of bleeding) attracted the alert attention of a Queen Alexandra Nursing Sister going off duty from the Night Shift. She hastened over to my stretcher. I was unable to speak as my lips were sealed with dried blood – she managed to moisten my lips with some grapes she was carrying, enabling me to greet her!

Very soon afterwards two shocked medical orderlies moved me into what we would now term Intensive Care. My fellow wounded seemed surprised and shocked, one bravely telling me I had come from the Mortuary Dept! After further specialist attention I was allotted a space on a plane, with attendant nurse and oxygen tube for the flight to the UK for urgent surgery.

Some are born lucky!

The close contact which existed between the gunners and the battalion is highlighted by Captain John Talbot MC who, after his Battery Commander,

Major R.H. Dunn MC, was wounded in the attack at Lebisey, commanded 16 Field Battery RA until the division reached Holland:

> On the final assault on Caen on 8 July I was the FOO in my Sherman tank (it had a wooden gun! – to accomodate an extra wireless set!) with the Staffordshire Yeomanry in a sweep east of Lebisey Wood. After being bombed by some American aircraft we rounded the wood just as the first Norfolks emerged from the south edge of the wood and moved on to the high ground overlooking Caen itself.

On 9 July 9 Brigade with 33rd Armoured Brigade entered Caen. The battalion was pulled out of the line on 11 July and given four days' rest at Blainville, the first since landing. For the past month they had been living rough, existing on 'compo' rations. The first bread since D-Day appeared on 12 July – sixteen men to one loaf – previously everyone had been living on biscuits! News was received on the 16th that Captain R.C. Wilson had been awarded the Military Cross and Sergeant C. Parker the Military Medal.

After completing a course at the School of Infantry at Barnard Castle in mid-May 1944, Lieutenant D.B. Balsom, known to all, inevitably, as 'Friar', found that he could not rejoin his unit because it had moved into a sealed camp prior to Operation Overlord and, instead, was ordered to take charge of the first reinforcements for the 4th Battalion The Welch Regiment in 53rd Division. He landed at Gold Beach and marched to an RHU south-east of Bayeux. The unit he was intended to join had no need of reinforcements and he was asked if he would transfer to a unit which did. He agreed and so joined 1st Norfolk:

> I took over a platoon of C Company at Blainville-sur-Orne in mid-July. Fortunately after Lebisey the period was quieter and I had a chance to get to know my platoon and they to know me.
>
> 14 July saw the Battalion moved to the left of the British front prior to Operation Goodwood and the attack towards Sannerville and Troarn. We moved via 'Pegasus Bridge' across the Orne and its canal and through Ranville, where the huge gliders used by 6th Airborne still rested where they had landed.
>
> We took over the line in front of Ranville near Herouvillette. We also held the little village of Escoville – a salient in front of the main battle position. Two platoons held Escoville at a time, but as the approaches were in full view of the enemy, it had to be approached in the dark. Mine was one of two platoons of C Company to hold Escoville on 16/17 July – shelling and mortaring were frequent and any signs of movement brought on heavy fire.
>
> Fortunately platoon HQ had a good trench, the centre of which the previous occupant (from 51st Div.) had covered with a heavy steel sheet. It somehow gave a feeling of security. There was however one drawback. In the village much of the livestock that had not been killed wandered loose. When the shelling became particularly heavy, a smelly billy goat

took cover in the trench. Have you ever tried to push backwards a stubborn billy goat? One had to brave the shelling, get out and push from the back. It never occurred to anyone to shoot it. It took its chance with the rest. The same thought must have occurred to the soldiers who previously had gone around all the rabbit hutches and let them all out – all precious domesticated breeds. It was a little incongruous to see, hopping around what was left of the gardens, rabbits of all hues – blue, white, beige and a variety of spotted specimens.

In the period to the end of June 1944 the total number of battle casualties suffered by the 3rd British Infantry Division was 3,508, approximately one seventh of the total battle casualties of 2nd British Army which by that time comprised the equivalent of almost twenty divisions. This high proportion of 2nd Army losses gives a very clear indication of the strength of the opposition against the division and the severity of its tasks. The majority of those casualties were suffered by the infantry battalions.

The major problem facing the Allies was that of supply for while the assaulting troops were self-sufficient at the time of landing they could not remain so for long. All troops, equipment and supplies had to be brought across the Channel, the convoys relatively safe from air attack, for the Luftwaffe was rarely seen, but subject to E-boat and U-boat attack and threatened by mines which alone accounted for the loss of twenty-one ships in the first ten days.

Preparations had been made since 1942 for the assembly of artificial harbours from blockships, concrete caissons and floating roadways, towed across the Channel to form permanent harbours off Arromanches and Omaha Beach. These were codenamed Mulberry and the first units arrived off the coast on D+1. The major requirement for each Mulberry harbour was to construct a breakwater of immense concrete boxes, manufactured in Britain, each 200 ft long, 60 ft high, each weighing over 6,000 tons, manoeuvred into position and sunk to provide shelter.

To ensure fast unloading, floating roadways and pierheads were also built and towed across. The harbours were operating from 15 June, and for the first four days more than thirty thousand troops and 25,000 tons of supplies were brought in daily. On 19 June, however, the wind increased and a full gale blew for three days, creating havoc in the harbours and reducing the landing of troops and supplies to one third. The Mulberry harbour at Vierville, intended for use by the American forces, was completely wrecked. This set-back left the Americans with only three days' supply of ammunition and the British short of three divisions. By this time Hitler had been persuaded by his generals that there would not be a second landing and began to concentrate a greater proportion of his reserves against the Allied forces.

By the end of June eight hundred and seventy-five thousand men had landed in Normandy, sixteen divisions each for the American and British armies.

CHAPTER FOUR

Break-out

After the brief rest at Blainville the battalion moved to Ranville and Escoville on the left flank of the bridgehead previously occupied by 6th Airborne Division and 51st (Highland) Division, returning to shelling and mortaring by day and night. The *Battalion History* records that 'At Ranville we made our HQ for three days, with a company detachment at a really horrible place called Escoville. This place was shelled and mortared regularly day and night, and was the local centre of patrol activity. It reeked of death.' Operation Goodwood started on 18 July, aimed at breaking out on the left of the front, again with hundreds of bombers 'softening up', this time at dawn. That evening at 2100 hours 1st Norfolk attacked the given target, Manneville Wood, but was not able to secure it before dark and found, at dawn, that the enemy had retreated during the night. Major H.M. Wilson MC takes up the story again:

Eventually that evening we were told to attack and occupy an orchard area known as Manneville Wood. Hubert [Major H.R. Holden] went off first with D Company and got right up to a high wall beyond which the enemy were still active. After further treatment the enemy decided to pull out, which was just as well for all concerned, leaving us in occupation on a sticky flank of the main armoured thrust. Next day we found we were occupying a well stocked racing stable with some horses still boxed up and of course beside themselves with fear. Here we became the target for regular shelling and mortaring which went on at all hours. It also rained hard and long turning our slit trenches and the Command Post into a complete bog. It was a particularly trying time for all and it was only the Battalion's sense of humour combined with good discipline that we got through this bad patch.

After several weeks of constant exposure to shelling and mortaring the first few cases of battle exhaustion were experienced but, as CSM Catlin MM points out, 'with straight talking we were able to overcome the problem.' The *Battalion History* records dangers often unreported:

Everyone had a narrow shave somewhere: the CO was having an afternoon nap when a shell landed three feet from his slit; one of the Intelligence section was buried by a direct hit and had to be dug out,

Company HQ, Manneville Wood, July 1944.

fortunately only knocked out or stunned by blast. The one-time orchard was reduced to a mass of broken trees – in fact the hand of war had passed over this one-time lovely spot and left its usual devastation.

Lieutenant Ken Wilson, one of four Canadian officers seconded to the battalion, remembers clearly 'how wonderful it was to get an hour or two of sleep. It seemed that patrols, stand-to and 'O' groups were interminable with very little provision for shut eye.' Wounded in Normandy and after his return again wounded in Germany, he recollects:

> After about six weeks in Normandy I believe that John Squire and I were the only remaining of the original platoon commanders. Then one night near Manneville Wood we were both wounded. We were both on stretchers on a jeep being evacuated and we agreed that at last we may be able to get some sleep. Lots of sleep I got, interrupted every three hours by a nurse with a very large needle of penicillin.
> The same thing happened the second time around when a sniper pipped me at Brinkum.

All who were wounded echo his feelings with regard to the necessary but tiresome course of injections which continued for five days, day and night.

Dennis Bell was on loan from the Carrier Platoon and back in A Company, as second-in-command, for the big break-out in mid-July:

The one thing, above all else, to stick in one's mind about that day, must be the massive raid by the combined Allied bomber forces – thousands of them – wave after wave. At first it seemed impossible that bomb loads could be released so far behind us over the Channel, so it appeared, pass over our heads and still land a long way out in front, on target.

Being in support it was a question of 'follow my leader' through the plains of standing wheat, of being shelled and stonked from both sides, meeting John Piccaver coming back on a Jeep, informing me that he had been hit in the chest and that I had better get up front as it was *now all mine.*

July 19th found us inside the orchards at Manneville, digging in. We were constantly shelled and stonked for hours on end, the effect of which, together with the huge craters left by carpet bombing, the broken and mangled trees etc, left the orchard looking like a scene from World War One. There was one particularly nasty bit of armament that regularly pumped its massive shells in. It was one of these that landed a bit too close. I vaguely remember being pulled out of the slit trench, taken to the medics in the kitchen of the big house, evacuated to field hospital and, in spite of protestations to the contrary, being flown out to Lyneham in a Dakota.

Throughout the accounts in this book run two very strong themes: first, the numerous narrow, almost miraculous escapes from instant death experienced by many and secondly, the care and compassion of one man for another. Sergeant Ted Carr gives some idea of the responsibilities of a platoon sergeant and, in so doing, contrary perhaps to the popular image of a sergeant-major, shows the concern of a CSM for his men:

End of July I was sent, in charge of my platoon plus 2 or 3 signallers, to Ranville to guard the bridge over the River Orne. As I had no other senior NCO with me, I felt I could leave no one else in sole charge, so had little or no sleep for 9 days.

The day I was relieved and back at the unit, the CSM came up immediately, and said I was to collect ammo. at 1500 ready to move later in the day towards Caen. I said I was tired and would get a few hours sleep. This was about 1000. I got down on my ground-sheet. The next thing I knew was the CSM waking me up. I thought he wanted me to collect the ammo. He said it was 1700 and to get the platoon ready to move. I had slept solidly and did not hear anything – not even the Bren carriers moving close by. When it was time to collect the ammo. the CSM had apparently said, 'Let him sleep'.

On about the 4th August I was called to a CO's briefing which was about 100 yds from the roadside where we were dug in. While there, one of our own unexploded shells went off just over the hedge from where our platoon was dug in. One private was killed by the blast. Maybe I had a lucky escape.

Frank Staples mentions the humorous side of a constant problem which never finds its way into history books:

The Battalion had been stuck in Manneville Wood for some days under what seemed to be permanent shell and mortar fire. I was with Carriers at the time and one afternoon, during a particularly heavy bout of shelling, I felt the 'call of nature', in fact nature did not 'call' as such, more like a sergeant-major's yell.

When it subsided a little I spoke to Corporal 'Stud' Baker, who was my carrier commander, about the possibility of going somewhere to relieve myself and he agreed that I could.

I left the slit trench and in a crouching run I found a large shell crater and, remembering my father, who fought in the First World War, telling me that shells never land in the same place twice, I decided this was the place for me. Halfway through answering the call of nature, with my trousers round my ankles, the shelling recommenced with more fury than ever and shells were dropping very close to my 'toilet'.

I instinctively dug my head into the side of the hole, and terror must have given me extra strength because I pushed so hard that the rim of my tin hat got stuck in the earth and I had to get my knife and cut the chin strap to release my head.

To this day I have a mental picture of myself with a white posterior stuck up in the air and my head stuck in the ground; not funny at the time but if the German gunners could have seen me in that position they may have got the message, 'Blank, blank to you!'

On 20 July Hitler survived an attempt on his life when a bomb, left by a German officer in a conference room, exploded killing four but not harming Hitler, who was protected by the table under which the bomb had been placed. The conspirators, believing him dead, attempted to take control, but without success, and were quickly arrested and killed.

Operation Cobra was launched by the Americans on 25 July to break out of the Cherbourg peninsula following the British and Canadian assault against heavy opposition into and beyond Caen.

The battalion moved from Manneville Wood to Cazelle on 25 July; before leaving the position the RAP received a direct hit wounding the MO, killing one stretcher-bearer and wounding two more. The *Battalion War Diary* records the beginning of the next, most important, phase; the movement forward from the bridgehead which ended with the encirclement of many thousands of enemy troops in what came to be known as the 'Falaise Gap':

2.8.44 Move with Brigade group to new area N. of Caumont to come under command 15 Scottish Division. All preparations made to take over from 9 Cameronians.

3.8.44 Moved almost as per plan, but orders changed once more. Under command 11th Armoured Division as an extra Infantry Brigade. Very little happened today as far as we were concerned. After many changes we finally settled down into a position for the night prepared for what may come in the morning, just S. of le Reculey.

4.8.44 Change of plan again to-day. Battalion attack on la Chapelle to push out enemy who had been infiltrating north through forward positions of 11 Armd. Div. Attack went fairly well, D Coy. badly messed about by 4 tanks. Finally consolidated the position but had to draw in our horns a bit so that medium artillery could shoot at la Bistière, tomorrow's objective. Weather excellent.

Names given to places where actions were fought are occasionally found to be incorrect; in this instance the action was at la Chapelle aux Huants but it has always been described as la Bistière. Similarly the battle known as Sourdevalle, which followed, was located at Pavée.
Battalion History:

The next day we attempted the attack on la Bistière, a small hamlet south west of le Reculey. Reports had stated that there was no armour there, others said there was some, so it was difficult to lay on an attack which would hit the enemy and not the air, and not to be hit by the enemy before we were ready. It virtually amounted to an advance to contact. That day, 4 August, was spent jockeying for a position with a limited attack by A and D companies, which unfortunately cost some casualties in dead and wounded.

Lieutenant E.A. Gray, commanding the Anti-tank Platoon, S Company, has clear recall of la Bistière:

The Battalion was soon sent into action against the hamlet of la Bistière buried deep in the Normandy Bocage, an area of great beauty made up of a patchwork of tiny, bank-enclosed fields, coppices and orchards, criss-crossed by little lanes and sunken tracks, which were arched by tall hedges and overhanging trees. Everywhere was lush and green and the countryside was bathed in a blaze of sunshine throughout most of July and August.

La Bistière straddled the Estry–Vire road and was held by a small pocket of enemy supported by a light tank. There I did my first reconnaissance patrol in a Bren carrier to discover whether part of the proposed start-line for the assault on the village was occupied. During the early afternoon a two-company attack, without artillery support, was put in on the village; but it failed due to the presence of the tank, and one of the companies was badly mauled. A little later the CO ordered me forward to see whether anything could be done about the vehicle which was preventing the advance by firing its machine-guns at any movement. I set off with a corporal (Coburn) and one of my lads and proceeded by a sunken lane to the forward companies' areas, immediately facing the hamlet. At the entrance to the lane stood a Daimler armoured car with its engine still ticking over. It seemed to have been abandoned and was undamaged.

Further along the lane, the body of a newly-dead German soldier, shot in the chest, lay in our path. Some yards further on, as we emerged from the lane into a field, we were fired on as we crossed a gap in a hedge near the forward company positions. A riflemen on the opposite side grinned at our dismay and said the fire had come from a small cottage about fifty yards away. Coburn cursed him solidly for failing to warn us, as he had seen our approach.

Both hamlet and tank were almost entirely obscured by the thick and enveloping foliage of the surrounding hedges and trees. We had fleeting glimpses of the vehicle as it trundled slowly back and forth on the road just beyond. However, it was clear that no action could be taken to render it harmless, as the banks against which the men of the forward companies were pinned-down were far too high to get the muzzle of a 6-pounder over the tops, and there was no chance of digging through the solid mass of roots supporting the hedges.

On our return to Battalion HQ by a different route, we passed a number of Norfolk dead, some of the casualties of the earlier abortive attack on the hamlet. I found my companions of Platoon HQ in the orchard nearby. The Platoon Sergeant ('Bidi' Holmes) had things well organised: the carrier was camouflage-netted and drawn into a nearby hedge and a couple of slits had been dug. More important, the petrol-cooker was hissing, and I was soon handed a very welcome mug of strong, sweet tea.

Private W.H. Holden, Anti-tank Platoon, S Company, who has been back to Normandy on a number of occasions and was largely responsible for the 1st and 7th Battalion memorials which have been erected there in recent years, here recounts his memories of the action named as la Bistière:

We were waiting on a track not far from the village of le Reculey, our section sergeant, Sgt. Bert Burling, had been asked to help to recover an anti-tank gun, not far away, in a position being fired upon by a very well concealed tank, believed to be a Tiger. He went down to the position, talked to the men and suggested that they rush down to the gun, close the trailer legs, hook it on the carrier and away in one mad rush.

At Bert's command they did this but on reaching the gun they received a direct hit from HE. They were all wounded except Cpl. Goward who was in charge, Pte. Green lost his leg from the hip. We were sitting on the Bren carrier, with our gun, waiting for Bert to return and eventually he came down the track towards us – he had a field dressing round his head and blood had run down his face from his forehead into his eyes and on to his tunic. He was limping very badly and I think he had one or two small wounds in his arms. As he got near the carrier he gave a big broad grin and said, 'Hello lads, I've got a Blighty, could I have my small pack and my walking stick?' Bert always had a walking stick.

We found his small pack, gave him his walking stick, he wished us all the very best, and said, 'I'll be back, I'll see you later' and he hobbled off down the track. Three weeks later we heard that Sgt. Burling, our section sergeant, was dead. He had died at sea. The hospital ship on which he was travelling either hit a mine or was torpedoed, nobody knows which – his name is on the memorial at Bayeux.

L/Cpl. Jack 'Tubby' Pratt then took charge of our gun team – we had been ordered to support D Company and Jack ordered me to drive down the track so we could catch up with D Company. I went down the track, turned left on to a lane, then into a gateway on the right of the road opposite a farmhouse. The meadow beyond was narrow at the gate but widened to our left at the bottom, shaped like a rough triangle – I drove across the meadow, towards the thick hedgerow. Further down the hedgerow I saw a soldier, laying on the ground with a gas cape over him. Reaching the soldier we stopped and spoke to one or two of D Company and overhead it just seemed like thousands and thousands of crickets chirping – they explained it was from machine gun fire, the noise was uncanny, firing from our right, the fire coming across from the corner of the meadow. They said that there had been, previously, a German armoured car down the road, machine gunning the meadow, and we decided to move further to see if we could get a crack at it. Tubby and I went to move the soldier's body, I lifted the gas cape and I had a great shock. The soldier was a sergeant, Herbert Wilson, nicknamed 'Tug'. His home was only a hundred yards from my home in Norwich – I had been to school with one of his younger brothers. Sgt. Wilson was a regular soldier and had served in India, I knew him very well as we had spent three leaves together in England.

We lifted him to one side and I could see no mark on him, no blood, anything, whether he had been hit in the back I have no idea but I placed the gas cape on him again and drove down the meadow. We had not gone very far when some of the D Company lads stopped us and advised us not to go any further as the machine gunning in the corner of the field was horrendous and they'd had quite a number of casualties.

We started digging slit trenches, the ground was extremely hard, and we'd only just got the top grass off, no more than about two or three inches of soil, when a Cromwell tank drove into the same gateway as I had, straight across the meadow to the rear of us, poked his barrel through the hedgerow and immediately we were very heavily mortared.

We carried on digging our slit trenches again when all of a sudden I heard Jack shout and saw him start running towards the centre of the meadow. I thought 'My God, he's gone dulally [crazy], he's gone!' He was waving his arms, and I saw two old ladies and an old gentleman, who had obviously come out of the farmhouse, crossed the lane, through the gate and into the meadow, running directly towards this ferocious spandau fire. Jack was running to stop them, shouting and waving his arms and I thought, 'I should imagine this is just what he does when he's rounding up the bullocks on his father's farm at Hemsby.' The old people slowed, stopped, then turned, he waved his arms again and they ran back into the farmhouse. Without any doubt he saved their lives.

Bill Holden describes how machine-gun fire and mortaring continued for the rest of the day and that, with the approach of dark, they were ordered to take up position near the farmhouse. There were just the four of them, Lance-Corporal Jack Pratt, Private Howes (nicknamed Bogey), Private White (obviously nicknamed Chalky) and himself. They found that they would have to remain forward, in this isolated position, throughout the night:

We decided that two men should sleep and two men stand-to. We drew lots and paired up for the duties throughout the night, Bogey Howes and Tubby Pratt would be together and Chalky and I would do the first duties. We sat on the trailer legs of the gun and Jack and Bogey went through the hedgerow to lay down.

We sat quiet for some time, it seemed like hours but it was probably only minutes. I'm sure everybody, at some time in their life, has had that feeling that somebody was watching them. I suddenly had this feeling and I knew that somebody was watching me – I could feel the goose-pimples coming up and the hair stand out on the back of my neck. I turned round slowly, very, very slowly, and there, in a little gap in the hedgerow, was a figure dressed all in white. The figure had white hair and was dressed from head to foot in white. I thought, 'My God, boy, you've seen a ghost, you're looking at a ghost!' and I sat staring at this figure for what seemed ages, but must have been at least a minute, when suddenly the figure tiptoed down the bank, across the shingled driveway and into the back door of the farmhouse and I realised it was one of the little old ladies that Jack had turned back in the field that day. Shortly afterwards she came out of the back door with a bundle which looked like blankets, tiptoed across the shingle and disappeared through the hedgerow.

I sat there for some time, Chalky and I didn't speak, we just sat. We'd turn and look at each other now and again, and I was just quietening down, feeling a bit better, when we both heard a footstep on the shingle in front of the house. Chalky and I looked at each other and he pointed to the front of the house, I nodded, he cocked his Sten very, very slowly and I lifted the Bren, which was across my knees as I sat on the trailer of the gun, on to the top of the gunshield, cocked the Bren very, very slowly and took aim on the corner of the house. The footsteps were still coming but they sounded in slow motion as though someone was raising a foot and waiting before they placed it down again – but they still kept coming on. I waited and thought 'The person who puts his head round that corner is going to lose it.' All of a sudden a big white cow poked its head round the house. Chalky and I let out a little sigh.

The battle of la Bistière tends to be overshadowed by that which followed but for those who were involved it was a bitter fight. Major I.A. MacGillivray, commanding A Company, rallied his men when heavily shelled during the approach march and later urged them to their objective. Major H.R. Holden, commanding D Company, also led his company to their objective against spirited opposition from four tanks – both officers were awarded the Military Cross for their leadership in this action. Sergeant C. Hansen, in command of the leading platoon of D Company at this time, was awarded the Military Medal for his outstanding bravery.

Battalion History:

At dawn next morning la Bistière was finally attacked under a proper artillery barrage, but unfortunately the enemy tank which had been the chief source of trouble the previous day had fled in the night, so could not be brought to account. This attack was entirely satisfactory and the position strengthened with an Anti-tank layout. The enemy had had enough at that point in the line.

CHAPTER FIVE

Turning Point

The strategy of the campaign in Normandy was to present the greatest Allied threat on the left of the front in the region of Caen to persuade the enemy to focus the major part of his forces against that threat and, when reserves of troops, equipment and ammunition had built up in the bridgehead, to make a break-out on the right against a lesser concentration of the enemy. This happened as planned, although perhaps not as quickly as some would have wished. However, by the end of July 1944 movement forward had commenced. On 25 July American forces moved forward in Operation Cobra to break-out on the extreme right (west) of the bridgehead, striking for Avranches. On 30 July British 2nd Army commenced Operation Bluecoat from a 10 mile front in the centre of the Allied line in the vicinity of Caumont to drive south towards Vire, some 20 miles distant.

Positioned on the right of the British assault, on the boundary with the American troops, VIII Corps of British 2nd Army, comprising the Guards Armoured Division, 11th Armoured Division, 6th Guards Tank Brigade and 15th (Scottish) Division. By the evening of 31 July American forces had entered Avranches and the British thrust had made progress south, covering about half the distance to Vire by the end of the following day but not without experiencing considerable resistance in places.

The advance of VIII Corps, ordered to push ahead at utmost speed but not to enter Vire as the capture of this town was to be an American responsibility, continued throughout the next day. At nightfall on 2 August the Guards Armoured Division was located to the south-east of la Féronnière, a village 7 miles from Vire on the main road to Caen. 11th Armoured Division, on the right of the Guards, had driven south through le Bény-Bocage and its forward units were located in the area of Forgue, Présles, le Bas Perrier and Pavée, its orders to make for the Vire–Vassy road little more than a mile forward of Pavée. The route of advance had been through le Reculey, la Bistière, Forgues and Burcy and this constituted the only line of communication to the forward units at Pavée.

The ground over which this bitter fighting was taking place composed two ridges running roughly west to east separated by the valley of the River Allière. The Estry ridge to the north carried the road from Vire to Estry to the north-east, with Forgues situated at its western end; the southern ridge, Perrier, about 2 miles away, overlooked the Vire–Vassy road. Pavée (midway

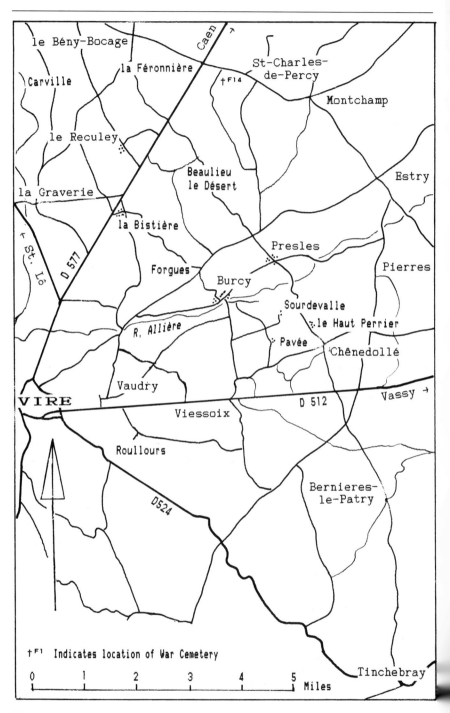

Map V: The Bocage.

between Sourdevalle and la Jarrière) and le Bas Perrier were located on this ridge with Prèsles situated just north of le Bas Perrier and Burcy downstream little more than 1 mile to the west.

159 Infantry Brigade, an integral part of 11th Armoured Division, comprised 3rd Battalion The Monmouthshire Regiment, 4th Battalion The King's Shropshire Light Infantry and 1st Battalion The Herefordshire Regiment. The Monmouths were forward at Pavée, the Herefords at Forgues with Brigade HQ, the KSLI 2 to 3 miles to the north-east, each relatively isolated but supported by armoured units and with call on artillery, subject to enemy attack from west, south and east.

On 3 August savage attacks began from enemy forces of 9th SS Panzer Division striking at la Bistière from Vire to get behind 11th Armoured together with attacks on the British left flank from Montchamp and Estry and the tip of the salient at Pavée from Viessoix in the south. The 3rd Division now took up positions on the right of 11th Armoured to fill the gap which existed between American and British forces; 185 Brigade was placed under command 11th Armoured. The following day the enemy continued to attack from the west with 3rd Parachute Regiment joining 9th SS in the fighting at la Bistière with further pressure from Montchamp in the east.

On 5 August 1 Norfolk attacked la Bistière to find the enemy gone. 185 Brigade was scheduled to relieve 159 Brigade which, by now, had been fighting continuously since 30 July and had suffered numerous casualties. 2 Warwicks had moved forward to the le Bas Perrier area and were fully engaged. The enemy continued to attack strongly on all three open sides of the British positions while American troops gained Etrouvy, to the west and 5 or so miles north of Vire.

The main effect of the break-out by VIII Corps and consequent heavy fighting on the Perrier and Estry ridges was to induce the enemy to withdraw divisions from the Caen front and the Pas de Calais and to concentrate those forces in the centre of the Allied front thus weakening their own defence on both flanks. By 3 August the equivalent of four panzer divisions were committed against the VIII Corps thrust, by 6 August five panzer divisions were assembled south of Vire and, in addition, 9th SS Panzer, in immediate contact with 11th Armoured on the Perrier Ridge, was joined by 10th SS Panzer.

This movement of armoured divisions to the centre of the Allied front was the enemy's answer to what the German High Command perceived as the major threat, leaving only infantry formations facing the American thrust on the right which were no match for strong American armour. On the left of the Allied front a similar situation prevailed so that, on 8 August when the Canadian Army commenced the move forward to capture Falaise, its advance was resisted only by a German infantry division bolstered by the hastily moved 12th SS Panzer Division. The Allied armies still faced severe fighting before the movement forward from Caen towards Falaise on the left and the encircling movement of American Third Army on the right to the German rear culminated in German defeat in the Falaise pocket and the subsequent Allied drive to and beyond the Seine. There can be little doubt that the disposition of the majority of enemy panzer forces at the centre of the front to meet the threat posed by British forces on Perrier Ridge made a considerable contribution to the overwhelming success of the Allied break-out.

Major H.M. Wilson MC describes the situation in more personal terms:

On the night of 5 August I was sent off to make contact with the Monmouths who were reputed to be sitting on a ridge miles away and in quite a different formation to ours, 11th Armoured Div. Lammas, my batman/driver, and I set off in our 'pick-up' truck since my jeep was off the road temporarily and around midnight I made contact with Brigadier Jack Churcher who pointed out a burning ridge in the distance and said: 'There are the Monmouths, or what is left of them, be careful how you go as we are only in wireless touch with them. Be prepared to take over from them by first light as there may be an attack from beyond the ridge.' Lammas and I made our way, after a wrong turn in Burcy which could easily have been our end since we drove through some Teller mines quite by mistake, and duly found a very weary CO in a Command Post who painted a rather grim picture.

The CO of 1 Norfolk received orders during the late afternoon of 5 August that the battalion relief at la Bistière would be completed by 07.30 hours, 6 August, allowing his men some rest before taking over from 3 Monmouth near Sourdevalle during the night of 6/7 August; however, early on the 6th, the relief of 3 Monmouth was brought forward, to commence immediately.

The weather over the past few days had been very good, hot sun and clear skies after early morning mist. The morning of 6 August dawned with a heavy mist blanketing the ground until towards midday when, as the mist cleared, the Norfolk's column was disclosed toiling across the valley through Burcy.

B Company (Major E.A. Cooper-Key MC) headed the column down a long forward slope to Burcy in the valley, and from there up a hill to the enemy-held summit, behind which was the 10th SS Panzer Division. The enemy immediately subjected the column to intense shell and mortar fire – they were sitting targets. A Company (Major I.A. MacGillivray MC) detoured trying to avoid the death-trap of Burcy, and lost two officers and fifteen other ranks in so doing, not arriving at Sourdevalle till after the counter-attack which followed the relief of the Monmouths. C Company (Captain H.J. Jones) also got badly hit coming up, losing some key personnel.

By 17.15 hours relief of three of the Monmouth rifle companies had been completed – 1 Norfolk dispositions were: B Company left, C Company right, D Company left rear. Many of the Monmouths had not left the position when at 17.30 hours the enemy laid a heavy artillery concentration on the rear of the battalion position catching most of the 'F' echelon vehicles and setting them ablaze. The two COs agreed that the imminent attack should be met by both battalions, totalling some 550 men, which represented only about 75 per cent of normal battalion strength and came to be known as the Normons. Fifteen minutes later first reports came through of enemy troops approaching from the front. At 18.15 hours B Company's right forward platoon was engaged and two sections overrun; ten minutes later C Company reported engaging the enemy; at 18.30 hours B Company was ordered to counter-attack their forward platoon position with the assistance of C.

By 1900 hours the situation in front of B had been restored but enemy pressure increased against C and the Monmouth company at the right rear. Within thirty minutes conditions had deteriorated further and by 20.30 hours C Company reported that they were down to thirty-five all ranks. At 2100 hours, however, they mounted a local counter-attack. To add to the commotion cannon-firing Thunderbolts mistook the Normon position for that of the enemy and shotup the area. The Normons' forceful defence carried the day; at 21.30 hours brigade was informed that 'the battle was as good as won' and by 22.15 all companies reported their areas clear.

Throughout the battle the Normons had the close support of a troop of Sherman tanks of the Fife and Forfar Yeomanry and of combined anti-tank forces apart from very considerable back-up from divisional artillery. *The History of the 3rd Division*, written by Norman Scarfe, describes the most noteworthy deed of the battle thus:

The hero of the Sourdevalle epic was Corporal Sidney Bates, ['B' company] whose VC was the first to be awarded to a member of the Division during the campaign; but, alas, it was posthumous. It would be impossible to imagine a worthier, finer 'descendant' of John Bates, Shakespeare's typical young soldier with Henry at Agincourt, who in the end says of his King, after the usual misgivings and apprehensions as they wait for the trumpet to sound in the cold dawn: 'and yet I determine to fight lustily for him.' The citation of Sidney Bates' supreme gallantry and self-sacrifice, submitted to and approved by the King, reads thus: the attack in strength by 10 SS Panzer Division near Sourdevalle 'started with a heavy and accurate artillery and mortar programme on the position which the enemy had, by this time, pin-pointed. Half an hour later the main attack developed and heavy machine-gun and mortar fire was concentrated on the point of junction of the two forward companies. Corporal Bates was commanding the right forward section of the left forward company which suffered some casualties, so he decided to move the remnants of his section to an alternative position whence he appreciated he could better counter the enemy thrust. However, the enemy wedge grew still deeper, until there

The memorial erected in 1986 to the memory of Corporal Sidney Bates VC by the 1st Battalion D-Day Veterans Association. The plaque reads: ON AUGUST 6TH 1944 DURING THE BATTLE OF PERRIER RIDGE IN A FIELD BEHIND THIS MONUMENT CORPORAL SIDNEY BATES AGED 23 YEARS, OF B COMPANY 1ST BATTALION ROYAL NORFOLK REGIMENT FELL MORTALLY WOUNDED IN AN ACTION AGAINST 10TH SS PANZER DIVISION FOR WHICH HE WAS AWARDED THE VICTORIA CROSS.

were about 50 to 60 Germans, supported by machine-guns and mortars, in the area occupied by the section.

Seeing that the situation was becoming desperate, Corporal Bates then seized a light machine-gun and charged the enemy, moving forward through a hail of bullets and splinters and firing the gun from his hip. He was almost immediately wounded by machine-gun fire and fell to the ground, but recovering himself quickly, he got up and continued advancing towards the enemy, spraying bullets from his gun as he went. His action was now having an effect on the enemy riflemen and machine-gunners, but mortar bombs continued to fall around him.

He was then hit a second time, and much more seriously and painfully wounded. Undaunted, he staggered once more to his feet and continued towards the enemy, who were now seemingly nonplussed at their inability to check him. His constant firing continued until the enemy started to withdraw before him. At this moment he was hit for the third time by mortar-bomb splinters and sustained a wound that was to prove fatal. He fell to the ground but continued to fire his weapon until his strength failed him. This was not, however, until the enemy had withdrawn and the situation in this locality had been restored.'

He died of his wounds two days later. His memory is not likely to fade from the minds of the men who knew him; indeed that is true of all men who die fighting.

On both sides tank losses were considerable – the German 'Tiger' tank was superior in fire power and armour to any British or American tank. British anti-tank guns made little impression on the Tiger with the exception of the 17-pounder, mounted in only a relatively few Shermans. In many instances German armour was knocked out only by the heavy British artillery concentrations called up by FOOs with the leading troops or by the British tank units.

This battle is known by a number of names – Sourdevalle, Pavée and Perrier Ridge. The actual location was close by a farm named Pavée. Major H.M. Wilson MC gives his memories of the occasion.

About 6 o'clock on this cloudless day the enemy came for B Coy in a big way. Cpl. Bates, one of the leading section commanders, was the first to receive this onslaught. His buddy was killed alongside him which was more than Cpl. Bates could stand. He seized the Bren gun and set about the advancing enemy. Not content with killing quite a number of enemy Cpl. Bates proceeded to charge them getting badly wounded in so doing.

This enemy attack was in fact a feint as the real one came out of the sun about 7 o'clock and fell on C Coy, or what there was left of it, and some Monmouths. Our Gunners saved the day here together with Sgt. Hopkins who personally knocked out some Tiger tanks with a PIAT until he himself got badly hit in the legs. Both Cpl. Bates and Sgt. Hopkins deserved the VC – Cpl. Bates got it posthumously and Sgt. Hopkins the DCM. The Fife and Forfar Yeomanry came up and stayed with us all that night refusing to go back. It was a very hard fought action throughout and all eyes were on Sourdevalle as the holding of that ridge was the key to the Vire–Vassy road and so the Falaise pocket.

The battle of Sourdevalle as we always called it was perhaps the biggest and most important battle the Battalion ever fought. The whole Battalion was battle experienced by then and so were our supporting arms. Almost everybody had the opportunity to shoot at the enemy and there is no doubt that there were many acts of outstanding bravery which could not be written up. The Norfolk soldier is remarkably good on these occasions, keeping his head and doing what he has been taught, he will always go on if his officer tells him to.

The Padre, Jim Green, was a tower of strength. He went round as many slit trenches as he could talking to the men, with one man he had a long discussion on divorce whilst all hell broke out around to which he paid not the slightest attention.

Private F.A. Staples, in the Carrier Platoon, has a memory which, he says,

. . . always makes me very sad even after all these years.

I hail from Camberwell, the same area that Sid Bates VC was raised in, I am a Londoner but since 1944 have considered myself an honorary Norfolk man. I joined the 1st Battalion in Manneville Wood 18 July 1944 and after a series of frightening experiences in la Bistière, le Reculey and, of course, Manneville Wood itself, which was no picnic, I found myself at Perrier Ridge on August Bank Holiday Sunday 6.8.44. After a hair raising journey through Burcy where some of my platoon took shelter in a graveyard of all places and I got covered in bits of coffins and gravestones, we arrived alongside 3rd Mons about tea time.

The main attack commenced early evening and I was dug in rather too close to my Bren Carrier which received a direct hit from what I consider to be an 88 mm gun – I did not hear it coming, the carrier was demolished and I was buried and on fire. I was completely disorientated, stone deaf, my left eardrum had burst and there was quite a bit of blood from flesh wounds which were nothing at all really.

I was helped out of the hole by a large 'Norfolk Farmer type' man, Pte. Nichols (5776762), helped along a hedge to a slit trench where he stayed with me for quite a long time till I gathered myself. My hearing slowly returned and I entered the real world after about an hour – we communicated in some kind of sign language and he made it quite clear he would not leave me until I was able to fend for myself, which I did and stayed in the line till we left that spot after about five days and nights.

The sad thing is that shortly after that a shell struck Nichols' trench killing him outright, I saw his face, and I was one of the four men detailed to carry the body to a collecting point for burial.

He now lies in Tilly-sur-Seulles Cemetery.

That man's kindness to me has remained with me all these years – I can see his face as clearly now as I could then, never have I, before or since, known such care from one man to another, and to think he was killed so soon after.

Captain C.P. 'Pat' Bennett RAMC, landed in Normandy on the morning of D-Day with the Brigade Field Ambulance with which he continued to work for about a month until he joined the 1st Battalion at Manneville Wood after the MO and the RAP had been knocked out – the fourth medical officer to join the battalion since D-Day:

My family often accuse me of having enjoyed the war. This is untrue, but stems from the fact that one tends to remember so much that was good in the war years and only a few horrors. Padre Jim Green was running the RAP at the time I took over and various untrained infantrymen were unwillingly drafted to me as stretcher bearers – they very rapidly became trained and motivated and excellent chaps they proved to be.

At Sourdevalle the RAP was certainly not far from the seat of fighting, and here we were really up against it. We nearly intercepted a direct hit as we approached the area when a shell landed a few feet in front of our truck before we arrived at the orchard which was Battalion HQ. Here we worked with the Monmouthshire RAP team in a small barn in the middle of the orchard, but were being shelled and mortared and when the barn caught alight we moved to a small cutting which was near a hedge and led down to the road. From then on everything happened and we worked incessantly on the wounded who poured back. We had no means of evacuating them for a considerable time. During a lull I lay down in my slit trench for the first time and, at that moment, the RAP had a direct hit, the Mons MO was killed, and several of the personnel from both RAPs were wounded.

At last Major Paton, 2 i/c of the Field Ambulance, turned up with a couple of jeeps equipped with stretchers, having found a way to us down a little leafy lane which was not being shelled. The evacuation of all the casualties I was holding was started – who was to have priority was quite difficult to decide. At length the battle just seemed to stop, the firing died down, no more casualties arrived and eventually we left our orchard and retired out of the firing line for quite a prolonged period.

Sometime in the middle of all this I must have evacuated Corporal Bates VC but I have no recollection of him at all, and did not realise at the time that he had done something pretty stupendous. I was so lucky to have Padre Jim Green with me. He did all the documentation of the people who passed through the RAP, so that I could spend my time, with the wonderful help of the RAP personnel, doing my job of helping the wounded to the best of our abilities.

Lieutenant 'Friar' Balsom:

C Company were to take over from the right hand company of the 3rd Monmouth positions – they were well dug in and had a sunken lane to their right. Fortunately we were meticulous and detailed in our questioning before taking over as, before all our questions were answered, the enemy barrage and the attack had begun.

We were lucky that the Mons had sited their trenches well, as we had no time to dig others. We doubled up with them in theirs. Tanks and infantry followed the shelling and we could respond only with the weapons we had left. Most of the transport behind our position and many of the 11th Armoured tanks had been hit and were on fire. At one stage in the battle I saw CSM Catlin climb on to one of the tanks behind us to try to direct its fire. Before he could do so, both the tank and he were hit. At another stage I had crawled out of my trench to get a clearer picture of what was happening – I looked over the bank to peer through the hedge only to find a Tiger tank facing me from the other side. Against this my

Sten gun was of little use. In all 3 Tiger tanks reached the company position.

At last – after what seemed a very long time – there was no-one in front of us any more. It was as if our position had been the high tide mark for the waves of German tanks and infantry and then the tide had ebbed away. The attack had failed. They had had enough.

As evening drew on, we were able to take stock of our position and casualties. The wounded were helped to the RAP. There were many enemy dead in front of our position and in the sunken lane that flanked it, C Company HQ trench had received almost a direct hit.

Captain R.W. Hodd, OC HQ Company, wrote an article in 1985 entitled 'The Road to Sourdevalle (Pavée) and Back', from which the following is taken:

On Pavée the air began to cool as the classic summer afternoon moved towards evening.

Out of the clear blue sky came a hail of shells, rockets and mortar bombs. There was no warning. The air became dark with smoke and fumes. The noise was beyond description. Pillars of orange fire roared from flaming vehicles. Exploding ammunition added to noise and confusion. Petrol whooshed with searing heat. The merciless rain of steel pelted down in fury. A vicious blast hurled me to the ground where I lay dazed and immobile. I felt myself being dragged along and realised I was being shoved under a truck. The people who did this for me were trying to give me shelter but I recognised that it was a very dangerous place to be as with such heavy fire it was almost inevitable that the truck would be hit and I was on risk of being grilled beneath it. I slithered out as my breath returned. As far as I could make out I had not been wounded (days later I discovered a tear in my battledress and a shallow dried up scratch on my left shoulder – a near miss and the only 'wound' I suffered during the whole campaign). For the time being I was disorientated and my instincts drove me to seek shelter and regain my powers. Through the murk I saw a large solid building and I entered. Others were also sheltering. There was a massive deafening explosion and I seemed to be surrounded by fire. Panic stricken I fought my way out and staggered as far away as I could, eventually finding a small fold in the ground in which I lay prone, face down. I felt light headed and detached from the noise and the chaos and gradually my senses returned.

I moved towards the centre of the area looking without success for an empty slit trench. A cheerful voice hailed me: 'Come and join me!' – it was the 2i/c. Humphrey Wilson is one of those people who never flap, are completely untiring and perpetually cheerful. We wondered how far the German infantry would penetrate and I shared my .303 rifle ammunition with him. My batman, wearing his face splitting grin which always meant good news, arrived to announce that he had found me a slit trench and had dumped my basic kit into it. He said he was sharing a trench as usual with his good friend Bert Lammas. My new home was 20 yards uphill from the Bn HQ Command Post and once again I had cause to be grateful to Basil Twiddy who looked after me so well at all times.

More enemy shelling developed and I was summoned to the Command Post. Besides the usual staff there were three Lt.-Cols present ('Enough to organise a war, let alone a battle', somebody remarked): Lt.-Col. Orr of the Mons who was nominally in command, an extremely pleasant and helpful Lt.-Col. from the RASC (who was on temporary attachment to see how the Infantry lived in action) – I believe his name was Ralph Stockley – and our own CO, Hugh Bellamy. The position, I was told, was extremely serious and the next 20 minutes would be critical. If we could sit tight and repel attacks during that time there was a reasonable chance that we could survive.

Then help seemed to come from an unexpected quarter. Above the other noises we heard aircraft and looking up saw some US Thunderbolts. Good old Yanks! They circled and then swept down, spraying us with machine gun fire. When we recovered from our surprise we hurriedly displayed the ground/air recognition signal – a patch of luminous yellowish green celanese triangles. The Thunderbolts returned and this time treated us with bursts of cannon fire and then thankfully they disappeared presumably to report to base how they had beaten up a bunch of krauts.

Ronnie Hodd's account tells of a '100 per cent stand-to' all night and relates how, on the following day, when the Sherman tanks in the locality started up their engines to recharge batteries, the enemy thought a further attack was about to start and viciously shelled the position. The next day, Tuesday, he remembers:

The Padre said: 'Just down there beyond the dip there's a sunken road and on the other side a field in the lee of the shelling. I've got a burial party there and we're going to have a service in about an hour. Would you like to come?'

We stood with bowed heads and crossed hands as Jim Green said prayers. The bodies of our friends were gently placed in their graves. Each was carefully marked and the positions reported by Jim. The Service, though short, was dignified and peaceful. Any who read this who lost a loved one at Sourdevalle has my sincere assurance that he went to his resting place in an atmosphere of sadness and the deepest respect.

On Wednesday I started to have hallucinations. My ears buzzed and rang perpetually and I heard sounds and distant voices which came from nowhere. Colours were distorted. I had fits of shivering and seem to recall that several of us donned great coats although it was a hot August day.

During the afternoon we learnt that the enemy seemed to have given up the fight and the wonderful news that we should presently be relieved. During the late evening a Bn of Guards moved in gradually (they were later to describe the area as one of 'utter carnage and destruction').

I led my own party out at some time after midnight. Once again it was a pitch black night. We moved in file up a very narrow sunken lane. Every few yards I collided with a thick branch at chest or face or even hip level. There was a terrible smell which even our numbed senses found nauseating. The realisation came that I was not colliding with tree branches but with the stiffened legs of dead cattle which had no doubt stampeded into the lane for protection – unavailingly. We tramped painfully on until we reached our transport. We heaved ourselves into the backs of the three-tonners and after a short ride debussed. We had arrived back at the le Reculey orchards. Dawn was breaking.

I sat on the ground, then lay back and it was night again with whirling lights and roaring noises. . . .

Ernie Seaman MM, stretcher-bearer, B Company:

On to Sourdevalle, what a few days there, being surrounded during the night and then being bombed by the Yanks and losing all our transport. I will never forget one incident during the night when we were being shelled and I dived into the trench and a bloody great sergeant came and jumped in too, right in the middle of my back. Of course this is where Sid Bates won his VC; I and my partner picked him up but had no idea of what he had done.

CSM T.G. Catlin MM, C Company:

Our platoons took up position ready for the take-over, once the counter-attack started all thought of take-over stopped. In the early stage my company commander was evacuated so it fell to myself to organize company HQ. A Tiger tank penetrated the forward platoons and they sustained heavy casualties but the lads hung on under Sgt. Charlie Hopkins and Sgt. Charlie Rehbein. Charlie Hopkins was badly wounded in the leg but refused to be evacuated. He came back to company HQ for medical items and PIAT bombs, these he used to good effect and was able to delay the attack. Sgt. Rehbein's platoon also suffered heavy casualties – my only contact at this stage was by runner, L/Cpl. Chambers, who was later killed trying to make contact.

During this period 3 tanks of the Fife and Forfar Yeomanry moved into our area to support us, this helped boost our morale. Given the situation up front I decided to contact the tank commander and give him details of the Tiger tank. I jumped on the rear of one of the tanks and was in the process of giving details when the tank received a direct hit and I was blown off, receiving a shrapnel wound in the abdomen. In a very short time our 3 tanks were put out of action.

A short time after this we lost our Bren gun carrier, blown up by an 88 mm shell, losing our reserve ammunition and stores and once again I was hit by shrapnel. By now I was losing blood and becoming weak – an officer attached to Battalion HQ arrived to assess the situation and he took over, I was helped back to the RAP after seeing the Commanding Officer.

Eventually I was evacuated to a Field General Hospital, all I remember was waking up in a bed having been operated on.

The medical services attendant upon the troops during the campaign were highly competent and very efficient, as evidenced by CSM Catlin's memories following wounds received that day. After surgery at a Field General Hospital he was flown back to England and hospital. He says: 'To me personally, just a wartime soldier, it was an honour to have served in the Regiment with great people from all walks of life.'

Nevil Griffin remembers a friend at Sourdevalle:

I think the most traumatic time for me was when (Harry I think) Russell was hit during the Sourdevalle battle on the day Cpl. Bates won his VC. We were sharing a trench during the 'Moaning Minnie' attacks and he was hit by shrapnel in the area of his heart. He began bleeding profusely and I called for stretcher bearers while I began to try and remove his webbing and his battledress blouse. This was a very difficult thing to do in the confines of a slit trench, particularly as I was operating the 18 set at the same time and trying to keep both our heads down because of the shelling still going on! Stretcher bearers came and took him away – we at the time were a couple of fields behind where Cpl. Bates was being so heroic.

Lieutenant Eric Woodhouse, now commanding the Carrier Platoon:

I had a premonition something personally unpleasant would occur. A small incident during the advance lowered the tension somewhat. I was standing up in my carrier when I received one hell of a clout on my right shoulder from a spent piece of shrapnel or flat stone, luckily it did no great damage. Later that day we hardly had time to dig into position before Jerry decided to counter attack and began slinging over shells and mortar bombs. We had an ammunition truck near our platoon position, this caught fire and could have been an embarrassment when it brewed up. I managed to get aboard aiming to drive it away – my driving rather like a kangaroo hopping I'm afraid. I jumped on a motor bike to get round the platoon positions but my luck ran out and I'm afraid I 'flew through the air with the greatest of ease' as the truck exploded near by.

I must have been punch drunk but vaguely remember getting to Bn HQ looking like a scarecrow and apologizing for getting blown up. I also felt annoyed having to salute with my left hand, my right arm being useless.

No doubt Major Wilson, Bn 2 i/c, thought 'Here comes another b——y S Coy trouble maker', but being the perfect gentleman he always was, saw me safely via the RAP on to an ambulance for the rear Field Hospital. The Jerry gunners, not being gentlemen, fired at anything that moved in our area including the ambulances so we had a good send off.

Back in the rear hospital I vaguely remember some 'medical bod' saying 'we might have to take your arm off.' I remember thinking that's OK so long as you leave my head and other vital equipment intact.

Captain T.J. Harrison reports that during the takeover at Sourdevalle the radio network quivered with the following encouraging report:

'There's a Tiger tank approaching my position!'
'Make a rude face at it,' was the comment!

The close association between the battalion and the gunners and the essential role of artillery in the successful action at Sourdevalle was acknowledged by the award of the Military Cross to Captain John Talbot RA. He went forward with the battalion commander to Pavée where he at once organized the defensive fire tasks, visiting all forward locations under heavy fire from tanks on the Chênedollé feature.

The CO of 1 Norfolk stated that the artillery support received by the battalion was made possible by Captain Talbot's complete disregard for the enemy's accurate and heavy shell and mortar fire, in the open, beside his carrier, directing the fire of his guns. John Talbot recalls the action:

I was with Bn HQ at Sourdevalle throughout that 'busy' day and night when 10 Panzer attacked 1 Norfolk and 3 Monmouth – I had an eighteen year old signaller, Gunner Bridge, (later killed by mortars a foot away from me at Bn HQ near Nijmegen) whose very high voice could penetrate the static at night on the RT and we could therefore call for defensive fire when it was asked for by Hugh [Lt.-Col. Bellamy] – which seemed to be most of the night! Humphrey Wilson was as splendid as ever.

I had many talks with Hugh over this period – he was so very aware of the heavy casualties which arose from 1 Norfolk operations and deplored them; but of course he had a job to do.

Erik Gray, after a perilous journey through Burcy, continues with his account of Pavée:

The afternoon sun blazed down and I felt very thirsty after our dusty drive. I was longing for a swill of the tea that was just being poured when the scream of a salvo of shells and almost simultaneous explosions in the orchard put an end to my thoughts on the matter. We all dived for the slits in a heap, and I found myself sharing with Holmes and Rasberry in the part-dug hole that was barely 3 feet deep. We were hunched in a tightly packed knot with myself on hands and knees in the centre. More and more shells shrieked in and burst unpleasantly close. I felt the bursts go over my back. I told myself it would be over in a minute or so but the shelling increased in intensity until the ground seemed to shake in one vast thunderous and continuous explosion. Showers of earth, dust and splintered branches fell into and over the trench. I was aware of my teeth clenching as pieces of choking dust cracked between them; and I kept telling myself to relax. I desperately wanted a cigarette, but could not reach into my pocket. Searing blasts continued to sweep over us and not even the rush of incoming shells was audible any more. The incessant explosions continued, as the three of us, curled, arched and cramped, attempted to press deeper into the earth.

I do not know how long the barrage went on. After what seemed a lifetime, the indescribable noise and upheaval in the immediate vicinity lessened and I risked a sideways glance over the edge of the trench. Just yards away my carrier was burning fiercely, its steel side plates oxidised with heat. The water cans clamped to the rear were distended and hissing scalding steam, and nearby the motorcycles were a blackened and twisted tangle. Behind, both trucks were burning and flames from them had set fire to the hedge. The air sang with bits of flying metal, and small arms ammunition was popping and pinging in the wrecked vehicles.

The shelling around us continued, although not as fiercely as before, I shouted over to the other trench and, as I did so, saw a Sherman tank at the crest of the ridge rotating its turret right. The same instant, I spotted about a dozen enemy infantry running down the opposite side of a thin hedge just across the stubble. There was a long metallic burst from the tank's Besa, and the men disappeared in a cloud of dust with the body of one seeming to be thrown high in the air. The tank's machine-gun hammered several more bursts, as I watched across the smoking ash of the cornfield, but there was no movement where the enemy had been. I suddenly realised that the shelling had ceased and scrambled out to run over to the drivers' trench. Both men were dead: the blond hair of one was scorched and a huge blister covered his forehead.

Turning about I ran into the orchard. My voice sounded resonant, and I realised that my ears were singing and my hearing dulled. I had a blinding headache, felt numbed and exhausted and my back was very sore.

It was not until I reached Battalion HQ in the now shattered farm complex that I realised that the forward companies reinforced by the Monmouths had been attacked in strength by enemy tanks and infantry. Only then did it dawn on me that the enemy the tank had dealt with on our exposed right flank were part of the assault and had been intent on infiltrating to our rear.

Erik Gray's account explains how those left began to take stock of the situation and that he

. . . set off towards the ridge at the top of the orchard, in order to do the rounds. The positions seemed fairly compact and we did not have far to go, although by the time we reached the last crew it was getting dusk. There was still some sniping going on from both sides, and now and again we were obliged to crawl. From time to time, an enemy Spandau apparently firing on fixed lines sent a burst of fire zipping along the lane, and we had to make a detour towards the rear, in order to reach the company on the other side.

Eventually, after stumbling and tripping over fallen branches and debris in the darkness, we returned to Battalion HQ, and I went into the farm to report. The Orderly Room was crowded, and the Quarter Master ('Bandy' Howard) had just arrived from 'A' Echelon somewhere to the rear with a hot meal. He had apparently overheard my conversation with the CO about the loss of two guns. As I was leaving, he asked me for their serial numbers and severely choked me off for not being able to give them there and then, adding that I could not have replacements until I produced the numbers.

I remember asking King to take a look at my back when I took my shirt off the following day. I could not understand why it felt so sore and believed I had a sweat rash. Later the MO removed eighteen tiny steel splinters, including a larger one from the fleshy part of my backside. Finally, I recall the Irish Guards relieving us and my opposite number remarking that the stench of the place was simply appalling. We had almost become used to it by then; and, in the darkness, he was unable to see the bloated carcase of the cow lying nearby. 'Has it been bad here, Sorr?', asked his hefty sergeant in a thick Irish brogue. 'Not too good,' I replied, 'But it's a lot quieter now.' Leaving them, I got a lift in a carrier and was sound asleep before it reached Burcy.

The *Battalion War Diary*, in its matter-of-fact way, describes the day which followed:

7.8.44 Beautiful day. Certain enemy activity but no actual attack. Trouble from a Mk IV on our left which took a whole day to shift, and then it was not properly disposed of. Probably left of its own free will. Heavy mortaring of whole area during the day, caused several casualties, including the Adjutant. Conditions fair. Some casualties caused during the night.

On the night of 9/10 August the battalion was relieved by the Irish Guards – the enemy seemed to get wind of the move as intensive shelling started about 2000 hours. Several casualties were sustained including one officer, Lieutenant J.D. Drew, killed.

The various actions fought by the battalion between 4 and 9 August cost forty-seven lives and around two hundred men wounded. In addition to the award of the Victoria Cross to Corporal S. Bates, Sergeant C. Hopkins was awarded the Distinguished Conduct Medal and CSM T. Catlin, Sergeant (later Lieutenant) G.A. Smith and Corporal C. Thirtle were each awarded the Military Medal for outstanding devotion to duty and personal courage in the action at Pavée.

Charge of the Bull, by M. Jean Brisset, sums up the Pavée/Sourdevalle battle:

The High Price of 'Good Luck'

In retrospect, although one can say that it was a stroke of bad luck that the SS attack came in at just the moment when the Monmouths were being relieved by the Norfolks for, undoubtedly, there was some confusion while the handing-over was taking place, yet it was good luck that there were two battalions in place at the time because a single battalion could never have withstood the fury of 10th SS Panzer Division in attack. But the price was high. Of approximately 550 men who took part in this particular fight, 160 were killed and wounded. On the other hand, despite the fact that some positions were overrun, not a single man was taken prisoner.

About 80 British soldiers, Norfolks and Monmouths, who were killed in and around the village of Pavée from 5 to 12 August, were temporarily buried in a field opposite the Taflet farm house. The bodies have long since been removed but to this day the field is known as *Le Champ des Morts,* The Field of the Dead.

From an article in the *Eastern Daily Press,* 1945.

The Royal Norfolk Regiment will have a place of honour in every written record of the great Allied surge of liberation through the Continent during 1944. Among the first of the divisional signs carried across the Channel on June 6th was that worn by the Regiment's D-Day battalion. New glory was later added to the emblem of the county's troops by the epic of Cpl. Sidney Bates, VC, affectionately referred to as 'Basher' in countless tributes paid to him in talks I have had with his comrades in the past few days.

His was the first VC won for the division, and the award was an unforgettable link with the Royal Norfolks' part in the Battle of Sourdevalle during August – a victorious campaign against formidable odds presented by the enemy's crack 10th SS Panzer Division. It was of that battle that the Second Army Commander, in an Order of the Day, wrote that if the Royal Norfolks had not held their ground it would have made a great difference to the subsequent development of the battle.

By holding it they made possible the terrific breakthrough which came in August.

The depleted battalion of only two rifle companies moved south on 11 August, reaching Roullers in the evening. Late on the 13th those two companies were called forward to relieve the leading companies of 2 Warwicks at la Maslerie, leaving that position on the 17th for Tinchebray.

At Tinchebray the battalion could rest and recover from the losses of early August; reinforcements arrived, including, on 26 August, a party of 7 officers and 160 ORs from the 7th Battalion of the regiment.

The main body of the 7th Battalion The Royal Norfolk Regiment, in 176 Brigade of the 59th (Staffordshire) Division, landed in Normandy on 28 June 1944 with the Vehicle Party following the next day. On 8 July the 7th Battalion took part in the final assault on Caen, towards the village of Epron, to the right of the 1 Norfolk objective, Lebisey.

During the night of 6/7 August the battalion crossed the River Orne and established itself between Brieux and Grimbosq, meeting heavy opposition and fighting off a counter-attack. The next morning (8th) a second counter-attack started, the brunt of the fighting being centred on D Company. Captain D. Jamieson, the only officer left in that company, reorganized his men in tighter formation round the one remaining Churchill tank and although wounded continued to encourage his men while sending back, over his wireless, targets for the superb artillery support which was such a feature throughout the battle (the guns of 116 Field Regiment, RA fired about one thousand rounds each during this twenty-four hour period). The counter-attack was held and the enemy ultimately forced back. Captain D. Jamieson was awarded the Victoria Cross.

Reinforcements were needed by many units, manpower was short, 59 Division, as the junior division in 21 Army Group, was disbanded. On 26 August, the Battalion dispersed. D Company and some personnel of S and HQ Companies went to the 1st Battalion; B Company to 1 Suffolk, C Company to 1 Oxfs and Bucks, and A to 2 Monmouths.

Officers transferred to 1st Battalion included Major F.H. Crocker MC, Captain D.W. Glass, Captain T.P.K. Oakey, Captain E.H.T. Ridger, Captain W.J. Smart, Lieutenant P.W. Buckerfield and Lieutenant L. Dawson. Senior NCOs included CSM L.W. Brown (killed in action 16.10.44), CSM R. Fuller, CSM S. Flint, CSM E.J.L. Langford DCM, C/Sgt. E. Lacey, Sergeant J. Moore and Sergeant W. Paskell.

On the night of 6/7 August the Germans launched a counter-attack to cut off the Cherbourg peninsula but spirited action by American forces at Mortain deflected and broke the attack and within a week American troops had driven south as far as Nantes and the River Loire.

On 14 August an operation was launched by British 2nd Army to force its way to Falaise, south of Caen, while, at the same time, American troops drove south then east towards Paris, in the process enveloping large numbers of the enemy in a pocket located between Falaise and Mortain. The next day Allied forces, in Operation Anvil, landed on the Côte d'Azur, between Toulon and Cannes, forcing German withdrawal from southern France.

By 18 August Allied troops had reached the Seine; the previous day Russian troops had crossed the German border. On the 19th, in Paris, the French police force together with members of the Resistance occupied various buildings awaiting the arrival of the Allies but it was not until 24 August that elements of the American V Corps together with the French 2nd Armoured Division entered the outskirts of Paris and the following morning reached the centre of the city.

In what came to be known as the 'Falaise Gap', during a series of battles which continued until the 22nd, ten thousand Germans were killed and fifty thousand taken prisoner; enormous quantities of enemy equipment and transport were destroyed or captured.

The day that Allied units drove in triumph along the Champs Elysées British and Canadian troops crossed the Seine some 40 miles downstream from Paris, at Vernon, making for Brussels and Calais. On 28 August in southern France the Allies entered Toulon and Marseilles and, the following day, Châlons-sur-Marne and Reims to the north. The British forces driving north from the Seine crossed the Belgian border on 2 September, liberating Brussels the following day. On the 4th Antwerp was entered.

Hitler ordered that the Channel ports of Boulogne, Calais and Dunkirk, as well as the ground on both sides of the Scheldt estuary, should continue

Battalion HQ, Villers-en-Vexin, September 1944.

S Company officers enjoying an alfresco lunch at Villers-en-Vexin, September 1944. Left to right: Capt. W.J. Smart, Capt. T.P.K. Oakey, Lt. P.W. Buckerfield, Capt. J.A. Allen, Capt. P.G. Baker, Lt. E.A. Gray.

to be held by German forces in order to deny the use of Antwerp and the French Channel ports to the Allied armies, which were still being supplied from Normandy. In Normandy the enemy had lost half a million men, killed, wounded or missing.

The 1st Battalion, reinforced and re-equipped, continued training until, on 3 September, it moved across the Seine to Villers-en-Vexin, where, in and around a large chicken farm, (without chickens) it settled down again. Major H.M. Wilson MC, in his memoirs, recalls an example of military humour observed during that journey:

All too soon we were off again crossing the Seine on a Bailey bridge alongside which was an American Army bridge. A notice by the American bridge was large and verbose, stating that; 'This bridge was built by 123 Company of Engineers in 23½ hours, it is 300 feet long and will take 40 tons load, etc. etc.' The British bridge was labelled; 'This bridge was built by 23 Squadron, R.E. There is nothing peculiar about it.' A nice touch.

CHAPTER SIX

Moving Welcome

Operation Market Garden

During the late summer of 1944 the Allied High Command decided that the Airborne forces should be used to support the troops pushing north through Holland. The plan was to drive north then east round the Ruhr into the heart of Germany; this required that the bridges over the three main rivers, Maas, Waal and Neder Rijn should be secured. Three Airborne divisions would be required to land in a corridor running from the Belgian/Dutch border via Hechtel, Eindhoven, St Oedenrode, Veghel, Uden, Grave and Nijmegen to Arnhem, to secure the bridges and allow the ground forces to move forward at speed, then to reinforce and consolidate and strike east.

After a fast advance through northern France and Belgium, XXX Corps, under Lieutenant-General B.G. Horrocks, had reached the Meuse/Escaut Canal, south of Eindhoven. The American 101st Airborne Division was to land north of Eindhoven, the US 82nd Airborne Division beyond in the area between Grave and Nijmegen and the British 1st Airborne Division still further forward west of Arnhem. XXX Corps, comprising the Guards Armoured Division, 43rd Infantry Division and 50th Infantry Division, would move north meeting and linking the Airborne divisions along the corridor. XII Corps, under Lieutenant-General Sir N. Ritchie, formed of 15th Scottish Infantry Division, 53rd Infantry Division and 7th Armoured Division, was to strike forward to the west of the corridor, to protect its left flank and to advance on Utrecht, Rotterdam and Amsterdam. The task of VIII Corps, under Lieutenant-General Sir R. O'Connor, comprising 3rd British Infantry Division and 11th Armoured Division, was to move forward on the right flank of the advance, again to protect the main line of communication north.

On Sunday 17 September 1944 an air armada, accompanied by more than one thousand fighters and fighter/bombers, carried the airborne troops to their targets and the Guards Armoured Division moved forward reaching Valkenswaard, a few miles short of Eindhoven, that evening. On Monday further airborne troops landed and armoured forces entered Eindhoven; on Tuesday the first ground forces linked with paratroops at Grave on the Maas and moved beyond to Heumen. It was not until this day (19th) that

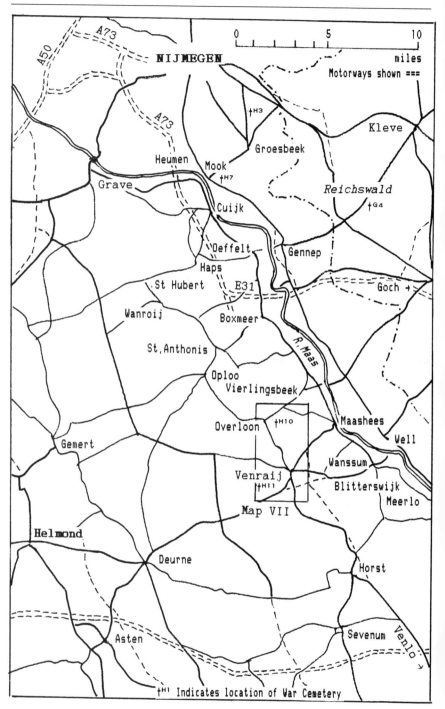

Map VI: Helmond – Nijmegen.

the first elements of 3 Division crossed the Meuse/Escaut Canal to play their part – the division had not been able to move from its location on the north bank of the Seine until the 16th because of a considerable shortage of transport. All supplies were still coming from the Normandy beach-head as Antwerp was not yet available as a port. The situation can be likened to an army fighting in Edinburgh being fully supplied from Southampton by road transport alone over second-class congested roads.

During this period, when the airborne troops were engaged in bitter fighting, bad weather and crowded roads slowed the ground advance. On Wednesday 20 September, however, the bridge at Nijmegen was captured, two days later than originally planned, and on Thursday 43 Division reached the Waal. The following day the division struck forward in an attempt to reach the Neder Rijn and so bring relief to the 1st Airborne at Arnhem, where bitter fighting still continued to prevent the enemy regaining the bridge. Strenuous efforts were made by the approaching ground forces to continue the advance north while the two corps on the flanks were meeting strong opposition over difficult ground and in bad weather conditions. On the 21st 8 Brigade occupied the town of Weert and 11th Armoured entered Asten. Enemy forces, during the entire advance, had been resisting strongly everywhere even to the extent, on 24 September, of cutting the corridor for a brief time, north of Eindhoven, near its base. The formations at the spearhead of the advance made every effort to reinforce the troops at Arnhem but without avail and finally it had to be accepted, after seven days of vicious fighting by British 1st Airborne, that all who could should be evacuated.

Of approximately 10,000 troops who parachuted or landed by glider near Arnhem only 2,398 returned to Allied lines; 1,400 were killed and some 6,000 were wounded and/or taken prisoner. Over the eight days of Operation Market Garden 101st Airborne suffered 2,100 casualties and 82nd Airborne 1,432; XXX Corps suffered 1,480 casualties and VIII and XII Corps between them 3,874 casualties.

The battalion left Villers-en-Vexin early on 18 September to stage overnight near Soignies and by midday the following day had arrived at Peer, in northern Belgium, some 30 miles due south of Eindhoven. This journey is still clearly remembered by certain subalterns. Convoy discipline on the previous journey from Tinchebray over the Seine had displeased the CO and for this move of about 300 miles it was decreed that certain officers from the rifle companies, riding motor cycles, should constantly monitor the speed and discipline of the convoy which must travel at 40 mi2h, i.e. 40 miles in two hours, an average speed of some 25 mph with halts every two hours. The first day's journey started early, encountered rain and consequent wet road conditions and finished ten hours later, after dark. For subalterns who had had relatively little experience of motor cycles and certainly no desire to wrestle with these infernal machines the resultant weariness, aches and pains are still clear in the memory.

German troops taken prisoner in Helmond by Dutch Resistance Forces the day prior to the entry of the battalion ('Michel').

Leading the advance of VIII Corps moving north to secure the eastern flank of the corridor towards Nijmegen, 11th Armoured Division crossed the Belgian/Dutch border and on 20 September reconnaissance units of the Inns of Court Regiment, probing ahead of the division, had reached the bridge at Someren to find it intact but strongly held. Attempts were made to capture it the next day without success and it was later found to be destroyed.

On 21 September 11th Armoured Division continued the probe forward. Last met in August at Pavée, 3rd Monmouths were ordered, during the latter part of that day, to move forward towards Helmond and two companies reached the village of Mierlo. The next day, 22nd, the Monmouths drove on into Helmond along the Mierlo–Helmond road, supported by the 3rd Royal Tank Regiment. Helmond is bisected by the Zuid Willems vaart (canal). Finding all bridges down, they were able only to occupy the western side of the town, with a strong force of the enemy still holding the eastern part. By the 22nd the Fife and Forfar Yeomanry and 1st Herefords had forced a crossing of the canal at Someren and a bridge had been built.

The 1st Battalion The Royal Norfolk Regiment arrived in Asten in very wet conditions on 23 September to take over from the KSLI of 159 Brigade. Two nights and a day were spent here – an uneventful stay marked only by the necessity to eat captured German rations. Ersatz cream cheese in tubes was a new experience, and the biscuits were harder than stone; transport was desperately short so the troops ate whatever could be provided.

The same day that 1st Norfolk arrived in Asten the Monmouths were ordered to leave Helmond and proceed some 10 miles south to Someren there to cross the canal and move on to Asten and Liesel.

Inns of Court patrols crossed the canal on the 24th finding considerable enemy movement on the Helmond–Deurne road caused by the opposing forces evacuating Helmond. The patrols eventually entered Deurne that evening. On 25 September patrols from A Squadron Inns of Court Regiment reached Bakel and another entered the outskirts of Helmond briefly before continuing the main thrust in the direction of Gemert and St Anthonis. At 0900 hours 1 Hereford left Vlierden to enter the outskirts of Helmond but finding no enemy left at 1100 hours.

Battalion War Diary:

25.9.44 Bn ordered unexpectedly to move to Helmond to take over from armour of 11th Div. We were the first British troops seen here. Reception was uproarious. Crowds almost prevented our entry. People drunk with joy made it almost impossible to take up a defensive position. Curfew at 1900 hrs cleared the streets. Weather showery.

A well protected recce party had set out that morning, hoping not to be ambushed on the way or sniped in the town; the battalion was to follow in TCVs (troop-carrying vehicles). The recce party did not know what to expect; indeed orders indicated that we might have to fight our way in. So we did, but in the happiest, most heart-warming way possible. I was in that recce party and can never forget that day. As a twenty-year-old subaltern, thought by some of his men to look too young to have left school (as I learned many years later), facing what I believed would be my first battle, the reception in Helmond was overwhelming. We had only a few miles to go and, ready to bale out of the jeep at the first sign of trouble, we found instead that, as we approached the town, the inhabitants came surging out on to the streets and soon we were driving slowly along a narrow path between what seemed like thousands of shouting, cheering, laughing Dutch people, many with orange flags or favours, all of whom wanted to slap our backs and shake our hands. In this carnival spirit we received an amazing and moving welcome which went on and on.

We eventually arrived in the town square where we waited while the CO contacted the Burgemeester. We were surrounded by masses of happy people – it appeared that the last German troops had left or been captured by the Resistance earlier and the Dutch were celebrating.

I stood beside the jeep, took my cigarette case out of my pocket and hands came from all around me clearing the case instantly. Those with some knowledge of English were talking with me, wanting to know so much, starved as they were of news.

I had for the past few days been growing a moustache, I thought it would improve my military image and I was quite pleased and not a little proud of its development so far. I had reached the stage of stroking it to encourage its growth. I wore a leather jerkin over my battledress and the badges of rank on my shoulder straps were covered. I was talking with a lad of about sixteen, who spoke good English, when he asked me, 'What rank are you?'

I replied, 'A lieutenant'.

He looked at me, paused, and said, with considerable emphasis, 'You're too young to be an officer, you don't shave yet!' His comment so damaged my ego that I shaved off the moustache that very evening and have never attempted to grow one since.

Lieutenant Paul Buckerfield, transferred from the 7th Battalion, a man with an ear for the Norfolk dialect, relates:

> English as she is spook. One of the lads, seeing his first Dutch telephone kiosk: 'Thass sensible spellin' a word the way you say it – Telefoon.'

Behind the recce party the whole battalion was on the move, the rifle companies in troop carrying vehicles. Passing through Deurne they came under enemy shellfire, a company from the 2nd Battalion The Royal Ulster Rifles were still engaged in clearing part of the small town. Turning west the column headed for Helmond but stopped about a mile short of the town where the rifle companies debussed and, headed by the carrier borne platoons, marched into Helmond. The carriers were told to push on as fast as possible – Bill Holden, driving the third carrier from the front, remembers that they entered the town through completely deserted streets:

> Suddenly many hundreds of people poured out of the houses, the column came to a halt, it just could not move. The Dutch people were so excited, slapping our backs, one man asked me to have a drink and produced a bottle of wine that had been kept from before the German occupation – his hands were black, he must have hidden the wine in the coal cellar! The wine was good.
>
> The Dutch asked for cigarettes so the section emptied two or three tins of cigarettes into a steel helmet and handed them round – within seconds all the cigarettes had gone.
>
> We were ordered to move on but made slow progress through the crowds then came out on to another main street which was Bindestraat and on into the Heistraat, stopping opposite a row of cottages where we unhooked the gun and manoeuvred the carrier into an alleyway. Children swarmed all over us, people were eagerly talking to us, more cigarettes were distributed, we had to remove the breech from the gun to prevent accidents with all the people milling around. The section set about brewing up some compo ration tea, which to us soldiers wasn't terribly good, the Dutch people asked if they could sample some and pronounced it wonderful; for the previous three weeks the only drink they had had was coffee made from acorns, the only food black bread and potatoes.

Civilians and soldiers examining a 6-pounder anti-tank gun in Helmond. Left to right: Capt. T.P.K. Oakey, Sgt. E. Seaman, Pte. Ely.

Bill Holden tells of being billeted in the front room of the house opposite the gun, and of the lady now known as 'Mother', who welcomed them and found a mattress for them to sleep on. They didn't know until years later that the mattress belonged to the two girls of the family, who then had to sleep on the floor. He describes the members of the family, how the children treated them like brothers and their parents like sons, how 'Mother' washed their shirts and darned their socks.

We had saved some of our rations during the campaign and now gave some of our store to Mother asking her to make a meal for both the section and the family. The first meal was a stew, she gave the troops a large helping each but only gave the family a small helping. Sergeant Newman said, 'We can't have this' and each soldier passed his large portion over to the member of the family next to him and took the small portion. The family were very moved by this.

When the son-in-law, who spoke good English, arrived we were able to have a long conversation and later his wife brought in the baby, a little girl called Enika. We had some powdered milk in the rations and asked if she would like some for the baby – later we all helped to bath the baby, just like home from home. I noticed that when they started to bath the baby they used a small cube of something like washing soda because they had no soap – I had a week or so before received a parcel from home containing amongst other things a bar or two of Imperial Leather soap, so

I went out to my pack on the carrier, got a bar and gave it to them. They thought it was wonderful and after the baby's bath, very carefully dried the soap and wrapped it up to keep for the baby.

On the third day we were ordered to move again, Mother found a piece of chalk and chalked a farewell message on the carrier, we never knew what it said; she was crying, father was upset, the girls were near to tears and sadly waved us goodbye.

At Tinchebray Lieutenant 'Friar' Balsom had moved to B Company to take over a new 11 Platoon consisting of those few left after the Sourdevalle battle, led by Sergeant G.A. Smith MM as platoon sergeant, a most able and efficient soldier, joined by a number of lively young men from Norfolk, especially the King's Lynn area. He quotes from a letter he wrote to his parents of the entry into Helmond:

We approached warily expecting to be greeted by guns firing – instead there were crowds cheering and giving us apples, flowers and tomatoes (the only food they seemed to have plenty of) and orange ribbons and rosettes. We were cheered right down the main street.

When we reached the hospital, the nurses turned out in their snow white uniforms and formed a long archway with their hands (as we play 'oranges and lemons') and we just had to walk through.

I was leading the platoon and tried to avoid the archway, but the crowd and the nurses would not let me. I expect I was blushing.

My platoon HQ was just off the Molenstraat at the Sobrietas Theatre, which was part of a complex run for the community by Capuchin Friars – an appropriate billet for one with my Regimental nickname – and I slept in the Superior's study.

When off duty the 11 Platoon members billeted at the Sobrietas were welcomed in the living room of the Jenniskens family which was behind the stage of the theatre. There rations were shared and I still have clear memories of the warmth and kindness of Mevrouw Jenniskens, of their friendly living room and of the lively music of their piano played by Johnny Wilson, the platoon pianist. Wilson was the name he used. We never asked his real name in case we gave it away inadvertently. He was a young Austrian Jew who had joined the army and fought with us despite the extra danger he risked if he was ever captured. His piano playing and his fluency in German became great assets to the platoon.

Here, if only for a few days, there was contact with normality – an experience that was to be repeated elsewhere but never with quite the same intensity as this first brief encounter. It is no wonder that links and friendship between the Royal Norfolks and Helmond remain after five decades.

Also in B Company, Lieutenant G.D.H. Dicks MC recalls unparalleled scenes of excitement within the town. The company had been assigned the task of defending the eastern end of the town having been assured by higher authority that the Germans would counter-attack that night and were most anxious to settle in and sort out fighting positions, fields of fire, etc. He remembers, after checking accommodation for the platoon:

. . . I turned to leave the house. I was immediately attacked by approximately 50 nurses who insisted that I come with them to the hospital opposite to give the inmates their first view of liberation. I had no option – in spite of the preoccupation of my mind – I was hauled across the road by each arm by a couple of lusty Dutch nurses, followed by at least eight of the lads being meted out with the same pleasant treatment. The scene inside the hospital, of patients waving white and feeble hands at a dirty, begrimed, equipped and armed British subaltern, would have been fit for any academician.

At last I made my escape and then had to sort out the others who had been hauled inside. I have often thought since about that bunch of boys – how happy they were at that moment – Cariello (killed March 1), Halls (killed October 14), Gorbell (killed October 14), McMorrine (wounded October 14), Taylor (wounded October 16).

Any soldier having the temerity to show cigarettes or chocolate was immediately pounced upon by the populace. I gave all my cigarettes away very early in the proceedings, and so, I think, did all the others. But their appetite was insatiable. It was in one of these 'distributing largesse' crowds that I started talking to an attractive Dutch lady named Leni

Heistraat, Helmond – civilians are crowding around one of the anti-tank guns in the background.

Meyer who invited me home to meet her husband Frans. I accepted, and Ray Hilton and I went along to see them.

Private A.H. Solomon, transferred from the 7th Battalion in August, presents another side of war – that in all circumstances the paperwork must be done. He became company clerk to Company Sergeant-Major Les Langford and one of his jobs was to keep the Company Roll up to date and list the casualties. This had to be taken to Battalion HQ daily and he recalls having to walk back with the lists two nights running. Alone – pitch dark – not a soul in sight. The Olympic time for the 2 mile walk was shattered – easily. He hated those walks. He goes on:

> Arrived at the outskirts of Helmond. Dismounted and marched into the town. That was a never to be forgotten experience. The march into town was incredible. The streets were lined with people all cheering and waving flags. (Still have one.) Finished up being billeted in a hotel. What a luxury – a bed! I could have spent the rest of the war there, no trouble. Two very nice young ladies used to come in and help us sort the mail. Of course we couldn't understand the feelings of the locals after so long under occupation, and at first we were quite horrified when men dragged women down the street, sat them in chairs in the square and cut all their hair off for fratting with the Germans.

Major F.H. Crocker MC retains a letter he received from the Dutch family with whom he talked when Helmond was liberated:

Helmond, September 28th [1944]

Dear Major,
  All the members of the family, who can't speak English so quickly, will try to wish you good luck in the battle.
  We are you and your company so grateful you have driven the cruel germans out of our town. Now we feel what it means to be liberated. It was a great pity that one of your captains came to fetch you.
  Now the Germans can't drive our husbands and fiancés and sons and brothers out of our country; now the Germans can't carry out our provisions; now the Germans killed and murdered the best of our patriots; now we need not duck!
  We liked so much to repeat our English, to hear (in the smoke of an English cigaret, that we missed for years) how you became successively the victories.
  We liked to hear the uses and the living in your native land as far as we could understand it. Every member of the family wrote a sentence of this letter as a sign of sympathy because you paid a visit to our family on September 27th and 28th.
  With kind regards.

The letter was signed by all eight members of the Duisters family.

A single-page news-sheet, a Dutch Resistance newspaper, dated 26 September 1944, was published in Helmond – *DE AABODE, Dagblad voor Helmond en Omstreken*. It contained the text of a telegram from Burgemeester Moons to the British Premier, Winston Churchill:

> The burgomaster and the citizens of the town of Helmond in the Netherlands give you and the whole British people best thanks for the liberation of the town by the gallant second British Army.

The following day *DE AABODE* published an article in English under the title 'Welcome'; the sentiments and feelings expressed in it are as true today in Helmond as they were then. In the final sentences it says, 'There is sun and freedom and orange and red, white and blue in our minds and in our hearts today; no more fear, no more cruelty, no more streams of blood . . .' and asks that we come back and be their guests. In the excitement of the moment, to provide a welcome in English was a happy, heart-warming gesture. In the same news-sheet was the announcement, dated 25 September, the day the battalion entered the town, of the birth of a baby son to H. Swinkels and A. Swinkels-Meulendijk. The baby's name was Tommie.

Captain E.H.T. Ridger recalls that day and a brief moment which admirably illustrates the feelings of the Dutch people:

> On the advance into Helmond I was travelling in the Signal Platoon jeep. As we entered the outskirts of the town through the cheering crowds a young man dashed up and asked whether I would go into the cellar of a nearby house to see his wife who had just had a child – she wished to clasp the hand of an Englishman. I duly obliged.

The Helmond newspaper *WEEKUIT,* dated 23 September 1989, featured a number of articles relating to the liberation of the town forty-five years before and included interviews with people who were there. This extract was translated by Mireille Geenen:

> People ran outside, to the English soldiers. Nelly with her orange skirt, her sister Riek in red, white, blue. Marietje van Eijk arrived too, together with many other children. Peter and Jan van Rooij were wearing sashes of their fathers. Midwife Van Rooij was also there, but only for a short moment because she had to do something very important.

Nelly Geenen:

> Only an hour before the liberation I was at the house of baker Swinkels in the Drietipstraat, because his wife expected a baby. She wanted to have a girl, but when I told her that the English soldiers were on their way to

Members of D Company with Dutch civilians at Heistraat, Helmond, 25 September 1944. The lady holding the child is Nelly Geenen.

Helmond, she wanted to have a boy and his name would be Tommie. Normally the delivery took three hours, but now she was so glad that the child was born in 10 minutes. When the tanks were driving through the Heistraat I shouted to the soldiers that a child was born and that he was named Tommie. 'A bag, a bag,' they asked but I didn't have anything with me. So they loaded my whole apron with salmon, soap, chocolate, cigarettes, etc.

And further? The excitement would last a little longer. In the streets and in the restaurant there were big parties. Everybody brought what they had in their house. They even brought gin, from before the war. Accordion music and English songs, 'It's a long way to Tipperary' and 'Roll me over in the clover'. White bread and biscuits in square tins. The first piece of good soap. Little Peter Geenen took his first piece of chocolate, but he spit it out! The high spirits lasted a little longer, but not so long. There was still another war, English soldiers had to go from Helmond to the front.

After reading Ernest Ridger's story and with considerable help from friends in Helmond in 1992 I met Tommie Swinkels, the baby boy mentioned above. He had been told of the events, and problems, of that time by his mother many years after when she asked him to take a gift to the doctor who delivered him on the doctor's retirement from practice.

He told me two stories which illustrate the contrasting faces of war. On 21 September 1944 his grandfather, who lived in Eindhoven, recently liberated, attempted to make his way to Helmond to visit his daughter. His grandfather travelled as far as Mierlo, a short distance from Helmond, where he had to take shelter from the battle in a house with a number of other Dutch civilians. This house was fired on by British troops who believed that it was occupied by German forces and, as a result of British fire, seventeen Dutch civilians lost their lives.

When Tommie was born he was the youngest of four boys; his brothers were aged 7, 5 and 3 at the time. Tommie's father told his brothers that Tommie had been dropped by parachute by the RAF and had been caught as he fell from the air. The three boys' main concern, as Tommie grew older, was that he would only speak English and they wouldn't be able to understand a word he said.

It was here, in Helmond, that Harrie de Rooij was recruited as interpreter for the battalion. Harry became more 'Norfolk' than anyone from our home county and insisted on wearing his Britannia badge.

This chronicle of the men of the battalion would be incomplete without the recollections of some of those civilians who welcomed the soldiers into their homes. It is very difficult for the British, who have not lived under an oppressor for a thousand years, to understand what 'occupation' means, to comprehend the intense happiness of liberation when it comes, and to appreciate the enormous relief felt when oppression is lifted. Here is the tender yet sad story of a fifteen-year-old Dutch girl; the memories of Mevrouw Carla Coenen-van Hoof:

MONDAY, 25 September 1944. About noon our liberators arrived. The first armoured car reached the Ameidestraat and stopped in the Market Place, on the corner of which stood our house. I jumped on the car and in my best schoolgirl English said to the driver, 'Oh, you look dirty!' I wondered afterwards if the man was hurt by my comments. I asked the soldiers, 'Please, chocolate for Mama (myself!?)' or 'Cigarettes for Papa' and then one of my friends said, 'Look at your house, the English have taken it over.' And there, on the first floor, pointing out of the window directly down the street towards the canal, I saw a Bren gun.

I went home immediately and there I met the officer, Terry Rourke, his sergeant, Ted Carr and Ron Palmer, Bernard Shepherd and others. Dad cleared the office so that all the soldiers could sleep there on mattresses. But what I remember above all else was the white bread and the corned beef. I still often buy corned beef and think about those days. And Dad and my mother were both very happy with Craven A and Woodbines! I was a non-smoker.

Each day the soldiers cleaned the office so well that my mother said that they set us children a good example.

On the third day that the Royal Norfolks were in Helmond, Terry told my father that the Battalion would be leaving the next morning on their

A recovery vehicle in the market place in Helmond, 26 September 1944. The damage to the roof of the building was almost certainly from British shells intended for the church just out of picture to the left.

way to battle. When I heard the news I started crying uncontrollably. When Terry came into our sitting room later on, he asked my father what was the matter with me and Dad answered, 'I think it's because you are leaving.' Terry was taken aback. But for me, a schoolgirl of fifteen, he had become very important in those three days.

As a consolation Dad went with me by bicycle to the Bakel Woods, about 5 miles from Helmond, where we had been told the Royal Norfolks would be spending the first night before advancing further north. We found Terry and he invited us to sit on the ground and have a drink. Another unforgettable memory. I was given a mug of 'lemonade' (so he told my father) but in fact it was whisky!

The next morning my father accompanied me again to Bakel Woods (he wouldn't let me go alone!). We arrived just in time to see them go. Terry, my idol, was sitting in the cab at the front of the vehicle and when he saw us he opened the door and waved to us.

At the end of October he came to Helmond on leave and stayed with my family for one night. Sometimes I received a letter and some chocolate as a sign that he still remembered me but it was not until 23 December that I saw him again. He was on his way to Brussels with another officer and could only stay a short while. How happy I was.

A jeep and 6-pounder
surrounded by excited
youngsters in Helmond.

We had just finished lunch and washed up the dishes when three German bombs fell very close to our house. Terry pulled me under the large table which was standing near the window in order to protect me from flying glass splinters. Then he pushed me into a corner and stood before me to protect me from further explosions.

That same day he gave me a present – a little silver cross to wear every day and remind me of him. I promised to do so and to pray every night before I went to sleep for his good fortune in that terrible war.

A week after, just before I returned to boarding school, another letter and chocolate and sweets arrived from Terry. I took it with me to school. In my free time at school I began sketching a photo which Terry had given me. I enlarged it about six times and painted it in light colours. I sent it home to my father so that he could in turn send it on to Terry by one of the Battalion drivers.

My last letter from Terry was dated 28 February 1945. I received it early in March, I kept Terry's photo by my bedside and thought how wonderful it would be if he could come and see me.

But it was not to be. My parents already knew, from a letter written by Sgt. John Slapp, a soldier of the Royal Norfolks, that Terry had been killed on 1 March 1945 at a small place in Germany named Kervenheim. Although John Slapp had never met our family he felt it his duty to write because Terry had often spoken about our house as his second home and about the daughter as his little Dutch Queen.

My parents told me the sad news a few weeks later. In 1947 when I was eighteen years old I went to London and stayed with the Rourke family for one month. The drawing that I had sketched at school and which my father had sent on to Terry, was framed on the wall of their sitting room. He had sent it to them the day before he was killed.

The activities of Dutch Resistance forces (Koninklijke Patrouille, King's Own Patrol – known by the people as the strong-arm squad) in the Helmond area during September 1944 are described here by 'Michel':

Telephone lines from the police and the German Army had been tapped and communicated with our headquarters. The tapped connections had been made by an official of the PTT (Post, Telefoon, Telegraaf), also a member of the resistance group. In the church tower at Bakel was a radio transmitter which was discovered by the Germans the day before liberation, too late to take reprisals.

Harrie DeRooij joined the battalion at Helmond to act as interpreter.

Information collected by our group came from Helmond and outlying villages. The group also carried out sabotage on the railway signalling system which disrupted rail traffic throughout the whole of Brabant and Limburg.

At the beginning of September the national railway strike started which surprised the Germans completely and soon after came the airborne landings near Son and Eindhoven was liberated on the 18th. The German troops retreated behind the Zuid Willems vaart (canal) and Helmond was split into two parts, on the west of the canal the English, on the east, which included the centre of town, the Germans.

I left the house where I had hidden to return to my parental home located at the town's abattoir. Here I was surrounded by the Germans because many were attempting to catch up on sleep in the stables (they had had very little sleep in the past few days) and, in addition, the cookhouse and German stores were in the same buildings.

Many groups of Germans left Helmond in the direction of Deurne with stolen bicycles, hand-barrows and prams. When the cook-house departed and very few rations were left behind (under guard) I knew that at most about fifty Germans were left in the town and I informed our commander by phone. That was on the 22nd.

On 23 September 1944 the group commanders received orders to clear the town of Germans the following day. On Sunday 24th this action

Somewhere in Holland. Capt. T.P.K. Oakey and Lt. P.W. Buckerfield during a move forward.

started and by the afternoon all the Germans were in our hands, captured by 3 groups each of 3 KP men, with the exception of two Germans (snipers) who shot out of a passage next to the church in the Veestraat who were killed with two hand grenades (of German origin). After this the OD (orde-dienst – police) came into operation to restore order and arrest members of the NSB (collaborators).

On 25 September the English troops marched into a freed Helmond and the day after our whole resistance group volunteered to serve with the Allied Forces, including our leaders, to fight together until the Germans had capitulated.

Any infantry soldier will tell you that such comfortable conditions would not continue for long. After all too short a stay the battalion marched out of Helmond early on 29 September to make way for other formations and the town subsequently became a base for numerous support units.

Lieutenant George Dicks relates that after the battalion moved out of Helmond, he and Ray Hilton walked back to the town and:

. . . we found that 2nd Army HQ had taken over, and on enquiry by Ray Hilton of a friend of his who was on the staff it transpired that Army HQ had ordered the evacuation of the town by the Royal Norfolks! Nevertheless we cadged a good dinner at the officers' mess, although we felt very scruffy in such a grand atmosphere – but we were a little irked by Ray Hilton's friend saying composedly 'Of course, you know, we don't get any of the fun that you chaps get'. Why must people with comfortable jobs think that the infantry has fun?

CHAPTER SEVEN

Infantry Battle

On 1 October the battalion made a further move north, over the Maas at Grave, through Heumen, and on to the area of Maldens Vlak. From there recce parties left at 09.30 hours on 3 October, followed by the battalion at 1300, to relieve American airborne troops south-east of Nijmegen.

The positions the battalion now occupied were in a wooded area at Kiekberg near Groesbeek on high ground which, on the right flank, overlooked the Maas in the distance. The ground was covered with thick scrub or planted timber, intersected by tracks. Patrols were constant. I remember taking over from an American unit; the body of a German soldier in the middle of the platoon position, his stomach blasted away; a listening post a hundred yards ahead of them, the furthest they had penetrated into the wood; the 'K' rations they left behind which we greatly enjoyed. My platoon position was around the point where rough tracks crossed. Patrols were ordered to find out what lay in front of us. One patrol returned to tell me that they had discovered a number of parachute containers untouched, which the Americans had not recovered, and suggested another expedition to examine the find. I agreed and before the day was out many members of the platoon were in possession of American sleeping bags, far superior to British Army issue blankets.

On 5 October I received orders to send out a recce patrol along a track to our front beyond any point so far reached, the object of the patrol not to seek trouble but to gather information. The patrol, under Corporal Gay, returned having located an enemy position and, on reporting the situation, I was told to mount an attack.

The plan was to take a Bren, together with two snipers and the 2 inch mortar for support, forward until the enemy was visible, hit the position as hard as we could and retire. I explained what we must do to those who were going with me.

'The Bren will be in the centre flanked by the snipers, the snipers will select targets and fire together. That will be the signal for the Bren to loose off a full magazine and when that's done get out of there as fast as you can. The mortar will be about 100 yards behind you. As soon as they hear you firing they will fire five bombs in rapid succession. The first bomb should land just after you finish firing so you've got to move fast.'

We set off. I led the way, with the ubiquitous Corporal Gay, along the downhill track in the wood until we reached the bottom of a shallow wooded

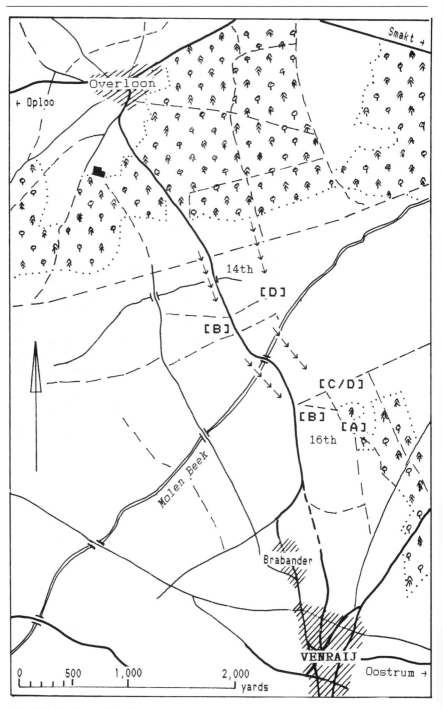

Map VII: Overloon – Venraij.

An anti-tank section near
Malden. Left to right:
Pte. White, Pte. Read,
L-Cpl. Pratt.

valley. There I placed the mortar team with a section to defend them and
went on with the rest of the party. I moved on, very cautiously, with
Corporal Gay until he indicated, through the trees, a number of grey-clad
figures, some in trenches, some standing on the track behind, clear against
the rising ground ahead. The machine-gun team and the snipers took up
their positions and I returned alone through the wood to the mortar party,
an action which, in the silence of the wood and the uncertainty of other
enemy locations, created a very uneasy feeling between the shoulder-blades.

Back with the mortar I gave the range, having located the mortar in the
most open part of the wood, conscious that bombs could be detonated by
tree branches over our heads. We waited, heard the firing to our front,
discharged the bombs and saw Corporal Gay and his men running towards
us as the last bomb left the barrel. Then we headed back up the track, not
wanting to linger.

The enemy reaction luckily did not come until after we had regained our
trenches, when we received a barrage of mortar bombs but no casualties.

Members of the Mortar Platoon cleaning up after an early-morning 'stonk' on the enemy. Wrecked gliders can be seen in the background.

The following day the company commander brought a war correspondent along to see us, at whose request we gave details of the previous day's patrol.

The war correspondent's dispatch was syndicated to numerous regional newspapers. Lance-Corporal Peter Gould, a member of the patrol, still retains a cutting from a Clacton-on-Sea newspaper. The *Eastern Evening News*, 31 October 1944, carried the report of this patrol conducted by D Company on 5 October.

Cpl. Leslie Gay, serving with the Norfolks on the Western Front, went on an early morning patrol in a wood and saw some Germans at their 'stand-down' after their all-night guard, writes a military observer.

'I was on a track which runs round a wooded bowl, and the German post was only about forty yards away,' said Cpl. Gay, who has fifteen years' Army service. His home is in Co. Donegal, Eire.

'I saw a German officer approach the post, heard him wish the men "Good morning", and then heard the rattle of their mess tins as they began to prepare for breakfast.'

The article then reported the subsequent raid on the enemy position at dinner-time.

Waiting for an 'O' Group in early October 1944. Left to right: Sgt. W. Paskell, Capt. E.H.T. Ridger, Lt. J.A. Allen, Capt. T.P.K. Oakey, Maj. F.H. Crocker, Maj. I.A. Macgillivray, Capt. R.W. Hodd, Maj. H.R. Holden, Maj. E.A. Cooper-Key (extreme right).

A story which made the rounds of the battalion at this time, creating much amusement, for who doesn't enjoy a laugh at somebody else's expense, is told here by the Adjutant, Captain T.J. Harrison:

The CO, Hugh Bellamy (hereafter 'H.B.') had some strong ideas about latrines and whereas the humble soldiery had to seek relief on the compo ration thunder box, H.B. required something more upmarket – ceramic, no less, and this had to be set up over a trench on cross-poles. Much depended on these two poles and what we always expected soon came to pass – a shell landed nearer than necessary, the poles were shifted and H.B. was deposited – guess where?
A man of uncertain disposition at the best of times, H.B. was absolutely unapproachable that day and I feel certain he suspected one of us as being responsible for this catastrophe.

Major H.M. Wilson MC relates one of many circumstances which defy explanation:

. . . Hugh Bellamy had just returned from the usual 'O' Group to our Command Post and was about to give out orders when it was discovered that we had all got the wrong maps. Everyone dispersed to ferret out the right ones leaving the little clearing in front of the Command Post empty.

Sure enough down came a neat little concentration of 81 mm mortar fire right on the spot we had just vacated, a driver sitting in a carrier some 50 yards away being the only casualty. Luck seemed to be on our side once again. Three minutes earlier or later and the entire 'O' Group might have been wiped out. We blessed those elusive maps and forgot Hugh's wrath that we had not brought them.

For a patrol carried out by 10 Platoon on 4 October, during which his Sten jammed and he subdued the enemy barehanded, fracturing his knuckles, Lance-Sergeant J. Shepherd was awarded the Military Medal. On the 9th the battalion left the woods to move back over the Maas and into the area of Cuijk, a riverside village to the south of Nijmegen.

Movement forward by the Allied forces had been halted short of Arnhem but a large pocket of resistance remained to the east, in the area up to the River Maas, and the intention now was to turn south and clear down to the town of Venraij. This was the task of the 3rd Division, with 185 Brigade in reserve initially. 1st Norfolk moved on foot on 11 October from Cuijk through Haps and St Hubert, on again the next day to Wanroij, St Anthonis and Oploo arriving north of Overloon on 13 October, occasional wrecked vehicles providing evidence of battle, which could be heard clearly in front.

Overloon and Venraij took a terrible pounding over a period of almost one month. The American 7th Armoured Division had launched an attack on Overloon on 30 September accompanied by British bombs on Venraij. Against heavy opposition the Americans advanced to within a mile of Overloon, from which the Germans had evacuated all civilians, by 5 October. The Americans were relieved by 3 Division, who planned to launch an attack by 8 Brigade to capture Overloon on 10 October which had to be postponed for two days because of bad weather and extremely muddy conditions.

On the 12th the attack started with a barrage of ninety thousand shells. Vehicles became bogged down, partly due to the fact that the enemy had closed sluices to raise the water level. The attacks of 14 and 16 October, of similar intensity to the first, caused further considerable damage to Venraij in addition to which the German forces in the town, on the 16th, blew up the church tower and other buildings including water towers before leaving the following day. The town had not been evacuated completely and many Dutch citizens survived in the cellars of the town during that period.

The battalion spent the night of 13 October in the woods around Overloon. The ground forward of those woods was flat and featureless apart from one or two small copses and sparse hedges. About midway between Overloon and Venraij ran a stream, the Molen Beek or Loo Beek, which formed a natural defensive barrier. Most of the enemy had retreated beyond the Molen Beek but from its far bank they had a clear view over a distance of 1,000 yd of British troops leaving the shelter of the woods.

At 0700 hours the next morning the two leading companies, B and D, led off. In support of each was a troop of Churchill tanks, along with flails,

AVREs and SP A/Tk guns (M10). The advance was a difficult one, as once through the thick woods there was very little cover and all the advantage lay with the defenders.

Lieutenant G.D.H. Dicks MC wrote a personal account of his experiences in May 1945 while convalescing from wounds received in March, of which this is an extract:

Next morning, 14 October 1944, we received our orders for the attack. B Company was to be one of the two forward companies having the thankless task of first bumping and locating the enemy. Friar [Lt. D.B. Balsom] was given the task of being the leading platoon, with company HQ next, then my platoon, then Ray's [Lt. R.S. Hilton] platoon. Ray and I would travel with company HQ.

Inevitably we soon came under fire from the German lines and Friar's platoon suffered casualties. Everybody took to the deep ditches either side of the road and crawled forward cautiously. I have a constitutional aversion to crawling so very soon I began to shuffle along using my hands and feet, with my knees off the ground. Result – one bullet through my haversack. I subsided for a time but soon my constitution overcame my caution and once more I raised my body. Result – another bullet through my haversack. I did not risk a third chance. Eric [Maj. E.A. Cooper-Key MC, OC B Coy] and his batman soon after rose and did a spirited dash forward to Friar to get information and then called us up to receive orders for the assault.

The plan was for Friar to remain where he was and by fire to keep the Germans' heads down. Ray and I were to form up on each side of the road – Ray on the right and I on the left.

I formed up behind a ramshackle farm-house and then moved out into the open on the left of the road with two sections in line as per battle drill with about five yards between each man. I felt as naked as the day I was born.

We moved forward at a walking pace with a Churchill tank rumbling along behind. A Spandau opened up and I saw the tracer bullets go through our ranks and a figure fall. It was Halls, 8 Section Bren gunner – shot (as I afterwards learnt) through the heart. He was on the extreme left of the section and the fire had come, I noticed, from a projecting copse on our left front. The sections had automatically gone to ground. Cpl. Smith recovered the Bren gun from the body of the dead soldier; and L/Cpl. Grimble, the other Bren gunner in the forward sections, was blazing away merrily although I feel he only had a vague idea in which direction the Spandau lay.

Rather than waste time telling him the exact position I doubled over to Eric and indicated the area to him, information which he immediately passed on to the tank commander who gave the wood a liberal burst from his Besa. Eric also ordered me to keep my platoon where they were while he ordered Friar to pass through me with supporting fire from my Brens.

Our initial objective was a cross road which had the code name 'Cartwright'. Friar had gone to ground about 150 yards in front of me, so Eric ordered my platoon to move forward once again, to pass through Friar and achieve 'Cartwright'. However, as I approached Friar he yelled that he had reached 'Cartwright', and I therefore ordered my men to ground about 70 yards short of him and reported back to Eric.

It was now about 10.30 a.m. and we had achieved our objective. My casualties up to that point had been one killed (Halls), one wounded (Hart – shrapnel in the forehead), and one bomb-happy (a soldier who rather surprisingly had broken down when we first came under fire).

I suddenly became aware that there was a German tank about 300 yards down the road near a blazing farmhouse and that it had been responsible already for knocking out three Churchills which were littered untidily over the landscape. At this stage Sgt. Parker became a little bored with ditches and decided to sit upright to see what was happening in the world. He immediately received two bullets for his pains, one in the side and one in the shoulder, a third just chipping the rim of Harry Blowing's tin-hat. Even this did not disturb his tranquility – he casually collected his haversack which he had taken off and walked off down the road in full view of the enemy in search of the RAP.

Artillery fire began to increase, and the cursed nebelwerfer opened up frequently and dropped clusters of shells in our vicinity in between ferocious displays by the German tank. Our troubles were increased by our own artillery who were trying to eliminate the tank. Running true to form some of their shells were falling short or hitting the tops of trees just in front of our position with the inevitable result that casualties occurred to our own troops.

I began to look forward rather eagerly to the hours of darkness, but the day seemed interminable. About 5 p.m. Gorbell in 8 section decided to leave his trench to urinate. As he crawled back he received a sniper's bullet in the back – and died within a minute. His last words were characteristic – 'The bastards have got me'.

Lieutenant 'Friar' Balsom describes the approach to the Molen Beek:

Between the woods near Overloon and Venraij the countryside stretched out as flat as only Holland can be and across this bleak, wet terrain, at right angles to our line of advance, lay a number of drainage ditches called 'beeks'. They were of varying widths, but all of them were obstacles to tanks etc. About halfway between Overloon and Venraij lay the biggest of them – the Molenbeek.

Dawn broke damp again and with light equipment only we took part in the Battalion attack – D Company to the left and we in B Company on the right. At 7 a.m. on that dull October morning we moved out of the woods. 11 Platoon was leading on the right near the road. We advanced until enemy fire began to become effective. We located one of their positions ahead of us, made our plan and using platoon covering fire moved quickly in to take it. I remember we passed through the remains of a still smoking and smouldering haystack. We raced on until we reached the line of a beek halfway to the Molenbeek – a position we had codenamed 'Cartwright' – our first objective. We had had little difficulty so far, but unfortunately L/Sergeant Stan Cook was killed by machine gun fire from a point far to the right of the road as he came to the 'O' Group for the final assault. It was the very day that he put on his sergeant's stripes.

Our position in that flat terrain was very exposed; 11 Platoon was forward, protected only by the bank of the ditch, and spent a very uncomfortable two days and nights. Slit trenches soon reached down to the water level and still it rained from time to time. There was frequent shelling and mortaring and movement – especially the bringing up of food, tea or ammunition – could only take place with any degree of safety after dark.

I wrote the account which follows some forty-five years after the event. It relates to D Company, to the left during this action. Subsequently comparing it with the narratives above, I was very pleased to find that my recall had not failed. Indeed, all accounts in this book show that experiences of battle remain most sharply etched in the memory.

Before dawn we had eaten breakfast brought up by the Company cooks and been given rations for the day. The sound of tanks moving up to join us was already attracting the fire of enemy 88s, a gun recognised by its whiplike crack and immediate shellburst, disliked by both infantry and tanks. A last-minute check of equipment and the platoon formed up near the track alongside the tanks. 0700 hrs. We moved forward with the tanks and reached the edge of the wood without trouble. Ahead of the troop of Churchill tanks attached to D Coy was a flail tank, a lumbering monster of almost medieval design with massive chains fastened to a revolving shaft at the front of the tank chassis which flailed the ground ahead of it to explode anti-tank mines. Movement through the wood by the tanks had been restricted but now, as we cleared the timber the tanks moved outwards, left and right, the platoon spread out behind them and enemy fire increased as we became visible.

Corporal Gay, commander of the right-hand leading section, seeing an enemy tank, ran across to the Churchill tank near him to use the telephone on the rear of the tank to ask its commander to engage that target – a mortar bomb burst almost beside him and knocked him momentarily unconscious without injuring him. He regained consciousness to find himself flat on the ground beside the tank, its tracks within inches of his face, the tank reversing over the binoculars still hung around his neck.

Within minutes some of our tanks had become casualties and the rest had retreated to the relative shelter of the wood, leaving us on our own, without support, but we continued to push forward, crouching, trying to use whatever scraps of cover we could find, of which there were painfully few, visible to the enemy and vulnerable to his fire. I was all too aware of the din of mortar and gunfire about me, of our own mortars and artillery engaging forward targets, of the enemy resisting our advance with machine-guns and 88s together with Nebelwerfers, 'Moaning Minnies', producing a distinctive and frightening sound when fired. To add to our discomfort the enemy was also using air-burst shells so that we were enveloped by the noise of explosions, the rip of machine guns, the crack of bullets. The platoon had suffered some casualties, that I knew, but could only press ahead to the illusory cover of hedges and scrub in front.

Without tank support progress became increasingly difficult and finally ground to a halt in light scrub about 200 yards short of our second objective, the lateral track ahead.

The platoon went to ground and I checked our losses. One of my platoon HQ, the PIAT man, had been killed and the 3 sections had suffered considerable losses. We seemed to be on our own, I could not immediately locate adjoining platoons. I was unable to contact Coy HQ by radio so I sent Barney Ross, my batman/runner, back to report the situation – before he had gone far he was badly wounded in the jaw.

The Company Commander needed to know what was happening so I went back myself using what cover I could from hedges, skirting round a blazing tank, reported the situation and a plan was made to continue the advance to the track ahead with the support of artillery and mortar fire.

Back with the platoon I found that L/Cpl. Stork, the NCO in Platoon HQ responsible for the 2 inch mortar section, had been killed outright by a shot in the head while I was away. L/Cpl. Stork was a married man with two small children, a kind and genuine man with whom I had often had conversations during which he told me of his family. To me he seemed a much older man, although only in his late twenties, compared to the average age of the platoon which was around twenty-one.

His death angered me so much that when the second attack started I can remember feeling only intense, savage outrage. The moment to attack again came, we got up and began moving forward. Enemy fire increased, I was shouting at my platoon, urging them forward, running with the leading sections, my only emotion cold, bitter anger. I saw a grey-clad figure disappearing into a wood ahead of me – I fired a long burst from my Sten at the figure, my anger making me want to kill in revenge yet at the same time realising that my Sten was unlikely to have much effect at that distance.

We were attracting a lot of fire – I felt a pluck at my right arm and saw a hole in the sleeve of my battle-dress. My immediate thought was 'I'm wounded, I'm out of this, I won't have to sleep in trenches any more.' But we were still charging forward towards the track ahead through the shell and mortar bursts.

We reached the track and with the surviving members of my platoon I took refuge in the shallow ditch. The ground in front was absolutely flat, the only cover a low and meagre hedge beyond the far ditch which itself was no more than 2 feet deep and wet, very wet. We felt extremely exposed.

I checked the platoon, we had suffered more casualties but had reached our objective. As soon as I could I rolled up my tunic sleeve and then my shirt sleeve – in both there were two holes showing where shrapnel or bullet had passed through but on my arm no mark at all. Then I realised that clothing on my right buttock was wet – again my immediate thought was 'I must be wounded – I'm bleeding'. My water bottle, hanging on my right hip, had a jagged hole in it about an inch from the bottom and most of the contents had leaked on to my trousers. . . .

Captain D.W. Glass joined the battalion early in October in the fringes of the Reichswald; his stay was all too brief. He describes here the action on 14 October:

I took over command of A Company, after Major Ian MacGillivray, the Company Commander, had been wounded in very bravely trying to dislodge a Tiger tank which had backed into some farm buildings and was holding up the Battalion advance. Ian showed me where the tank was before leaving for treatment to a nasty wound in his left shoulder.

I went forward to see a post of our men and on return saw tracer bullets flashing past me until one caught me up and hit me through my hip pocket in which I was carrying a New Testament; it turned out that the bullet had torn the Bible in half, but the strength of the India paper was so strong that it turned the bullet through a right angle and it came out between my stomach and my liver instead of passing through the whole of my body.

I was evacuated that evening, it was thought at first examination that I had been wounded in my stomach, but luckily this was not so.

Battalion History:

The next day we waited for other units to straighten themselves out and for a co-ordinated plan for forcing the Beek and the capture of Venraij. Unfortunately we did not get our orders till after dark that night and in the usual streaming rain with hooded torches we struggled to read our maps, the unhappy company commanders having then to make their plans. Again we had a troop of Churchills to each company, also a bridging tank and flails. REs were to assist in the building of the pontoon bridges, of which there were two, one on each side of the road. An excellent patrol was carried out and the site decided on before dark. That night the bridges were assembled as near to the bridge sites as possible, and by 0400 hours were in place without incident – a good piece of work.

The plan was to cross the Beek silently, if possible, with two companies, form a small bridgehead, bridge the road gap and then push on with the other two companies going through, supported by the tanks. Artillery was on call through FOOs. Being a brigade attack, we were not to push through to our final objective until the Warwicks were over their sector of the Beek, thus keeping the attack in step.

CHAPTER EIGHT

Memorable Advance

Continuing the advance towards Venraij, 185 Brigade was ordered to attack at dawn on 16 October across the Molen Beek. This was a stream between 10 and 15 ft wide with sloping banks about 5 ft high, an effective gap of about 30 ft. The approaches were difficult, with cratered tracks and water-logged ground. The area was extensively mined. The success of the operation depended on crossing the Beek silently by night, any attempt by day would be suicidal. As the road bridge was blown, it was therefore planned that the infantry would cross using kapok (floating) bridges while a bridging tank would lay a girder bridge for vehicles.

Battalion History:

At 0500 hours, 16 October, the leading companies, B right and D left, crossed without incident, it being established later that D Company had walked through a minefield of Schumines. Later, A Company did the same thing, without a single casualty: such are the fortunes of war.

A morning wash and shave near the Molen Beek, 16 October 1944. Pte. C. Wells on right (IWM B 11030).

By 0600 hours the leading companies were very anxious to be allowed to get on, as they were lying in the open in full view of the enemy and getting casualties. Unfortunately the Warwicks had not fared so well, and quite rightly brigade would not allow us to push on. In the meantime the bridging tank came up and started to lay its bridge. Under intense fire it made noble attempts. The first failed owing to the state of the banks, the second only when a flail was half-way across when the whole lot toppled into the Beek. In the meantime our Churchills had all been knocked out, which was most unfortunate, as by now the enemy tanks had withdrawn. At last, after what seemed to the unhappy leading companies to be years of waiting, we were allowed to go. It was now 0700 hours and both sides were slogging each other with all they had.

Sergeant E.W. Carr of A Company was closely involved in preparations for crossing the Molen Beek. Two kapok bridges were used, one each side of the road, one immediately available, the other arriving at the last moment:

October 15 at the Molen Beek I was in charge of a party to construct a pontoon bridge. This was made up during the afternoon in a small field just back from the beek behind a tall hedge for protection from observation. Later, under cover of darkness, this was manhandled with great difficulty through a gateway to the beek and placed in position. This we guarded until the troops went across next morning.

Major J.P.C. Searight, commanding S Company, wrote an article under the pen-name 'Yeoman' entitled 'Twenty Four Hours – or a Lifetime', which was published in the *British Army Journal*, volume no. 7, January 1952 and from which the following is reprinted:

. . . Suddenly two huge black shapes materialized, screaming quietly down the road. They were my 3-tonners. I leapt into their path for otherwise there was nothing to stop them driving past our forward posts. The drivers, men still in another world up there in their warm dry cabs, saw me and stopped. Two excellent Sapper NCOs jumped out. I suppose they were dressed in dirty, creaseless, battle-dress and leather jerkins like working sappers usually are, but they seemed more than smart compared with the men they were about to meet. They were rather expecting an Infantry working party like the ones they used to teach clove-hitches to at Chatham, or wherever it was. They got a nasty shock when 15 pl of C Coy rose from the ditch to construct the first bridge. These infantrymen were dirty, dishevelled, exhausted and browned off. If any man in that platoon had ever seen a kapok bridge before he kept it mighty quiet.

A slightly acrimonious discussion then threatened to develop on the question of the responsibilities of Infantry and Engineers. Luckily, just as he was about to invoke Field Engineering Vol II my Sapper Sergeant grasped the basic fact that either two bridges were to be put together before dawn or else a lot of lives would be lost unnecessarily. He realized that he had just been put down in a world he had never met before and he reacted splendidly.

The two platoons and two sappers then started unloading the lorries and laying out their bridges on the side of the road. The noise seemed bad but not excessive – a certain amount of bumping, of coughing and ceaseless swearing.

At last, at 4.30 we were beginning to get men on to their right jobs, when two company carriers with breakfast on board, crept into our midst – that appalling feature of Infantry active service; breakfast at 4.30 issued in the dark with two vast sandwiches to last you until death or the evening meal!

Just then I noticed a flash in the sky; followed an anxious moment, a powerful whistle and two explosions about 60 yards away. Only 75 mm, I think . . .

As it was, the shelling soon stopped and we felt that little bit stronger through having cheated it. The bridges were eventually finished with some time to spare. The clanking of mess tins reached its crescendo and slowly died out. The groups of shadows sorted themselves out round their bridges, picked them up and staggered off, still swearing.

It was approaching dawn and all was set for H-hour. I knew that war is a long game and it would be much more important for me to be fresh and ready when I was wanted than to try to be busy and useful in a few small ways at the present moment.

So I told the Signal Officer where I should be, then wandered over to a position recently evacuated by the mortar platoon. I climbed down into a good straw-lined weapon pit and slept.

George Dicks in B Company takes up the story:

We crossed the Molen Beek and then formed up, Ray left, my platoon right, with company HQ and Friar behind us both. I found in the dim light of the 'artificial moonlight' that the wood was in fact nothing more than a belt of reeds in the middle of which we had to take up position, at times sinking in the marshy ground and swearing and cursing under our breath in the manner typical of men in the Army. I deployed with 9 section left, 7 section right and 8 section in reserve and told the lads to lie up in the reeds until 6 a.m. the time scheduled for zero hour.

My batman was feeling very unwell and I had been in two minds about sending him sick. I knew him well enough to state that he was not shamming, but at the same time I felt that going sick at such a time would look very bad. I have never ceased to kick myself since for not sending him off to the RAP for he died of the injuries received in this assault at 7.10 a.m. that morning.

We had used the utmost caution in taking up our positions and felt reasonably safe that we had not been spotted. Our D Company were on our left and the Royal Warwicks on our right. Caution however seemed to be confined to the Royal Norfolks since the Warwicks made an infernal din in taking up position and I shall never forget hearing a stentorian voice shouting 'Cpl Hanson, move over to the left'. Within ten minutes Jerry had retaliated by placing some very accurate shells among the Warwicks. His nebelwerfer opened up and some of the shells landed uncomfortably close to us. The lads cursed.

At about 5.30 a.m. Eric informed me that zero hour had been put back one hour and that the artillery barrage would start at 7 a.m. We would get up and move forward to our objective at 7.10 a.m. I told the section commanders and we settled down to a cold, uncomfortable and tense wait. By this time we had become quite used to the wet in which we were lying – in fact, it only became uncomfortable when one moved.

After what seemed a very long time, 7 a.m. arrived and immediately all the field guns in creation opened up on the area of our first objective. From my position in the reeds between the two leading sections I was able to see the shells bursting and to our surprise and gratification we saw after about 5 minutes a white handkerchief being waved from one of the houses.

At 7.10 a.m. I shouted 'This is it!' and rose and moved forward accompanied in line by the two leading sections. Then I began to be aware that shells were dropping around me and that the Boche was firing his Spandaus in the direction of our advance. However we kept on advancing and were about 50 yards from the first farmhouse when we saw a German dart out and run across in front of us to the lee of another house. Immediately every gun and rifle in the two platoons seemed to open fire and the German fell riddled with bullets just before he reached safety. This second house for which the German had been heading was my platoon objective and we made a bee-line for it. Naturally my Sten jammed!

Just before we reached it I was astonished to see several men on my left halt and look very hesitant about proceeding further. I looked – and saw the reason. About 150 yards in front of us was a German Tiger tank in process of swivelling its gun in our direction. I swiftly moved the platoon behind the house but the tank evidently decided that it had had enough because, after firing a few shells at my platoon objective, it retreated.

As soon as we reached our objective about 20 Germans came out with their hands over their heads and we shooed them off back to our Battalion HQ assisting one reluctant type with the point of a bayonet. I started to take stock of my casualties and found about 7 people missing. This was a shock because I did not think we had suffered much. However three turned up from company HQ with whom they had joined on getting separated from the rest of us. The missing ones were Blowing, Hathaway, Taylor and Ball; and I soon found people who could tell me what had happened to them. Blowing had shrapnel in the side, Hathaway shrapnel in the bottom, Taylor a bullet in the leg and Ball had been a non-starter. So generally speaking I felt happy since none seemed wounded seriously. It was not until four days later that the padre informed us that Blowing had died in hospital.

In the meantime we thought we heard sounds in the house in whose small garden we were sitting and Pte. Capstick threw a phosphorus grenade into a room upstairs and shouted odd words – but there was no reply so we settled down once more into the slit-trenches we had taken over from the Germans.

After about a couple of hours we had received no orders to move and I was just settling down for a quiet smoke in my slit-trench when the cry of 'Kamerad' was heard coming from inside the house. I entered the house covered by L/Sgt. Larkins and found that the cry had come from the Dutch people who lived in the house and were hiding in the cellar. The old boy had a 6 inch long deep cut across his head and one of the girls aged about 12 was dead. The others – mother and a boy and two girls were OK except for their understandable grief. I ordered them out and told them to make their way to the rear but it appeared that the old man was too ill to move. At that moment a complication arose in that an incendiary bullet or perhaps the phosphorus grenade set the thatch of the roof ablaze. The boy – aged about 17 – got up on the roof and we handed pails of water up to him but as soon as the Huns saw him they gave him a burst – so he soon decided that there was no future up on the roof. Eventually I persuaded them to cart father off in a wheelbarrow, leaving the dead girl in the cellar and the roof blazing merrily [see below].

One other lucky escape must be mentioned. I had noticed, in turning round to encourage forward my men in the attack, that one man seemed to be alight somewhere around his waist and that he had collapsed to the ground. Sensations at such a time are so crowded in on a soldier that the memory of the incident is only fleeting; but I recalled it later when I was told the whole story. L/Cpl. Grimble had been carrying the Bren gun when a bullet had set the magazine alight – that is what I saw – the bullet had penetrated his blouse, AB 64 parts I and II, shirt, vest and smashed his identity disc and had then passed through his clothing again and out at the side leaving him unhurt. I should be inclined to disbelieve this story had I not seen the evidence – including the smashed disc. Just one more 'believe it or not' story.

George Dicks wrote an award-winning article which was published in *CHOICE Magazine*, September 1977. The article described the attack over the Molen Beek on 16 October 1944, the Dutch family in the farmhouse, the injured father, the dead child. It goes on:

Twenty-two years later, three of us, all ex-rifle company subalterns from the same Battalion met at a reunion and decided to visit the Dutch battlefields. Contrary to the generally accepted view, we had no difficulty in identifying our war-time line of advance. We crossed the Molen Beek and strolled up the road leading to the farm-house. An elderly man was standing by the door, sunning himself. I recognised him immediately. But he spoke no English; I spoke no Dutch. There followed some hilarious sign-language as a result of which I managed to persuade him to take off his cap. And there across his bald head was a long white scar.

Further gesticulations! We gleaned that he would like us to call the following day when he would arrange for his son to be present. When we arrived the next morning we were greeted by the family and by the local newspaper reporter who acted as interpreter. The boy who had been up on the roof was now a portly middle-aged man and the daughters were equally matronly. Mother looked rather forlorn and I had a sad feeling that our visit had brought back memories that had lain dormant for many years. But father was obviously delighted. After mutual expressions of good-will we went on our way.

In 1968, I received an invitation to their Golden Wedding. I didn't go but sent a bouquet of flowers and received in reply a very pleasant letter and a photograph showing the whole of the family at the celebrations – some fifty of them!

The farmer in this story, Wilhelmus Lambertus Wetterhahn, died on 6 March 1991, aged ninety-nine.

Also in B Company, Lieutenant Balsom recalls:

As we attacked, a German tank broke cover and started retreating ahead of us back towards Venraij and as it went it fired a series of Parthian shots in our direction; one unfortunately landed in the middle of L/Corporal Drake's section, immediately killing him and wounding others in his section. Despite this loss we moved on quickly and took our objective, cleared the buildings and made the area safe. Only when captured enemy stretcher bearers were recruited to help move casualties back to the RAP and they did not wish to walk through their own minefields, did we learn of the additional hazards we had escaped.

By evening the battle had rolled on and we just had shelling and mortaring to remind us that it was not far away. While moving around my various section positions, I decided to investigate further a German bunker that was behind our defensive area. In the gloom inside I turned over with my bayonet a piece of old carpeting and heard a groan. I found a badly wounded German soldier beneath it. We were soon able to get him back to our RAP.

To the left of B Company, D also made the same silent approach and experienced the same frustrating delay. Orders received had promised a very heavy artillery concentration for this attack – for the brigade front, if memory serves, something one thousand two hundred shells per minute. The leading platoons would be required to form up 100 yd from the barrage. My own memory of that day, in 17 Platoon, D Company, starts with breakfast organized and eaten in the dark, our only illumination from artificial moonlight – searchlights behind us angled low under the clouds. We moved off, slowly and silently, crossing the footbridge, following the marked path, then going to ground on a flat featureless field.

The next hour, from 06.00 hours, remains etched indelibly in my memory – it requires no effort to re-live my thoughts at that time:

Just been told that the Warwicks, to the right, have had problems and are not yet ready to move. We had heard firing from that direction. We are ordered to wait.

This is a very exposed position and dawn will come very soon. I can see silhouettes on the skyline of the farms left and right which mark the first objective. I crawl to the sections to tell them the situation. Time drags, the sky lightens and some movement can be seen, the enemy knows something is about to happen but I don't think they've seen us. What are we waiting for?

I can hear, behind and to the right, sounds of tank movement at the blown bridge – surely Jerry can hear it too? How much longer must we wait here?

The light is brighter although, thankfully, its a dull and dismal day – Jerry surely can't fail to spot us!

I see movement on the road to my right, the road runs on an embankment and two figures show plainly against the lightening sky. They must be Germans – B Company, on the other side of the road, must surely be seen. The figures walk back, away from us, apparently not having noticed anything.

It's getting lighter – we must move soon, we haven't got a scrap of cover and one spandau would get the lot of us. For God's sake let us move.

How much longer must we stay here, exposed and vulnerable?

As the day grew brighter the two leading companies, B and D, lay for an interminable hour within 100 yd of the enemy's forward positions, without cover, in full view, not daring to move.

Frantic efforts were being made to bridge the Beek as we hugged the ground, awaiting discovery every moment, not knowing what precisely was going on nor what prevented us from moving forward.

0700 hrs. An hour late. The barrage started, 25 pounders, heavy artillery, 3 inch mortars, heavy machine guns, the line of the barrage just 100 yds in front of us. A shell burst near me – I realised that one of our own guns in a 25 pdr troop was firing short – those guns were close enough behind for me to identify the sound of each one firing.

I lay there, listening to the four guns in the troop, counting them fire. One, two, three, FOUR – shrinking as I waited for the fourth shell to explode nearby. Something slammed into the ground between my right arm and my ribs. I moved slightly to see what it was, to pick it up. It was the brass nose-cap of a 25 pdr shell, too hot to hold.

One, two, three, FOUR – a shell burst within feet of me. In the belief that a second shell would not land in the same place I rolled the few feet into the fresh shellhole.

One, two, three, FOUR – another shell exploded very close. Will I survive?

One, two, three, FOUR – God, when will this end?

For an eternity of ten endless, interminable minutes we pressed ourselves to the shaking ground, deafened, battered, helpless. When, after a lifetime, the barrage lifted I called my platoon up – and out of the hell of that brutal, vicious ordeal those men who could get up wrenched themselves off the ground.

We ran forward in a ragged line. To my right I saw the Bren gunner of that section prone beside his gun – he was a reinforcement who had joined us only the evening before and with no previous experience I thought he might be scared and intended to help him. I shook his shoulder and called his name. He was dead. I took his Bren and ran forward. Just in front was a mound of earth and on its far side an entrance covered by a camouflaged ground sheet. As I approached, a grey-clad figure drew the ground sheet aside, saw me and ducked back in again.

I registered a young, pale, frightened face but my only thought was that I could not leave an enemy soldier behind our backs as we moved forward. I took a 36 grenade from my belt and attempted to pull the safety pin but my hands were too cold to close the ends of the split pin before withdrawing it. I sheltered against the bank of earth while it seemed to take me an age to press the ends of the pin closed against my belt buckle so that I could pull the pin and throw the grenade into the dugout. I waited for the explosion but had no time to see the result and ran on until we gained the ditch alongside the track.

To my left was a farm which was the objective of 16 Platoon and beside it I could see a Tiger tank which was pinning that platoon down. I looked around for the PIAT, the only weapon we had of any use against tanks, but its operator, who had replaced the man killed two days before, had been wounded and it had been left somewhere behind us. None of our tanks had yet crossed the Beek, we were without support and I was powerless to do anything.

Of some 30 men who had comprised 17 Platoon just two days before only a dozen were left. Near me a slight, quiet soldier of about nineteen was shaking uncontrollably, pleading to be sent back. I had no alternative but to tell him, roughly, very roughly, to stay where he was, to pull himself together.

On my left 16 Platoon had reached the farm, on my right B Company had reached another farm, the roof of which soon was blazing. Behind us we could hear the churning of tank tracks as the bridging tank repeatedly attempted to lay its girder bridge over the Beek, bringing considerable enemy fire down on that area.

Hubert [Maj. H.R. Holden MC OC D Coy] came up to learn the situation, told me that Roger [Capt. R.S. Elford] had been killed then went on to talk to 16 Platoon. The CO later came up also and I was talking to him just as Hubert came back along the ditch towards us – the ditch was interrupted by a bank over which Hubert had to dash – as he did so he was hit by a sniper's bullet and fell into the ditch at our feet. The remaining few members of Company HQ had joined us in the ditch, including the wireless operator and, at the CO's request, I later found out the strength of the Company and radioed it back.

Of more than one hundred men who had formed D Company just over two days before only thirty-three were left.

Lance-Corporal Ernie Seaman MM, one of only three stretcher-bearers in the battalion who survived, unhurt, to the end of the campaign:

. . . the big battle was Overloon and Venraij, a very sharp battle and bad conditions, very wet, a lot of casualties – the main one for me, of course, was Major Hubert Holden, for whom I got my MM; a lovely man and a good soldier – he had a terrible wound for a man but I met him at one of the dinners years after and I asked him how he got on after leaving the battlefield – he surprised me by saying he was the proud father of three children and that was after this very serious wound.

This was where I had my luckiest escape – L/Cpl. Drake got a direct hit from an 88 mm shell, but the unluckiest soldier there was Driver Bill Reynolds – I had him loaded on the jeep to go back with an ankle wound when he was killed by an air-burst. I had a very good jeep driver by the name of Jack Whiteside from Preston, he saved me a lot of carrying and walking by coming well up the front line.

The article from the *British Army Journal*, written by Major J.P.C. Searight, continues:

Somehow I sensed it before that beastly message woke me up. 'Sunray Mike 4 (poor old Hubert) badly wounded. Sunray Mike 5 (me) to report at once to Tac HQ to take over D Coy.'

I rose from my trench, shook the sand from my hair. I changed my socks, then gave my big pack to my batman/driver whom I would leave in S Coy, God bless him. I took my map out of its rather smart S Coy map board and put it with my beret inside my battledress jacket. Then I put on my tin hat and set off along the edge of the road to Tac HQ – thank God there was a nice little ditch along that edge. . . .

I suppose it was only a few hundred yards to the Colonel's forward command post but it seemed a very long way. It was behind what was left of a big hedge and I heard the Colonel's infectious laughter ringing across the emptiness before I got there.

The attack had gone well, he said, in that D and B Coys had captured their first objectives but not their second. D Coy, which I was to take over were now standing firm at a spot he showed me on the map. It appeared to have no military significance or advantages. (C Coy might continue the attack through us later in the day.) He showed me the best way to get to the Company, very exactly, detailed my new Coy runner to accompany me and wished me good luck.

'Mind the snipers,' he said.

Pte. Jordan and I walked on down the side of the road. Soon we were in full view of the whole enemy position. I could feel dozens of hostile, unfriendly eyes gazing at us. When would someone shoot at us?

We walked on over the tank bridge across the dyke. The whole place was absolutely deserted. I might have stopped, thinking we had gone too far but Jordan knew the way and on we went (Poor Pte. Jordan was killed on his way back to Bn HQ after showing me the way to D Coy HQ, I heard months later).

Suddenly we came on B Coy HQ and several friendly, smiling officers dug in under a thicket beside a ruined house. My morale, which had been descending, went up with a jerk. So there were real live human beings in this dreadful landscape after all.

We discussed the local situation and they pointed out where what was left of D Coy HQ was to be found – in a shallow ditch about 70 yards to the flank. There was no stitch of cover between where we were and the ditch and they warned me to look out for snipers while I crossed that open bit.

That seventy yards felt like half a mile. I jumped breathless into the little ditch, with my new Company.

'Keep down, sir,' shouted several voices. 'There's a Spandau got a line just here.'

Well there I was and there was my new command. One platoon was spread in a straight line along a shallow ditch with, I understood, Coy HQ at the far end of it. The other two platoons were not visible.

Coy HQ appeared to have been reduced to L/Cpl. Marshall the company clerk and two signallers. John Lincoln whose platoon was next door in the ditch was more or less keeping an eye on things. Morale was very low. Several men were just huddled up, shivering in their gas capes. The shivering I knew was not only from the cold.

I felt that I ought really to go and visit the two forward platoons. The only trouble was that the ditch ended at Coy HQ and it was in running across that open space that both Hubert and one of the Sec Comds had been shot when within a yard of Coy HQ. That made it a discouraging prospect. . . .

. . . I decided to crawl behind a low bank along the route Hubert had chosen to run.

It was a very long and anxious crawl. I discovered afterwards that the enemy sniper who had shot Hubert and two others had in the meantime been spotted and killed by my leading platoon. This was just as well for me and I decided that in future I would rather risk death more obviously and run.

At last I found a man from 16 Pl, a Bren gunner beside his gun. I asked him where his section commander was. There was no reply. I asked again. Then I saw that he had been shot in the head and must be dying. Oh, what to do now!

Just then a voice called to me from behind a hedge. It was Cpl. Davies of the leading section of 16 Pl and somehow I had got between him and the enemy. We discussed what to do with Wilkinson, the wounded man. We decided that we would have to leave him there and evacuate him the moment it started to get dark.

Eventually I got round my platoons. . . . They knew roughly where one or two enemy LMG posts were but they had only seen one living enemy. When C Coy made a limited advance through my left hand platoon about thirty enemy were captured only 100 yards in front of Coy HQ. I could hardly believe my eyes and was thankful that they had not made an Aunt Sally out of me. We can only assume that they were as tired and frightened as most of my men were. . . .

The remnants of C Coy came under my command to form one company and I prayed for dusk. . . .

Eventually dusk came; also rain, the CQMS with a big supper, and some enemy hate. Wilkinson was dead. We made ready for the night. It was good to stand on the road above our ditch and talk with John as though we owned it anyway.

Night closed on us, long and cold and damp. Many bushes moved in the dark but no enemy. We sent out no patrols, not because I did not want to but because I did not know who to send.

Just before dawn I decided to move my HQ to the lee of a haystack, which was more central and convenient. Another battalion was attacking across our front and we were moving about more freely in our company area.

The other battalion's attack seemed to have gone well so I went back to my trench for a nap. I was just settling myself in my straw-lined trench below the haystack. At last I was confident and comfortable, and happy to chat with Bill [Capt. W.J. Smart], C Coy's only surviving officer. We had only been in my trench a few minutes when that screech from hell made by a German multiple rocket launcher went off a short distance away on our flank. There were some terrific explosions. Coy HQ in their shallow trenches were in terrible confusion, and I found I could not see. Bill was luckily alright.

I was led back to the RAP and after washing the dirt out of my eyes the MO decided that I had a small cut on the white of my eye and must go to hospital.

While I was waiting at the RAP my old batman came up with a mug of hot, sweet tea.

'I should keep away from those rifle companies if I was you sir,' he said.

Nevil Griffin, in charge of D Company signallers, recalls that day clearly:

Our Company Commander Hubert Holden was injured in the battle for the Molen Beek crossing in October 1944. As it happened I was just behind him when he was hit. I later discovered I too had been hit but the fragments were so small that they had just penetrated both my battledress trousers and the top layer of skin on my buttocks and the backs of my thighs. I wasn't aware of it at the time and only discovered it when later I was in the shower and felt pricking feelings which on investigation turned out to be the tiny fragments. The last came to the surface in 1963 while sitting in the bath!

Another very disturbing event happened – the Coy Commander and we two signallers were standing with our backs to a haystack. My colleague who was the middle one of the three was hit and wounded – another lucky escape for me! I can't remember what number out of 10 colleagues he was but I think about number 8. No wonder towards the end colleagues began to get a bit uneasy about coming out to D Company with me!

Battalion War Diary:

16.10.44 . . . Heavy fighting against very stiff opposition. Several casualties are caused by shelling, mortaring and sniping. Nevertheless Bn becomes firmly established. In evening CO announces that the Bn's achievements far exceeded the expectations of the Higher Command and issues his congratulations to all ranks on their magnificent, if costly, effort. At least 65 P/W taken during day and great havoc caused to enemy. Heavy rain.

Lieutenant P. Buckerfield, S Company, recalls a moment when a practical philosopher established a principle which has remained with him ever since:

In the Molen Beek battle I was standing by a house near Bn HQ, in the rain and the din of our bombardment while the wounded and prisoners came in – and here I would like to mention some of the bravest men I have ever met, the company jeep drivers who spent the whole time driving up and down the axis of advance bringing the wounded in. With me was the Provost Sergeant, whose name I regret having forgotten since he taught me a philosophy of life which I have ever since lived by – that is, never to envy *anyone anything* and never to forget one's own good fortune to survive when so many better men didn't.

The sergeant, a big tough Londoner – nowadays I suppose you'd describe him as the 'minder' type, said:

'D'you know the first thing I'm going to do if I get through this lot? I'm going to dig a slit trench at the bottom of my garden. And any time I'm feeling browned off, brassed off, fed up or hard done by, I'm going to go and sit in it . . . and I hope it's pissing with rain at the time.'

An example of sharp eyes, steady hands and cool courage is recalled by Paul Buckerfield:

After the Molen Beek battle Sgt Moore with his Carrier Platoon section was collecting bodies of fallen comrades when Pte Stitt trod on a Schumine (literally shoe-mine – a small wooden box about 6 inches square by 3 inches deep, designed to be capable of blowing off the foot of anyone treading on it. As I recall, the only metal in it consisted of the firing pin and spring and so it could not be found by mine-detectors).

Sgt Moore spotted the cuts in the turf made by the minelayers and their pattern – staggered rows. He guided his stretcher-bearers by picking up each man's foot and placing it, for every step they took to get to Stitt and carry him out.

Private R.G. Freeman, 17 Platoon, D Company, known as 'Barrel', remembers the attack over the Molen Beek and how, after losing his mates from 'Moaning Minnie' bombs, he took shelter in a trench. He tells of the shock of battle and the consequences, to the infantryman, of living rough for days on end:

The mortars came in rows of eight. The first one came very close but by the time the last one had dropped it had hit the Bren gunner and his mate, they had been blown to pieces, all we found was a hand. We knew it was the Bren gunner's hand because it had freckles and he was a very freckled man indeed. What a waste of life – it is very embarrassing and upsetting even today to relive those awful moments!

My boots had been on for such a long time and my feet were absolutely soaked and very sore. I decided to take my boots off and found that my once grey sock was now drenched in blood! I waited until it was dark, then made my way to the RAP, I remember there was a full moon with just a few clouds here and there. I found the RAP but it was deserted, I crept around to the rear, as I turned the corner the moon disappeared behind a cloud. Everything was so dark, I stumbled and fell over something, as the moon reappeared I realised I had stumbled over a dead German soldier. I stood there just staring into his face. Panic set in and I ran and ran, forgetting all about my sore feet.

I did finally soak my feet and was given clean socks. It was unbelievable, I felt like a new man!

He speaks, as so many do, of his mates and of his emotions when visiting the graves of those who didn't survive and ends his memories with a sentiment many of us echo, 'I consider myself a very lucky man to be alive.'

Assault Division:

The Infantry kapok bridges were a success; the tank bridges – through no fault of the Sappers, whose pluck was beyond praise – were with one exception a failure. The last consignments of kapok were received by the Infantry at 4.20 a.m. The assaulting troops carried it forward to the *beek* and launched it with the aid of the Sappers. 185 Brigade crossed first, silently, and by 5 o'clock the Norfolks had two companies across beside the Overloon–Venraij road, the Warwicks two

An overturned bridging tank at Molen Beek (SNNO-V, Overloon).

companies across half a mile along to the right. A small counter-attack against D Company of the Warwicks was beaten off after a hand-to-hand fight.

If the Sappers were not lucky, the Norfolks certainly were. They began by advancing straight across a minefield, without realising it, and miraculously without a single detonation. Until the Warwicks had beaten off the counter-attack against their D Company, the Norfolks had to wait in very exposed marsh, accumulating casualties. Then the Warwicks A and C Companies crossed the *beek* and both Battalions advanced. This was at 0700 and the Divisional Artillery laid down a barrage for them. The German guns and mortars were already firing as fast as they could reload. . .

Farther along, on the extreme left, the Norfolks had advanced a thousand yards, to reach the woods outside Brabander. Since they joined the battle two days earlier they had been hard hit, losing 211 casualties, including five Company Commanders. . . .

This was an Infantry battle. As a demonstration of the way an Infantry Division fights in adverse conditions it was eminently successful. In cold and wet and mire and sand-dunes and dark pine-woods and minefields that were a perpetual nightmare, but with the fullest support from all the supporting arms, the Infantrymen advanced and took every objective. That was all that mattered to them.

A Special Order of the Day was issued by Lieutenant-General Sir Richard N. O'Connor KCB, DSO, MC, Commander of VIII Corps, as follows:

3rd British Division
I would like to congratulate you all on the very fine performance you have put up during the recent operations against Venraij.

All of you have taken your share in this success, but I must particularly congratulate 185 Brigade on the magnificent performance of bridging the Beek north of Venraij with all the elements against them.

In this fighting you have shown grit and determination, and you have gained the knowledge that you are a better man than the enemy.

It is probably the first action of a good many of you, and I feel that you have made a great start and have thereby gained my full confidence.

[Signed] R.N. O'CONNOR
Lieutenant-General,
Commander,
VIII Corps.

16 October 1944

Captain George Haigh MC, RA, of 16 Battery, 7th Field Regiment RA, who says he 'walked many a mile with the Norfolks', remembers, in Holland:

Probably on the outskirts of Venraij in Holland; the Company having suffered a fairly severe mauling were resting in a ditch by the side of the road. A steady tramp of feet is heard and some rather smart looking soldiers are seen coming up the road.

Norfolk Sergeant: 'Who the bloody hell are you?'
Smart Soldier: 'The Royal Warwickshire Regiment.'
Norfolk Sergeant: 'They're the lads.'

Only an old soldier can appreciate all the subtle shades of meaning in that last remark.

Captain Haigh continues:

A Company Commander pointed out to me a windmill, which we both agreed would make a very good OP for me to look a few miles ahead. He suggested a few of his company and myself went to it to see what the possibilities were. We did this rather quietly, knowing the Germans were not far away and after a while returned to the company. Down the road, partly hidden by trees and about 400 yards away was a Tiger Tank and within about half an hour, the gunner inside, starting at the top of the windmill, put about fifteen shells straight through the building, rather like buttons on a waistcoat, ending up a yard from the ground.

Between 13 and 18 October the battalion suffered forty-three fatal casualties including Captain R.S. Elford, Second-in-Command, D Company, and almost two hundred wounded. Lieutenant T.M. Rourke was awarded the Military Cross for his reconnaissance prior to and his work in subsequently establishing the kapok bridging over the Beek before the attack. Lance-Corporal E. Seaman was awarded the Military Medal for his work as a stretcher-bearer in this action.

On the 19th the battalion was relieved and moved to an area south-east of Heikant. On the 21st the commander of VIII Corps visited the battalion to offer his congratulations on the recent successful attacks.

Only those who have experienced the conditions which troops of the infantry battalions had to endure can know the terror which the soldier controls and masters, consciously or unconsciously, as he submits to the conditions about him. And it says a great deal for training and morale that cases of battle exhaustion were relatively few. A genuine example from my own experience:

19 October. We were relieved and moved back, into reserve, settling down that afternoon in a farmhouse a few miles back with most of the Company under cover in the farm buildings. Late that evening one of my platoon came to fetch me. 'Will you come quickly, sir, . . . is in a hell of a state and we don't know what to do!'

I went out to the barn where the troops were settling down to sleep. In one corner, surrounded by members of his section, was an NCO I liked and respected, laying on his blankets, having to be physically restrained by his men. He was delirious, raving and when I spoke to him began to curse me, blaming me for a problem we had all encountered, because of the conditions under which we had been living, that of sand and grit getting into Bren magazines preventing the smooth operation of the gun. Even in his demented state his concern remained centred on his responsibilities as an NCO and a soldier. It was an indication of the strain under which all of us had been and which affected different people in different ways. I felt a great sympathy for him, he had supported and encouraged his section through all the bad times and now, when pressure had eased, he could hold on no longer. He was taken off to hospital and rejoined us again some months later.

The *Eastern Daily Press* published a series of articles written by R.M. Gray, who visited the battalion in January 1945, of which this is an extract:

A tour I have just made of the area in which the Royal Norfolks bore the full brunt of a desperate four days' battle between Overloon and Venraij, gave proof enough of the hazards they were called upon to face in flat, featureless country, identical with so much of East Anglia's fenlands, so familiar to Norfolk men here from the extreme west of their county.

. . . Post and wire fences hurriedly slung across some of the fields and along most of the roadside verges are hung with small red triangles, warning soldiers and civilians who have resumed their normal occupations against the countless mines with which the territory was strewn by the Germans before the Royal Norfolks launched their memorable advance.

One of the miracles of the battle is the fact that two forward companies of the battalion, who fought their way over one of the most heavily-mined of these fields, did not suffer a single casualty from the mines, although later there were men seriously wounded by them.

The main objective of the Royal Norfolks was the establishment of a bridgehead over the Molen Beek. It had to be bridged at all costs, and it was done by the gallantry of men of the county regiment in weather conditions that were appalling.

The first attempt to bridge the Beek failed owing to the state of the banks. A second bid also failed. . . . The lot toppled into the Beek, where it lay until recently, a grotesque monument to the tenacity and endurance of the Royal Norfolks in their advance on Venraij, a town mostly battered to ruins, like so many others in the path of this battle. . . .

On the left of the road from St Anthony [sic] to Overloon is a little cemetery containing the graves of a score of men who helped make

The memorial at the Molen Beek. The 1st Battalion the Royal Norfolk Regiment D-Day Veterans Association raised a memorial at the Molen Beek, between Overloon and Venraij, which was dedicated at a ceremony in 1988, the land on which it stands being gifted to the regiment. It marks the battles of 14 and 16 October 1944, described in Chapters Seven and Eight, and is located approximately on the line of advance of B Company during the early hours of 16 October. The bridge spanning the Molen Beek can be seen to the left of the memorial. The ground over which D Company attacked is beyond the belt of trees, and the farm which was the left forward objective of D Company can be seen, in the distance, to the right of the memorial. The materials for the memorial, which is in the form of a pyramid to represent the sign of the 3rd British Infantry Division, include Norfolk flints and was built by Bill Holden and a friend, with considerable help from local inhabitants.

possible the crossing of the Beek. I saw the white crosses to-day, grouped in the clearing of a pleasing plantation.

They were buried there during a solemn little service in which bareheaded men of the Royal Norfolks, tarrying in their advance to the next town, clustered around Padre F.J. Green, whom men of the battalion have described to me as one of the most serene men seen on this front in the height of battle and one of the busiest too, ministering to comrades in need.

CHAPTER NINE

Doing the Rough Stuff

After a very few days resting, recovering, re-equipping, the battalion moved to the northern part of Venraij on 26 October taking over from 2 Suffolks. By the next day the town was empty of its civilian inhabitants, its eastern edge forming the front line. We could enjoy the relative comfort of the abandoned houses.

In Venraij, rifle companies changed location every four or five days in order to relieve tedium, to keep all alert and on their toes. On 27 October a patrol master, Captain R.C.Wilson MC, was appointed to coordinate all patrol activity, the need for which increased when, on 1 November, it was learned that an attack by the enemy was threatened in the region of Horst, about 5 miles south-east. The next day, 2 November, the posthumous award of the Victoria Cross to Corporal Sidney Bates was announced – the CO issued a Special Order of the Day. On that day also the first V2 rockets were observed being fired to the east.

George Dicks describes here the life of a rifle platoon at that time:

My first fighting patrol of several was on the third night after our arrival and followed reconnaissance patrol carried out by another platoon which had heard movement in a certain farmhouse. We were about 15 in number, naturally it went without saying that all normal precautions were taken; faces were blackened, plimsolls were worn, rifle slings removed and all personal documents left behind.

Cpl. Mason and L/Cpl. Hopkins were usually my scouts since I found they were best fitted for the job. On this first occasion our role was to approach the farmhouse and, if enemy were within, 'to deny the use of the farmhouse to them'. We went very cautiously preceded by our scouts and lay up in a field full of stooks of corn about 20 yards from the building. There undoubtedly were some noises coming from it – partly from something moving inside and partly from the swinging and banging doors typical of these houses which have been damaged by shell-fire.

Eventually I got tired of lying and getting colder so I advanced with my two scouts to the house itself leaving two Bren gunners to cover our movement. We went right round the house and looked into the stables and it was obvious that animals were the full cause of the noise since as we retreated we were accompanied by unmistakeable porcine snorts. We

Lt. D.B. Balsom (on left) and Lt. G.D.H. Dicks at St. Anna's Hospital, Venraij.

continued our journey to examine a second house but, finding that deserted, we returned to Battalion HQ to report.

After about three weeks of fairly comfortable existence we moved into a street of small houses at the west of the town and prepared to settle in for a week or so – but we were, of course, to be disappointed again because we stayed exactly two days and then were pitchforked again into the line in another position.

And during those two days of 'rest' I had to undertake a reconnaissance patrol. I forget all the details of the route which I was intended to follow because I never managed to complete the circuit owing to the fact that it was pouring with rain, all the ground was waterlogged, and the going was so heavy that we had to report back to Battalion HQ at the end of time allotted without completing our job. Was I wet!

I took L/Cpl. Hopkins and Pte. Plain with me and the journey was eventless apart from Hopkins insisting that he had seen a patrol of 5 Germans pass us about 20 yards away. But the rain was so insistent that listening was out of the question. To add insult to a very comfortless night's work I returned to my billet to find that my batman, Pte. Long, had allowed the fire to go out and consequently next morning my clothes were still drenched.

Patrols were the priority at Venraij. I remember a recce patrol in late November/early December after a briefing from Robin Wilson, the patrol master, at Battalion HQ, explaining what the task would be. He gathered information from every patrol and, as time passed, accumulated a mass of detail available for each new sortie. On this occasion he proposed a rectangular route, starting and finishing at D Company positions, and listed the various hazards that had to be faced – principally trip-wires triggering flares or grenades, which were equally dangerous to us as to the enemy – and gave some idea of what might be seen and heard:

'On your way out, to your right, here, there's a farmhouse where water drips from a gutter on to a corrugated iron roof which sounds exactly like someone using a spade.' He gave me the password for the night and then took me forward through the town to a barn in the roof of which the intelligence section had established an observation post.

There, through one of the many gaps in the tiles of the battered roof, he pointed out features on the ground that could be identified on the map and I could see through binoculars part at least of the ground I would have to cover in the dark.

Returning to my platoon I asked for two volunteers and L/Cpl. Gould and another man came forward. L/Cpl. Gould was young, neat in appearance, slim and spare, his companion older, similar in build. During the afternoon I had plenty of time to go over the details with them, to go back to the observation post and point out the ground and answer their questions as best I could.

After the evening meal and a nap we prepared for the patrol. A recce patrol seeks information, not trouble, so we were only lightly armed. We wore black plimsolls so that we could move without noise, our faces were blackened with burnt cork, woollen cap comforters on our heads, over our battle dress leather jerkins turned inside out so that there would be no shine from the leather. We wore no equipment except a belt which, in my case supported a revolver tied to my thigh and small pouches to contain compass and revolver ammunition. We each carried a Sten with a spare magazine and the odd grenade in our pockets which were otherwise empty. We were particularly careful not to carry anything likely to make a noise.

It was not completely dark because we had the advantage of artificial moonlight, which was a mixed blessing for, whilst it obviously helped us to see and shone into the enemy's eyes, we still had to use what cover we could to prevent being silhouetted against the sky.

Passing through our last outpost with a whispered 'Good Luck' from the men on watch we moved forward and then to our right, following the line of a shallow ditch. This was flat farming country we were in, few hedges, lots of ditches little more than two feet deep. The bottom of the ditches were no more than a foot wide, muddy and puddled – our plimsolls were immediately soaked and our feet cold, yet we paid little heed to that discomfort, our senses were directed only to what we could see and hear. I led the party, conscious that at the post and wire fence ahead I must turn left and before I made that turn I must locate a trip-wire across the ditch which activated a flare. The trip-wire would be at about knee height, the flare at a distance in the field and while accidental discharge of the flare represented no personal danger to us it would alert the enemy. This safely negotiated we went on, turning towards the enemy – a few yards along here was another trip-wire, this one connected to a 36 grenade which, if I triggered it, could be fatal to any one of us. I could not make it safe or mark it as both these options would render it ineffective so, again, I approached with caution, feeling in the dark for the wire itself, careful not to make any sudden movement. The same procedure as before, guard it as the other two step over and then move on.

We continued our slow progress along the ditches; in front, to our right, I could see the outline of a building from which came a sound made, I would swear, by someone using a spade. But I have been warned of this, water dripping on a tin roof is causing it. Do I believe the evidence of my ears or do I accept the information I have been given? I compromised and waited long enough to satisfy myself that the sound is so regular that it cannot be made by human hand.

Moving slowly on, beyond the limit of previous patrols, we saw marks on the road of very recent tank tracks which alerted us to possible enemy. We crept on to the farmhouse ahead, if the tank was near it would be concealed beside the house. I saw that the bottom part of the first sash window at the front of the house was open, indicating perhaps that the owners have left but that the Germans had a gun position in the room. I moved along the wall and stood beside the open window, I could hear no noise, no evidence of movement in the house, all was very silent.

After a long, long moment standing beside the open window, listening intently to assure myself that the house was empty, I moved to the open window and, just as I looked in, the most dangerous moment of all, for if anyone is waiting inside I am dead, a clock chimed in the room.

Almost anything else I was prepared for but not that – I was startled and crouched by the window, my heart racing – after what seemed, in the circumstances, something very akin to the crack of doom, nothing stirred, all remained quiet.

The Germans must occupy the house by day, I reasoned, and rewind the clock then. My heart-beat slowly, very slowly returned to near normal, the house appeared empty; we looked around the outside and then moved on to begin our return by another route.

More trip wires to find and negotiate and we arrived back, safe but cold, wet and weary, keyed up after hours of concentration of all the senses, exhilarated yet thankful it was over. And returned to the luxury of dry socks, a hot drink and sleep.

On 14 November, at an investiture conducted by Field Marshal Mont-gomery, Lieutenant-Colonel R.H. Bellamy received the Distinguished

Men of C Company pictured during a break on the march to Wanssum (IWM B 12156).

Service Order, Major D.W. Smith and Captain R.C. Wilson the Military Cross. Sergeant S. Allen, Corporal C. Thirtle and Lance-Corporal C. Shingfield received the Military Medal. For his activities during patrols at the time Private J. Parsonage was subsequently awarded the Military Medal.

The battalion, even in what may appear as a static situation, was constantly pushing forward. On 23 November it moved east to the area of Oostrum and the following day D Company patrolled forward to Wanssum. On the 25th Wanssum was occupied as described below by George Dicks:

. . . we sallied forth through the streets of Lul and Oostrum with Friar leading followed by me and Ray. The plan was for B Company to approach Wanssum at its northern extremity while A Company would enter from the south. Wanssum was a long narrow village running North – South and it was anticipated that in searching the houses we should meet halfway through the village. A Company was able to march straight along the main road whereas we made our way through woods and fields until the houses were in sight.

We then received orders to lie up while Friar moved forward to search the first few houses. We could see that we were under observation from a large church tower on the other side of the river and we confidently expected to see some hostile shells. In this we were not disappointed because Friar's platoon ran into a number of explosions, mortar shells I

Lt. C. Barnby leads his platoon of C Company into Wanssum (IWM B 12155).

think, which wounded two of his men – but the fire was desultory to say the least and Friar was able to reach the first houses, ensure there were no hostile inhabitants, and receive one or two rounds of small arms fire from the other side of the canal (which split Wanssum in two).

My platoon took over the house clearing, with instructions to concentrate on the main street. I was soon able to confirm the fact that there were no Boche on our side but it was obvious that they had not yet decided to abandon that portion of the town which lay over the canal. The church was now a large pile of masonry and I moved one section into it with instructions to watch through any gaps for the source of the machine gun and rifle fire which was disturbing us. The section must have been seen getting into position because bursts of Spandau fire began ricocheting round the ruins.

We continued to search the houses in the street running parallel with the canal. On one occasion Cpl. Hasler's section were ordered to run to the next house and clear it, and in so doing Pte. Bridges was wounded by a bullet in the biceps of his right arm. He looked very forlorn, but the only comments he received from the others were derisive rather than sympathetic – 'Why, you're laughing – you'll be home in a few days, you lucky old man'. He persisted in looking miserable, I shunted him off to company HQ.

History seldom, if ever, relates the routine, mundane matters of war, for example, cleanliness. The Army provided periodic washing facilities in the form of a mobile bath unit – multiple showers, erected in a marquee or ruined building, fed by pumped water heated by an oil burner. When conditions allowed, a party of men would be withdrawn from the line to shower and be issued with clean underwear. Sometimes the marquee would be set up in a field and although duck-boards would be laid on the ground under the showers and from the changing area there never seemed to be enough of them. In Venraij the bath unit was located in a single storey building where all the windows were shattered and icy winds blew from all points of the compass.

Having stripped naked in cold, muddy, draughty conditions, the troops would start soaping themselves under the showers, probably having to share each shower-head, finding it extremely difficult to retain their footing on slippery duck-boards and totally unable to control the temperature or volume of the shower. Without warning the pump fails and thirty naked men are left, soaped and shivering, without water. It needs no imagination to guess their reaction and their comments to the poor unfortunate who is tending the machinery.

After finishing the shower the duck-boards had to be traversed again, where a slip meant squelching into icy cold mud, to a table where a clean towel and clean vest and pants, woollen, long, or whatever, would be issued. These might not be quite the right size or could have been over-boiled in the laundry and have the texture of thick felt.

Most demeaning, on occasion, was to have to submit, before getting dressed, to a cloud of insect powder from an oversize Flit spray, required by order from on high to prevent livestock problems – which never did occur.

Lieutenant E.K.A. Hastings, joining the battalion in November, describes the process of getting there, the long slow journey by train to the port of embarkation:

The next day we sailed, uncomfortably overcrowded in a converted liner. The weather was atrocious, and after many hours at sea we had to return to port, unable to land at the other side. There followed several days of agonising waiting, and finally we managed to cross the Channel. Then came a long journey through France, Belgium into Holland. At Louvain, in Belgium, which was a huge 'sorting' centre, I remember staying a long while in a deserted café, listening to a very old man playing Bach most beautifully on the piano. Eventually several Royal Norfolks were taken by 15 cwt truck to join the Bn, which was resting at a place called Haps.

It is not easy at this distance to recall just how very apprehensive one must have been; we had been well trained, and no doubt had the confidence of youth, completely unjustified because of our lack of experience. My introduction to, and speedy integration with my platoon, company and battalion was made easy by the presence of three men. I met D Company commander, Philip Searight, who was washing and shaving 'al fresco' (it was November and very cold). His experience, friendliness and total lack of pomposity were at once apparent. He introduced me to 16 platoon which was temporarily commanded by the platoon sergeant, Sgt. Kay MM. How fortunate for young officers to have such men to assist them, especially when they arrive 'green' when others have much battle and general war experience behind them. Sgt. Kay was a very relaxed senior NCO. He knew all the ropes – not only had he been there, he'd seen the film, read the book, and even had the 'T' shirt. He had won the MM in Normandy but so far as I know he never mentioned it to me or discussed it with anyone. He made it easy to take over command of some 37 soldiers – I have the exercise book still in which I wrote down their names, numbers, next of kin, etc. Then there was the fortunate coincidence of being in the same company as John Lincoln, who was No. 17 platoon commander. We had been at Norwich School together, with another Old Norvicensian J.F.J. Williams, who had been killed soon after D-Day. With the tremendous help and advice of these three men I gradually came to be a 1 Royal Norfolk officer and grew to be so proud of 'my' men, 'my' company and 'my' battalion. As the smallest unit of an Infantry battalion, the rifle platoon mostly led a very detached existence in those days. Whether living in dug-outs, barns, stables, ruins or anywhere else, the platoon was very much a family unit, living very much in each other's pockets, detached from the rest of the Bn for longish periods. The platoon commander was always the one to whom his men should be able to turn for advice and help – for example with writing letters, and dealing with problems 'at home'. One had to preside over problems and arguments, and never show any favouritism. Always pride in appearance, cleanliness of person, uniform and weapons, cheerfulness, pride in being in the Battalion, high morale – these were the priorities. The result was a unit, multiplied by many others, which I believe made the British Infantry the finest in the world.

Robin Wilson, recovered from his first wound, relates an incident which shows the fierce pride the fighting soldier (the emphasis is on the word 'fighting') had in his unit and his regiment:

Looking back on the mutiny. . . . No, of course this wasn't anywhere near 1 Norfolks, but in Northern Ireland. Some genius had ordained that before any officer who had been wounded in Normandy could rejoin his unit, which we were all intent on doing, he must first do a spell with a training unit. So after I was passed fit from a wound acquired at Manneville Wood I found myself, in company with a number from 6th Airborne and other fighting Divisions, posted to a battalion of the South Lancashire Regiment at a place called Castlewellan. This wasn't at all to our taste, and I'm afraid we were a shade unco-operative. The first evening we were assembled for a talk by the CO who began by saying: 'You're all now members of the South Lancashire Regiment, so tomorrow you'll appear wearing our badges, and you fellows in the red berets will exchange them for the regulation type.' With one voice we said: 'We aren't going to. What are you going to do about it?' Wise man, he decided that a lot of trouble would be avoided if he arranged our immediate postings. I spent just three days in Northern Ireland, and rejoined the Battalion just as the battle for Overloon began.

When, after Venraij, things became rather static for the winter, with the Battalion manning positions along the River Maas, I was sent off to do a spell as an instructor at the Divisional Battle School in Helmond. Thus while others were living in cold and damp dugouts in places such as Blitterswijk, I was having quite an easy time. Not quite so easy on one particularly foul day. The weather forced the commandant to cancel the planned exercise, and he said to me: 'You'll have to take them indoors. Give them an hour's talk on street fighting while I arrange something else for the rest of the time.' Not a lot of street fighting had then come my way, but I thought I could remember something from those training spells in Aberdeen. Hardly had I begun when in came the Divisional Commander, General 'Bolo' Whistler, who said: 'Mind if I listen for a bit?' Never mind, the general was probably busy and wouldn't stay long. He wasn't, and he did. I received a message to keep going for two hours, and he stayed right up to my despairing; 'Right, are there any more questions?' To my relief he was most complimentary, and said he'd learned a lot! I think it might have been this incident which turned my mind towards teaching as a career. I remember a 'What are you going to do when it's all over?' conversation with Jack Dye at around this time. He was thinking of staying in. Reckoning that my luck couldn't hold for ever, I decided to come out. We all know of the distinctions Jack went on to achieve in his subsequent career.

20 October. Aachen, first German city to be captured, surrendered after a seven day seige.

1 November. Week-long battle started to capture island of Walcheren.

22 November. American and French forces entered Strasbourg. Three days later Metz was taken.

28 November. First supply ships entered Antwerp.

Early in December a scheme was announced to provide leave in the UK for troops of the BLA (British Liberation Army) and those who had landed on D-Day prepared to return home for a seven day break.

16 December. Germans launched a massive counter-attack towards the Ardennes, between Luxembourg and Malmédy, breaking through a thinly-held line, in an attempt to strike first west towards Liege and Namur then north to Antwerp, to deny its use to the Allies and to cut off the Allied armies fighting in Holland. Initially the attack was successful and by the 20th the Germans had surrounded the town of Bastogne. There was considerable confusion caused by a relatively small number of German commandos dressed in captured American uniforms and driving jeeps, and Allied troops were greatly angered by the murder of some seventy American prisoners-of-war near Malmédy.

In snowy, misty conditions the Germans forced their way forward for almost 60 miles but by 24 December their advance had been halted. Heavy losses of men, tanks and aircraft were sustained, in bitter weather conditions, in holding and then driving back the enemy – by mid-January the Germans had retreated.

The Platoon Commander, indeed all officers, were required to perform a reluctant chore – to censor troops' letters to ensure that they didn't give away vital secrets. This job was thoroughly disliked by all but it had its lighter side as shown by this comment from George Dicks:

Naturally the sudden rest resulted in unexpected literary talent among the men and our evenings were partly spent in deciphering and censoring innumerable letters. It seems that some soldiers are incapable of writing a letter without sealing it with a series of letters which may to the uninitiated seem like censorable codes. Such hieroglyphics as S.W.A.L.K. – Sealed With A Loving Kiss; and I.T.A.L.Y. – I Trust And Love You – are known all the world over. Less known are B.O.L.T.O.P. – Better On Lips Than On Paper and G.U.T.S. – Get Up Them Stairs! And N.O.R.W.I.C.H. – I'll leave you to work that out.

This was a period of constant patrolling, change of positions, brief intervals of rest. Lieutenant 'Friar' Balsom:

. . . what I most clearly recall was the week we spent in a position overlooking the Maas at Oeffelt. The Germans had here been completely cleared from our side of the river, but there was easy visibility across it and observed movement was punished by both sides. What made Oeffelt memorable was that it boasted two windmills which afforded excellent OPs. B Company was to gain a reputation for finding good OPs. The Germans of course knew we used them and often fired at them. Somehow most hits were in the middle so the observer at the top escaped. The stairs inside, despite getting steadily more rickety, remained passable for the time that we were there.

It was at Oeffelt too that we heard for the first time the steam tram that the Germans used along a line on their side of the river. It was only used at night and we could hear it chugging and clanking along. We were to hear it first at Oeffelt, later in the winter we were to hear it going through Well and later still even further south we heard it from opposite Arcen. I am sure artillery shots were called on it, but it always seemed to keep going.

On 20 December, 11 Platoon with others from the company moved forward from Tienraij to Ooijen Kasteel – from here we were to guard and patrol the river front. The flat fields stretched towards the river from the Kasteel and there were scattered copses and some reed beds and, as always, drainage ditches. There was frequent shelling from across the river and at night we could still hear the steam tram.

We were to spend Christmas 1944 in this position – the first time I had spent Christmas in a castle – even though it was not a very big castle, more a moated manor house. It had a great advantage – it was tall enough to afford a good view over the river – another B Company OP. It also had strong, capacious cellars. Movement by day had to be made with care and most patrolling was at night.

Christmas Day was for us a day like any other – same routine, same rations. I remember it quite well, as late on Christmas morning we received a bout of heavy shelling.

The battalion spent Christmas in the line knowing that festivities must be postponed until New Year. Attached to the battalion at this time were two companies of Dutch Resistance men, armed and equipped by the British, sharing the task of holding the line yet with little or no military training. Just before Christmas I was seconded to one of those companies as liaison officer and adviser, as were other officers in the battalion at other times. The Dutch were extremely keen and of course very excited both by their freedom and their wish to hit back at their recent oppressors. I was with them on Christmas Eve when they received Christmas rations – that night, without waiting for Christmas, they had a terrific party, consuming all the extra food and drink, enjoying themselves as they had been unable to do for years. Their happiness was infectious and I could understand a little of what they felt. Having eaten all the goodies, our Christmas dinner next day was bread and bully beef.

On 29 December the battalion withdrew to Horst, and the next day was spent preparing for Christmas. The CO offered a prize of a hundred bottles of beer to the company which provided the best Christmas dinner. The moment we settled down at Horst my job was to make sure D Company won the prize. So I set off searching Holland in the company commander's jeep trying to locate sufficient crockery to provide a memorable meal. After months of eating out of mess tins, plates would be a luxury. I eventually located a NAAFI depot in Eindhoven where I was promised that plates could be collected on the morning of the 31st. The traditional Christmas meal would consist of tinned turkey and vegetables with plum pudding and a bottle of beer apiece – if we won the CO's prize our beer ration would be doubled. We planned an entertainment in the evening and with Eddie (Lieutenant E.K.A. Hastings) I wrote a script following the pattern of a popular radio show 'I want to be an actor'. The only character whose name I can now remember, the villain, was called Count von Spitzenfarz.

On the evening of 30 December all officers had been bidden to HQ Company Officers' Mess for a celebration and D Company officers duly turned up for the party. Next morning some of us (and that included me) were not at our best but the day had to be organized. In the small factory at the back of the house were trestles, lengths of boarding and a variety of odds and ends. We constructed tables and seats, built a small stage and decorated the room as best we could. Everything was ready except the plates. The meal was ready, the CO had arrived but still no plates. Regretably we had to use mess tins in the end, but this didn't detract from a fine meal with the company officers acting as waiters. And the CO awarded us the prize.

We had borrowed a piano, and that evening Eddie provided all the music needed. The show was a huge success ending close to midnight with everyone joining in all manner of songs. Never has 'Nellie Dean' been sung so loudly.

The plates did eventually turn up, too late, and were returned to the NAAFI depot. More than a year later, in Egypt, I received a letter from NAAFI requiring me to account for two or three hundred plates which their

The traditional, but delayed, Christmas Day football match, Officers v Sergeants, 30 December 1944. Left to right: Capt. T.J. Harrison, Capt. M.C. Wiggins, Capt. H.J.H. Beeson, Maj. W.E.G. Bagwell (back to camera), Lt.-Col. R.H. Bellamy.

The ruined church at Blitterswijk after an enemy attempt to create a bridgehead over the Maas.

records indicated had not been returned. I wrote back in no uncertain terms and the correspondence was terminated.

The *Battalion War Diary* records that the morning of 31 December started with Church Parade. The CO visited each company while Christmas dinner was being served. Small children gathered round at mealtime to collect oranges. 'So ended 1944. Most of the Bn. slept the New Year in.'

Lieutenant Eddie Hastings also has his memories of that time:

There was a Christmas party where I met some of the other officers for the first time, and quite a party it was. Somehow or other some bottles of brandy and champagne had been acquired, and this lethal mixture in the form of champagne cocktails was my undoing. Completely unused to such exotic drinks, I was soon enjoying myself far too much, and helped to provide some of the music by taking over the piano in the small band which was formed by some 'other rank' musicians. The next morning I had to appear before the CO, Lt-Col Bellamy – feeling absolutely dreadful. I was severely told off – not for being drunk as I had anticipated, but for mixing with other ranks in such a manner!

Major H.M. Wilson MC describes another aspect of our Christmas celebrations:

New Year's Day was spent playing a comic football match in fancy dress to the horror of a couple of enemy fighters who zoomed over us at 0 feet in their new jets en route for a scrap over the Ardennes offensive. Clearly they thought we were silly civilians or else a lunatic asylum.

Lieutenant D.B. Balsom:

I remember Blitterswijk which we took on 5 January. A German bridgehead had been formed nearby. It was to be eliminated by 3rd Div and our task was to move into Blitterswijk. I don't think I have ever seen a village so devastated – not a building had a complete roof and there were people surviving among these ruins to be moved out. Some who were in buildings down on the river bank were difficult to move, especially if they were sick. Blitterswijk is a memory of destruction, shelling and patrols.

I don't think I have ever felt so cold as when we moved to the Hooge Heide. It was open heathland, bleak in the driven snow. We robbed haystacks to find a warm lining for our slit trenches and had white snow suits for patrolling. I remember coming back at some ungodly hour in the middle of the night, when an icy wind was blowing and the thermometer must have plummeted. 'Posh' Price, my batman at the time and an old soldier, produced for me a thermos flask with a steaming hot drink. I swear it was Bengers Food. How he got it, or even the flask, and how he heated it in the bleak and empty wilderness I never found out. I am sure it saved my life.

Eddie Hastings continues:

The winter of 1944/5 was one of the worst for very many years. In Holland, moving up to the River Maas, it was bitterly cold. Much time was spent watching and patrolling; living for long periods in dug-outs or exposed to the elements was hard. We were forever grateful for our support services, especially those provided by Quartermaster 'Bandy' Howard. How they were able to feed us all so regularly and well under such difficult conditions is a mystery – but how it helped to keep up morale. Patrolling was an exhausting business; to be worthwhile it had to be done thoroughly – in depth, nearly always at night, always in absolute silence. On two or three occasions I recall we had some 'trigger happy' soldiers behind us in support – they were from a Dutch unit which was helping us to liberate their country – nice people but anything but helpful to the patrol ahead of them! It was difficult to grasp where our little unit fitted in to the 'grand design'; difficult to explain to the soldiers at the time exactly why they were there, doing what they were doing, in cold and miserable conditions.

Major H.M. Wilson MC recalls the CO's departure and the arrival of his successor:

Tea at Hooge Heide with members of 18 Platoon, D Company. Left to right: Sgt. Crichton, Pte. Woods, Cpl. Simpkiss.

Snow came early in the New Year and Hugh Bellamy left us to command 6 Air Landing Brigade. Peter Barclay arrived and we firmed up on the Maas all in the space of ten days. Hugh had been a very good CO but no one was happier to see Peter back to lead us than I was as we were old friends and I could see a lot of fun ahead. I suppose there are few more gifted natural leaders than Peter. His enthusiasm is wildly catching, his energy enormous. His eye for country was exceptional and this undoubtedly saved his life on many occasions. It was said that when he laughed, which was often, it could be heard in the next county.

As usual everyone's morale stayed high, even those who lived in dugouts lined with hay near the wrecked village of Blitterswijk or 'Blitzmequick' as the troops called it. Whilst the ice and snow of January still held we managed to get an assault boat over the river *(Lt L. Dawson, 27.1.45)* which was something of an achievement as the enemy were actively patrolling their bank day and night. News of this success spread and just before the thaw we were asked to sponsor a party of Free French, who wanted a bit of fighting, to get across. We duly got everything set, with two assault boats up a tiny creek blind to the enemy and were just about to launch them when a fairly accurate spandau opened up from the opposite bank. I said, 'No crossing tonight' firmly but the gallant French officer thought I was very wet. The real trouble was that his men just could not keep quiet which was the whole essence of success or failure and a quite unjustified loss of life would have followed had we gone on.

Men of 14 Platoon, C Company, at practice for crossing the Maas by folding assault boat, led by Lt. L. Dawson, 25 January 1945 (IWM B 14148).

The account written by Lieutenant G.D.H. Dicks MC refers to the enemy crossing the Maas to occupy Wanssum Wood and the resulting decision to move the battalion forward again:

. . . back in the line, this time a few miles further north than Ooijen Kasteel and Wesserhof, two miles south of Wanssum in the town of Blitterswijk, held by a company of the Suffolk Regiment. I went along with Teddy [Maj. W.E.G. Bagwell MC] and others to look over the town and found a very troubled company commander in a cellar. He stated that he had been under intense shell-fire for four days and had had very little sleep. It appeared self-evident that the enemy was deliberately shelling the town as part of the plan of occupying Wanssum Wood, the road through Blitterswijk being the obvious way to approach the wood without unnecessary exposure.

Our next move was to take us to an area lying back about one mile from the river, an area of wood and scrub called the Hooge Heide. We were in dugouts and the snow was about 9 inches deep. During this period we devised another method of keeping the feet warm. Sandbags filled with straw were pulled over our boots and tied up with string. This certainly had the desired effect, in fact, in some cases, caused trouble arising out of hot feet – not to mention the soreness attendant on walking about on such an insecure foundation.

After a few days in reserve at Meerlo George Dicks found, to his horror, that the next move would be to Wanssum Wood:

The plan was to occupy the wood with two platoons by night and one platoon by day, the remainder of the company being about half a mile back in two farmhouses which we cleaned up.

My share of the occupation was four nights and two days – and during that period I achieved the greatest degree of coldness from which I have ever suffered. The temperature during the period was consistently low – the bottom point registered being −1° Fahrenheit or 33° of frost. Our shelter was simply open dug-outs and we carried one blanket in addition to our clothing and equipment. The Hooge Heide seemed like the Ritz compared to Wanssum Wood.

The first evening of our occupation Mike Hodges occupied the left of the wood and I occupied the right, with Teddy and company HQ at the rear. It was arranged to put out a standing patrol on the edge of the Maas just by the ferry crossing, and Teddy suddenly announced his intention of going out and putting it in position instead of leaving it to Mike whose platoon was affected. We had been warned by the previous unit of the presence of Schumines near the river but we had heard so often these warnings that few of us took much heed of them.

A patrol from 17 Platoon, D Company, setting out from Wijnhoverhof.

Just after Teddy had left me, a message was received that we were to expect the CO in our area because he was out having a look at the Maas himself. I warned both platoons and had returned to company HQ when suddenly there was a loud bang followed by a shriek. Both Mike and I realised that somebody had trodden on a Schumine so we phoned for the MO to be on hand and for a jeep to come down. To our amazement we found that the casualty was none other than Teddy.

About an hour after he had been evacuated there was another loud bang and once again we realised that a Schumine had been exploded. Soon after the CO appeared on the scene a little irate for no apparent reason other than that one of his bodyguard, a corporal from A company, was lying injured on the banks of the river. A search party immediately went to look for him but could find no trace. Later, Mike took out another party to look for him but in spite of the fact that they searched along the river for about a mile they could not find him. Early the next morning a crawling figure was observed by a standing patrol of A Company in Blitterswijk about 2 miles away from Wanssum and the poor lad was brought into the RAP. He had crawled all the way from Wanssum and his hands and feet were terribly frost-bitten in addition to the severe wound which one of his feet had received in the explosion.

On 19 January Lieutenant-Colonel F.P. Barclay DSO, MC, previously second-in-command of the battalion until April 1944 when he left to command the 4th Lincolns, arrived to take over command of his old battalion. The weather was bitterly cold, it was stated that this winter was the coldest in living memory – it certainly seemed like it. Private A.H. Solomon relates his experiences:

Winter. Lots of snow. In a town in Holland not far from the Maas river. One night on guard duty outside Coy HQ saw some figures in white camouflage going across the end of the road opposite me. Enquired if we had patrols out but was told 'No', so if they weren't ours they must have been 'theirs'. Wondered if they went back and told Adolf they had seen me!

Before this we had had a very bad day. Coy advanced early morning. I stayed back with Coy HQ so didn't see all that went on up front, but casualties were high – very high. Some I was told were caused by mines they walked over. I accompanied some of the casualties on the jeep driven by Sandy Sansom to a first aid post a mile or so back. Helped carry the first stretcher case into the tent and the first Medic I saw was a friend from Oulton Broad. How far you have to go and in what circumstances you meet people you haven't seen for years. I recall vividly that evening seeing CQMS Lacey by the roadside with his band of cooks getting the meal ready. The news of the very heavy losses hit him hard. He was such a caring man and always brought up the evening meal with a cheery smile and encouraging word even in the worst situations.

GOC VIII Corps. Lt.-Gen. E.H. Barker CB, DSO, MC (on right) and Lt.-Col. F.P. Barclay DSO, MC (commanding 1st Battalion The Royal Norfolk Regiment) coming out of the HQ of A Company in Blitterswijk (IWM B 14163).

Then to another farmhouse where we made Coy HQ, very near the Maas river, where in one of the lighter moments the daughter of the house tried to teach me how to milk a cow.

Lance-Corporal E. Seaman MM, carrying out an essential job, does not forget the bitter cold of that winter:

Remembered to this day is Blitterswijk, a lively little place on the River Maas. I dreaded going on those night patrols round those old farm buildings; being a stretcher-bearer meant always being last man and I always thought of a German's arm round my neck – never did happen, thank God.

Just fancy lying outside now, in the snow, at night, for six hours in the middle of winter; creeping out of your dugout in the morning, breaking the ice to shave in, the same water for 15 people.

On the banks of the Maas it was bitterly cold and instructions were given to take all precautions against trench foot and frostbite. Only when out of the line would we have the opportunity to take off our clothes – often we would live and sleep in battle dress for weeks at a time, with clean underwear only if we could get to a mobile bath unit. We were provided with woollen underwear and we wore sweaters, greatcoats, leather jerkins. Feet and hands suffered

Sgt. E. Kay MM (on left),
and Maj. J.P.C. Searight
about to go on
reconnaissance at
Wijnhoverhof.

most. We received a limited issue of cold weather clothing, sea boot socks, rabbit fur waistcoats, and were provided with a grease to prevent trench foot.

Patrolling was constant. One typical patrol, each man dressed as warmly as possible in every item of clothing he possessed, made its way into Blitterswijk and then, more carefully, along a farm track north to an area of marshland where the curve of the river produced a prominent bulge in the front line, remote from our forward posts. On arrival the patrol lay down on the snow either side of the hedge-lined track, what ditches there were had been flooded and were now frozen. The night was still, misty but bitterly cold, the range of vision not great so the patrol had to depend on hearing which necessitated quiet at all times, no talking, no movement. They stayed there for seven hours, senses constantly alert, gradually becoming colder and colder, their only consolation that they would be relieved at midnight. Just before midnight a commotion was heard in the distance to their left and behind them, firing they could not identify but which came from the direction they were expecting their relief.

The patrol continued to wait, cursing their relief for not turning up, now intensely cold and still unable to move about to keep warm. The leather uppers of boots, after days of walking around in snow, had become saturated and were now frozen on the feet, the leather itself solid as iron.

It was not until after 0400 hours that the relief arrived, delayed by enemy fire and casualties – the patrol had spent almost twelve hours lying in snow, unable to move to keep warm, the temperature subsequently reported as more than 30 °F of frost. That they survived the cold without any ill-effect says a great deal for their fitness and ability to adapt to all conditions.

On 8 February XXX Corps, under command 1st Canadian Army, launched an attack south from Nijmegen to clear the area between Maas and Rhine and establish a hold on the west bank of the Rhine facing the Ruhr.

A visitor to the battalion was Howard Marshall of the BBC who broadcast on the Home Service on 18 February 1945, as quoted in the *Listener*:

The Soldier on the Maas
I have just come back from Holland, that watery country: at least it's watery now – and even worse than that – so muddy we cannot appreciate what it means in this country – mud so thick on roads which have cracked and buckled after the thaw, so thick that jeeps almost disappear into it; and, incidentally, now that the covering of ice and snow have gone, we are beginning to discover mines in roads where we had travelled safely for weeks, mines which the icy covering had neutralized. And troops are living out in the mud. I have been living with them for a time, men of the Norfolks and Warwicks, troops who were living in the open 'within spitting distance of the Boche' as one company commander put it. And he was not far wrong; they were holding a stretch of the River Maas when I was there, a few miles south of where our attack is going on now. They were close enough to hear the Germans talking; there was only a river between them, and not a wide river at that. They had been over since D-Day, hammering away, never far from the Germans; fighting most gallantly in the woods and narrow lanes of Normandy; battering up through Belgium and Holland to this sector of the front, where as usual they were doing the rough stuff – quietly, solidly doing it. . . .

What is it like on the Maas? Well, to begin with – and this may seem odd – it's quiet. I don't mean peaceful. It's deliberately quiet; the further forward you go the quieter it is; and the more sinister the quietness is, except for the crump of a mortar now and again, or the crackle of a German spandau, or the sudden wallop of guns putting down a stonk on enemy movement. For instance, the other afternoon (and I tell you this because it's the daily routine for the men up forward and it may show you something of the job they have been doing since D-Day) I wanted to have a look at the Germans, so I called first of all on a battalion commander in his headquarters in a farmhouse, to get the picture; a colourful character he was, with a red scarf round his neck, sitting in a not over-warm room, planning a fighting patrol across the river. He said he had had a glorious walk the night before along the river in brilliant moonlight. He could see a sheep at four hundred yards; through glasses he could see Germans moving in houses five hundred yards away. But unfortunately he had had a company commander and his escort wounded; the escort had trodden on a mine and had his heel badly hurt. He had been told to stay where he was till the stretcher-bearers came up, but the Germans had opened up on him with spandaus, and he had crawled back to headquarters. There was still snow then; two hours it had taken him, and when he got in his hands and feet were frostbitten, but he was still cheerful. 'He ought to have stayed put', said the Colonel, 'but he had guts.'

Howard Marshall spoke of his journey forward under enemy observation to Blitterswijk:

. . . We drove a couple of hundred yards to a village which had been completely flattened; it was just a heap of rubble. And down below the rubble in a dark cellar, we found the platoon command post. It was so dark but for one carefully shaded lantern that I didn't know there was a

Capt. A. Dines of London, with his most-forward Salvation Army mobile canteen, serving men of C Company including Maj. S.T. Murcer (centre) and Capt. J.B. Dye (right) (IWM B 14143).

man asleep in the corner until he began to snore. There the fire plan for the fighting patrol was fixed, and we went on to the river's edge to look at the ground on the German side which the patrol would cover that night. That meant putting on a white snow-suit as protective colouring over our battledress; rather a tight fit I found it and very warm. We set out on the last two hundred yards, moving warily along a wall and through an orchard, stepping over trip wires, crouching along the bed of the stream, a final little sprint across an open patch, and we were there – on the edge of the Maas.

Other white-clothed figures were there, snipers and observers reporting back German movements in whispers to the company commander and the mortar officer. They had just seen two Germans moving along a hedge a hundred-and-fifty yards away. You had to whisper or you would be heard by the enemy. Well, they had heard the Germans: three Germans, for instance, arguing about Hitler. One said Hitler was a great man; the other disagreed bitterly. And there was one shot, and then silence. And they had heard and reported a group of Germans moving, and orders being given by a sergeant-major – and when they were asked how they knew it was a sergeant-major, they said they would know a sergeant-major in any language in the world. And there's a steam train the Germans still operate, bringing up food probably – and they swore they could hear the conductor say: 'Full up inside, mum; one on top.'

. . . So, the summing up from the front line is the usual one – 'Mustn't grumble; might be worse.' That was their summing-up, those infantrymen, those men of the Norfolks and the Warwicks on the Maas. But the observer adds to it a tribute to the magnificent job they and their like are doing. When the full story of the campaign comes to be told, the gallant part played by these infantry regiments will surely rank very high indeed.

During January the battalion had been visited by R.M. Gray of the *Eastern Daily Press* and his dispatches, reprinted from various issues, were published in booklet form by the newspaper and a copy subsequently given to each member of the battalion. He wrote of the 'indescribable magnitude of the organisation which lies behind all that our armies have accomplished since "D" day' and of the daily existence of the Dutch people 'indifferent to the roar of guns', living in shattered homes. He reported the quiet dignity and strong will of the Dutch people and that '. . . Nothing is too much effort for these people if it will help the men of the Royal Norfolks.'

He reported Army humour:

Which reminds one there are no half measures about the way Norfolk men do guard in this part of the Western Front. There is the story of the HQ officer making his way in the night to his office, a bundle of battalion papers under one arm. 'Stick up your arms,' yelled the sentry who had challenged him, and the officer put up one hand, clinging to his papers with the other.

'I said both your arms and put 'em up quick,' insisted the guard, interspersing the demand with sanguinarily colourful adjectives in the Norfolk dialect. The officer reluctantly let his papers flutter to the ground, and mentally pictured the smile he could not see on the face of the challenger, for he had recognised the voice of his batman, a dryly humorous character whose home is in Briston. With language and such dignity as the occasion demanded, the officer gathered up his papers and made himself scarce.

On the night of 8 February the battalion was relieved and after a long drive settled into billets in and around Rekem, further south and upstream on the River Maas. It was required to produce a complete operation order and staff tables for an assault across a major river obstacle using 'Buffaloes' and other amphibious vehicles after finding out their capabilities and limitations. Obviously, the task at Rekem was to plan, test and train for an amphibious crossing of the Rhine – an operation that everyone knew could only be a few weeks away. Training started on 15 February on the nearby River Maas where, by night, loading and landing from 'Buffaloes', armoured troop carriers based on tank chassis, was practised having earlier tried out various drills and formations on dry land. The river was in flood, the 'Buffaloes' had yet to be tested in battle and at times were difficult to handle in the swollen river.

Lieutenant D.B. Balsom:

We were all made very welcome at Rekem and found comfortable billets. I had a neat and tidy upstairs room at the home of Mme Kuypers and her family in a small house in the middle of the town. She gave a motherly welcome to a number of my platoon and I remember that Cliff Human was a particular favourite of hers. I was delighted to find her 45 years later still living in Rekem with members of her family around her and to take her flowers.

During our stay in Rekem it fell to me to organise a dance for the troops in the local hall. I had to negotiate with the parish priest and guarantee the safety of the young ladies. I am very pleased to report that all went well and that it was a most enjoyable occasion.

The winter of 1944/5 was a time of extreme hardship for the Dutch in that part of Holland not yet occupied by the Allies. The Germans paid little, if any, attention to their basic needs and at least eighteen thousand Dutch people died of starvation in spite of air-drops of food by the RAF. Ernest Ridger tells here of a recent experience:

Some two years or so ago my wife and I were staying in Bognor, and we decided to visit a friend who had been Matron of an RAF Hospital in

Aden during the war. She was living in the RAF Home 'Sussex Down' near Storrington.

We arrived about lunch time to find a reception being prepared for Dutch friends, and we learned that each year the Dutch came over and dropped cheeses by parachute as a 'Thank You' for the efforts of our RAF in dropping supplies of food during the Autumn and Winter of 1944 – these supplies in fact kept them alive until the port of Antwerp was opened.

A lovely gesture we thought so long after the end of the war.

During almost six years of war, seven thousand Allied planes crashed in Holland, most of them returning from operations over Germany.

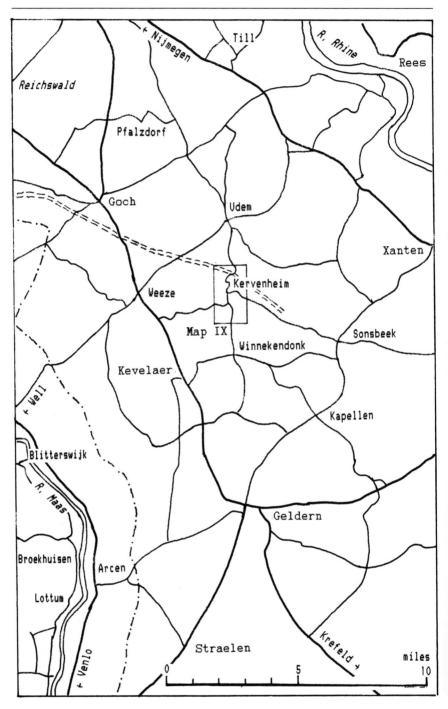

Map VIII: The Rhineland.

CHAPTER TEN

Not a Place of Happy Memories

The battalion entered Germany on 25 February 1945, passing through the town of Goch which had just fallen; the front line ran some 4 miles east of the town. To the right was 53 Division, which was battling in the direction of Geldern to the south-east, to the left the Canadians were going for Udem, and 8 and 9 Brigades had just relieved 15 Scottish in the line. Coming up from the south was the American 9th Army, the gap between being only 23 miles.

The country the battalion was facing comprised thick woods interspersed with boggy, low-lying ground and arable fields on the approach to the small town of Kervenheim, held by a strong force of German 7th Para Regiment and known to be the pivot on which the enemy defensive system was based. Roads were very bad, the weather cold and wet.

By 27 February the battalion had concentrated in the woods south-east of Goch; unfortunately the pioneer officer, Lieutenant J.R. Williams, was killed by an 'S' mine while recceing and clearing a path to follow the next day.

Battalion History:

Eventually, at 1300 hours on 28th February, the marching troops moved off to an assembly area about a mile along the brigade axis. The brigade plan was for the KSLI and Warwicks to secure the flanks, and the battalion was then to pass through to assault the town of Kervenheim. . . .

The CO, quite rightly, decided to stay put where we were till 0400 hours and get everyone fed and rested, and then move up to a forming-up place under cover of darkness and wait for a proper artillery plan to be put into operation before launching the battalion under this in daylight. . . .

A patrol was now ordered to go forward and find out all that could be ascertained about positions and strength of the enemy. Lieut. Rowe led this patrol, and went right into the outskirts of the town, returning after dawn with some valuable information. A most gallant and well-conducted patrol. [Lieut. Norman Rowe was killed in action later that day.]

At 0415 hours a long snake of men wound their way along the track to the assembly area. Before dawn on 1st March the battalion was dug in complete with command post in its forming-up place. By 0800 hours our tanks had arrived and the final link-up was completed. At 0900 hours the leading companies crossed the start line and the battle was on. The start line was the edge of a wood beyond which lay open fields with no cover of any sort. To the right were two groups of farm buildings, it was from these that we suffered our initial set-back. A company on the right suffered badly. Major D.W. Smith MC, was killed, shot clean through the head, all the platoon commanders were either hit or badly wounded, only the gunner FOO remaining to control what was left. B company had got on a bit better, but were still being troubled by the farther farm on the right. They did not know exactly how far A company had got and called for fire. This was answered by an 'Uncle' target but the enemy still held firm.

The gunner FOO mentioned in the preceding account was Captain George Haigh MC, who later wrote, as quoted in *Assault Division*:

My operator and I were watching the battle from a shell-hole about seventy-five yards away from the farm. We were neither of us in very good form, having had about an hour and a half's sleep the previous night. Before long the Company Commander and two of his officers had been killed, and the remaining officer I last saw with a wound in the leg being carried away by two of his men. I could count only fifteen or twenty men remaining, who with the loss of their leaders and so many wounded requiring attention were already coming away from the farm. I assumed command of the Company, and gave orders to the only remaining sergeant to organise a defensive position. After my operator and I had helped some of the wounded I returned to the carrier, and, after passing on what information I had, ordered the driver to 'brew up' straight away, and this being done, we took some tea round to the remaining men.

Sergeant E. Carr, the 'only remaining sergeant' mentioned above, recalls A Company's bitter experience in the assault:

At Kervenheim I was acting CSM. The frontal assault was a disaster. Very soon 4 officers and 103 ORs were reduced to only 35. The officers were all either killed or wounded. (Terry Rourke by blast from one of our own shells). I was the only senior NCO left and 34 ORs. The next day we entered Kervenheim unhindered.

Lieutenant Balsom remembers the move from Rekem over the Maas at Gennep, into Germany to the village of Pfalzdorf between the towns of Kleve and Goch, then on into the attack:

We began to advance according to our timetable through the wood. It wasn't very comfortable, as some of our shells seemed to be falling short and bursting in the trees above.

We persevered and moved out of the wood on to the long expanse of newly ploughed heavy clay. We moved out at a trot and the enemy small arms and machine gun fire was heavy. I could see some of our men being hit, as it was all so exposed. We had to get across before we could begin to attack the town.

Half way over I heard a loud crack, and thought I felt a push. I threw myself down and asked George Hardy, who had thrown himself forward at the same time, 'Have I been hit?' He didn't think I had. (I found out much later that the crack of the round had been loud as it had passed through the left shoulder of my jacket close to my ear.) So on we pressed and many of us reached a ditch and hedge that surrounded the edge of the town.

We collected ourselves and moved across an open space to a high wall that curved round for some distance to the left. There was no sign of our tanks nor any sound of them either to indicate that they had left the woods behind us. We did not have a radio to find out what was happening, as the company radio and company HQ did not appear to have got across. No platoon mortars appear to have got as far as us either to help us over the open ground with smoke.

As I appeared to be the only B Company officer left, I collected all remaining B Company troops and with what covering fire we could provide for ourselves we moved into the open gap. The enemy response was prompt and accurate and we had serious casualties especially in L/Sgt Moore's section, including L/Sgt Moore himself. There was no way round that way as fire was coming at us from many directions, including the far right.

We moved with survivors back under the cover of the wall and I went back to the gap to see if I could find another way round. All the firing I could see was from small arms. If the enemy had had tanks or heavier guns they would have used them on us.

Without support we could not move to the right, but if we moved round to the left we might find a way of infiltrating behind the enemy firing positions. I began moving all of B Company who were with me to the left. Very soon we found another of our companies (D) moving in front of us in the way we needed to go; I decided to ask for further orders. It was in fact this movement from the left which won Kervenheim.

It was a despondent evening as 11 Platoon and B Company had had many casualties and, although Kervenheim was won, we had not achieved what we had hoped. Of the several casualties in 11 Platoon the partnership of Taffy Wheeler and Wally Sowle, two old soldiers who were always ready to raise the spirit with their buffoonery, was broken up as Wally had been killed. So that night we all felt disappointed.

The account written by Lieutenant George Dicks MC two months after the battle gives a very clear description of an infantry attack:

At 9 precisely the barrage started and I had just time to see A Company go into the attack on the right before we set off through the trees. As we moved forward, the occasional shell from our barrage fell short (what again?) and exploded in the trees above our heads, causing us to duck involuntarily and to emit muttered imprecations! Eventually we emerged at the other side to see the roofs of the town of Kervenheim and the spire of the church about half-a-mile distant.

At 9.15, with Friar left and me right, the two platoons moved out into the open. Our rate of advance, dependent upon the rate at which the artillery barrage would be lifted, was set at 100 yards in 4 minutes so we had to move very slowly. I was unaware what luck had attended A Company's efforts; there was such a din going on that once more I experienced the sensation of hundreds of things occurring and being observed by me without any conscious effort of thought. I was therefore not surprised when my eyes, rather than my brain, told me that Gable and Capstick had obviously been wounded. Gable lying with his arm up in the air, and Capstick stretching a leg out painfully. A split second afterwards my brain told me that bullets were coming from the right, and my natural impulses were therefore to remove myself from the position in open country.

I ran forward past the end of a hedge on my left and observed another hedge about 150 yards ahead of me which looked as if it might afford some shelter for enough time for me to reorganize my platoon and continue the attack.

As I ran forward I saw many tracer bullets pass from right to left in front of me, and suddenly I felt a sharp stinging sensation on the inside of my left thigh, close to my groin. I staggered on for a few steps, examining my trousers at the same time but could find no break in the cloth. I therefore decided that I could not have been hit – and then I realized it was caused by blast from a shell which had fallen about 6 yards to my right. All these things happened within the space of a second, including the grim thought that it was probably one of our own shells.

I continued to run and eventually reached the shelter of the hedge in front of me. At least I thought it was shelter, but when I turned round to wave on and encourage those of my men who were following, I suddenly received a kick in the shoulder which hurled me backwards, threw up my left arm and rendered it completely numb and useless. I realized that I had stopped a bullet and so dropped back into the ditch alongside the hedge. This was filled with green slimy, stagnant water but I was very thankful to accept its cold embrace in comparison with what open country had to offer me.

Looking back I saw several of my platoon running across in my direction – Sgt. Larkins, L/Sgt. Smith, Cpl. Mason, L/Cpl. Hopkins and Pte. Blood – but I was as yet unaware of the fate of the rest of the platoon. I had started the attack with 22 men, rather a small number owing to my having several men on home leave and courses. As soon as the five soldiers reached me I heard the story – nearly all the others had been hit and Pte Cariello had been killed by a bullet in the brain. Sgt Larkins whipped out his jack-knife and sliced up my clothes, whilst I removed the cover of my field dressing with my teeth. The rest huddled in the security of the filthy water. We found that my wound was a small hole just above the arm-pit and bleeding had already stopped. Larkins put on the field dressing and I told them to push on round to the left where there seemed to be more cover. By this time other remnants of the company had reached me – I remember seeing Friar and L/Sgt. Moore from 11 platoon and Sgt. Smart and several of his men from 10 platoon. They all made their way up the ditch splashing the malodorous water as they went and responded to my orders to move over to the left for cover. Several of them grinned at me, knowing that I had got a 'Blighty', and I grinned back partly to cheer them up and partly because I too knew that I had got a 'Blighty'!

The enemy strongpoint at Murmannshof held off the attack by A Company, pinned down C Company and caused numerous casualties in all three companies. The only possible approach now to the town was from the left. D Company was ordered to work round to the left flank and was able to penetrate the north-western outskirts of the town being joined later by C Company. George Dicks continues:

I was hit about 9.30 a.m. and I had to stay lying in the ditch until about midday before there was a slackening in fire. Then I moved cautiously round to the left to find that D Company were in process of putting in an attack. I stood up and saw a Churchill tank at the side of a house about 100 yards away. I made a dash for the house, and ran into the arms of L/Sgt. Smith who assisted me round to the back of the house where I saw the disconsolate seated figure of Denis Millar [Maj. J.D.W. Millar OC B Coy]. He was very upset because he could not find out where the Company was and urged me, on my way back to the RAP to see the CO and explain what had happened. But this I was never able to do, because the Churchill which took me and several severely wounded back did not go to the Royal Norfolks area. Instead it dropped me with some Canadian stretcher bearers who quite obviously already had their hands full. Seeing that I could get no attention there I asked the way to the nearest RAP and, accompanied by McHugh, the soldier who had been in the ditch with me, I strode off down the road. The RAP was about half-a-mile away and no sooner had I arrived than a burst of artillery fire hit the road up which I had come.

I had a shell dressing for my wound applied by an MO attached to 15/19 Hussars and then started a series of ambulance drives back to home, sanity and safety via ADS, CCS and hospitals in Nijmegen and Tilburg. My morale was excellent throughout; I had none of the depressing symptoms associated with shock. I was flown home in a

Dakota a few days later having in the meantime had one operation and innumerable injections of penicillin.

It has often been said that the front line is the worst place to be when forming an impression of the general scheme of things; it is equally true to say that it is the best place to be to describe a minute part of the war – and if I have erred in the general I hope I have been exact in the particular.

Lance-Corporal E. Seaman MM, stretcher-bearer with B Company:

On to Kervenheim, what a place – this was where we really got cut about and the weather didn't help; drains full of water, where a lot of our people went to escape the shelling and machine gun fire. I think we started the morning with about 130 men and at night when the cooks brought the meal up we had about 26 to eat it – a terrible day for B Company. I can see us now, in the woods, very depressed as we had lost so many of our friends.

Captain Robin Wilson MC recalls the hectic hours of 1 March:

I was commanding D Company, which was initially in reserve. When it became apparent that the other companies were unable to get nearer to their objectives, I received orders to try to find a way into the town taking

The first men into the town of Kervenheim – L/Cpl. P. Gould and Pte. Duffill of 17 Platoon, D Company (IWM B 15046).

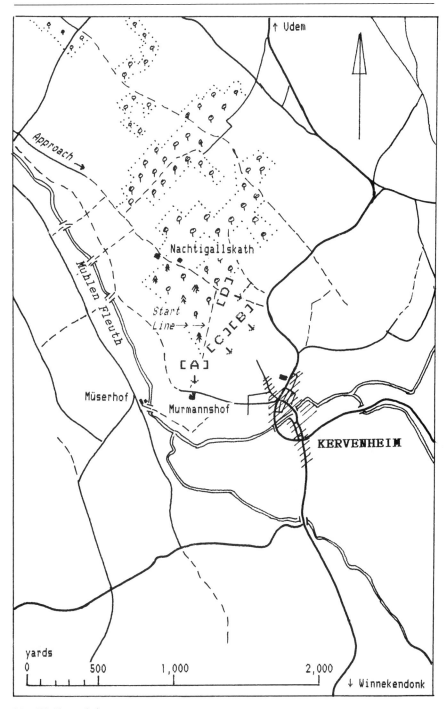

Map IX: Kervenheim.

a line further to the left. With the help of smoke from our mortars, and finding a modicum of cover here and there, we managed to advance without incurring many casualties on the approach. We got into the main street and occupied buildings on either side of it – a factory building on one side, and a group of houses on the other. To keep control of the company it was necessary on a number of occasions to sprint across the street to liaise with Leslie Dawson, my second in command, in the factory area. This was an unpleasant procedure, as snipers were active. I did it once too often and got a bullet through the thigh. I hung on for a while, but once our carriers were able to enter the town allowed myself to be evacuated after putting Leslie as fully as I could into the picture. To this day I regret not having stayed put as, though immobilised, I was still able to function after a fashion, while poor Leslie was killed shortly afterwards. No, Kervenheim is not a place of happy memories.

D Company, ordered to move forward on the left flank, gained the first foothold in Kervenheim. My own memory of this battle also remains sharp after so many years:

Robin gave out his orders to Eddie [Lt. E.K.A. Hastings], Jack [Lt. J.A. Laurie] and I in the wood to the constant accompaniment of shell-bursts, mortars, machine-guns, and 'Moaning Minnies'.

'The other companies are pinned down from the town and from Murmannshof and Müsershof'; Robin gave us all the information he could and we studied the maps we carried. 'We are to move into Kervenheim on the left, advancing along this track until it meets the road then along the road and into the town.' The map showed that we had to advance 400 yards to meet the road where it curved left and continue in the same south-easterly direction for another 400 yards until the road curved right and entered the town. From the map we could see that there were isolated buildings along the first stretch of road and after the final bend, beyond other houses, a factory built at a right angle to the road. This was agreed as the first objective, further movement to be determined according to the resistance we would meet. My platoon, 17, was nominated to lead.

I went back to my platoon, called the section leaders together and told them what we had to do. We would advance along the verges of the road, using the ditches we assumed would be there as cover. I gave the order to move and we left the relative shelter of the trees for the hazard of open ground. We had no close support, no tanks, no rolling barrage to flatten the opposition ahead of us. Just the will to get up and move forward.

The track was over flat ground, no ditches, no hedges, an occasional tree, nothing to prevent the enemy seeing us – luckily our advance did not seem to attract enemy shell-fire immediately.

We reached the road, which I crossed as quickly as I could to find a shallow ditch no more than two feet deep which gave an illusion of cover. We progressed slowly, carefully but without stopping, the leading section across the road from me, in the ditch on that side, I, level with them, in the ditch on the left of the road. The enemy must have seen us as I distinctly remember grit from the road surface being sprayed in my face as bursts of machine-gun fire hit the road and mortar bombs fell in fields close by.

We covered almost half a mile and were now approaching the final bend of the road beyond which were houses on both sides, built to the road, without gardens at the front. Some casualties had been suffered in the platoon but we were still pressing on. At the bend we came under fire from a spandau located at the cross-roads ahead and I knew that it would be suicidal to continue up the street, the ditches we were using ended at the houses and movement at the front of the houses would be in plain view of the enemy. The only way in appeared to be to the right using the factory building as cover.

I shouted across to the section opposite, warning them I was coming over then told my platoon HQ to prepare to cross the road under cover of smoke. I threw a smoke grenade ahead of me then ran crouching across the road. On again to the factory which was built end-on to the road with no entrance on our side although part way along the side wall a shell had made a large hole in the wall. The leading section flushed two or three German soldiers from this hole and we could only gesture to them that they should make their way back to our lines and get out of our way.

A quick look round the inside of the factory for other enemy then back out through the hole in the wall and to the end of the building leaving one of the sections in the factory. Peer round the corner briefly then run to the next building, a private house, probably the manager's home. Here I established one of the sections and platoon HQ while the third section investigated outbuildings.

We had achieved our first objective and were the first troops into the town. We had unfortunately received further casualties from 88s, mortar and machine gun fire and from the opposition we encountered from the centre of the town – I left the sections where they were, little more than 100 yards from the cross-roads, and made my way back to Robin. Mortaring was heavy at the time and, rounding the corner of the factory, a closer than comfortable group of explosions to my left caused me to drop on one knee. I felt a hard blow on my left hip, looking down I saw only a very small hole in my trousers. I got up and as I started to walk forward realised I had been hit for although I felt little or no pain from the wound I could not walk properly. Company HQ by this time was established in the factory through the hole in the wall and there I reported the situation to Robin also telling him that I had been hit. He told me to go back to the RAP but, for some reason, I determined that I should first go back to my platoon.

The section moves forward in Kervenheim (IWM B 15047).

I hopped and hobbled back and examined my hip. Very little blood, just a purplish puncture at the hip joint. Bound a field dressing over the wound, left the platoon in the charge of Cpl. Carter and made my way back to Company HQ where Robin asked me, on my way to the RAP, to report to the CO and give him the latest information.

A member of my platoon, a ginger-haired lad about my age and height, had been wounded in the arm and together we returned along the road and ditches we had used earlier. It was now well after midday and firing had not slackened at all, shelling and mortaring continued incessantly from both sides. I hobbled along, the pain at first not excessive but soon found that I was grateful for the support of my companion for we had the best part of a mile to walk before we reached Battalion HQ where I made my report. The CO was pleased to receive news of D company's advance, asked about my wound and sent me off to the RAP. There both Trevor, the Adjutant, and Jimmy Green, the Padre, had a word with me and the MO, after taking a look at my hip, gave me a shot of painkiller, put me on a stretcher and sent me off on a jeep to the ADS.

Lying on a stretcher above the jeep-driver's head I felt terribly exposed, painfully unprotected from shell-bursts as enemy artillery wàs shelling the approach route. The road was rough, part surfaced with logs to overcome mud and though the driver took the greatest care the ride seemed excessively bumpy.

I arrived in due course at the ADS, situated in the gloom of a disused brick kiln – I had parted with my trousers, underpants and boots at the RAP and as a result of the injection was in a somewhat stupid state so that, when I heard two doctors talking about me say something about 'ATS' my immediate thought was 'ATS girls so close to the front?' followed by 'but I haven't got any trousers on!' 'ATS' , I found, was not a promise of caring feminine hands from the Auxiliary Territorial Service but anti-tetanus serum, duly administered probably with more pain-killer for I remember very little of a long journey by ambulance to a hospital near Turnhout.

My platoon suffered numerous casualties, including Cpl. Carter, who I had left in charge of the platoon, wounded within minutes of my departure so badly that he remained paralysed from the waist down after a long, long stay in hospital. I was present at his wedding a few years after when, in a wheel-chair, he married one of the nurses who had looked after him in Stoke Mandeville Hospital.

Private K. Wilby, in D Company, has memories which he can never forget:

Before we entered Kervenheim we assembled in a small wood – when we came out I found that one of our men had been wounded a few yards out in the open. One of my mates, with a stretcher-bearer, went to fetch him with a stretcher but when they went out and my mate attempted to pick up the wounded man's rifle, the German machine guns opened fire and they dropped the wounded man and the stretcher and ran back to our position.

So we attempted it again, I volunteered to go with the stretcher-bearer and, as we went to pick him up, there was no firing, nothing, but we left his rifle alone and we got him back without the Germans firing again.

We went in on the left hand side over wide open spaces and eventually, in Kervenheim, after we looked round the first house we entered, when I opened the back door I could see several good places in the next house for German machine gun posts, such as open windows, and I got my Bren gun and sprayed all these windows and firing points that were of advantage to the Germans. I found out later that I had fired on the vicarage.

From that house we went out on to the main road into Kervenheim and eventually we came to this farmhouse, the whole platoon, under the command of Lt. Laurie. We entered the farmhouse and then went on into the barn, a few yards further up. Opposite the farm was a big tall building, we didn't know at the time what it was but we found out later that it was an asylum which the Germans had taken over and they were firing at us. We opened fire back through the windows and doorways in the barn and after things quietened down a bit the rest of the platoon withdrew to the farmhouse and I was left in the barn with two friends of mine, one had been killed outright, the other badly wounded – I stayed with him; after five or ten minutes he died.

After that, I was still stuck fast in that barn, the Germans were still counter-attacking the barn with only me in it. There was hardly any roof to the barn, but the Germans must have seen me through some hole or something and they kept throwing grenades over into the barn – they knew exactly where I was so I thought rather than stand here I'll go to the other end of the barn. This carried on for five or ten minutes, me dodging from one end of the barn to the other – it wasn't funny at the time.

When that finished I managed to get through into the farmhouse with the rest of the platoon – I got settled with them and put my Bren gun through the window. After about ten minutes the Germans with a Bazooka team came round the buildings and into the barn where I had been, they must have been looking for me. I saw this Bazooka team, switched from safety and lined up my Bren on the Bazooka man as silently as possible so that he couldn't hear me but he turned round and I fired straight away and killed him and wounded his No. 2.

Lieutenant Eddie Hastings, commanding 16 Platoon, D Company, recalls:

Robin Wilson was my company commander. He was wounded and waiting to be evacuated, sitting in some cover. I reported my position and situation – 'Have you got a plan?' I remember he asked. I had, but where was the cover? Somehow or other we managed to edge forward and as taught I tried to get a fire section down whilst other sections crossed the street under heavy fire (this is represented in the picture in the Regimental Museum). Severe house to house fighting resulted in heavy casualties before the day was won. But at what cost; John Laurie (soon to be killed at Brinkum) and myself were the only surviving officers of D Company. My platoon list, written after the Battle, contains only eighteen names. The British soldier, once again, had proved to be superior in morale, spirit and training – unflappable and 100 per cent reliable. No praise is too high for him. To have to write letters to next of kin was one of the most sorrowful tasks I have ever had to undertake.

The enemy strongly resisted the entry of D Company into Kervenheim and put in a counter-attack but were unable to dislodge the British troops.

Battalion History:

Our tank support had not been all that it might, and that intimate fire to help us on to the final objective was not forthcoming at the vital moment; it therefore became a purely infantry battle.

By 1500 hours the enemy had had about enough and C Company were able to back up D Company, and the key to the town had been won. Some house-to-house fighting still took place with a few suicide paratroops holding out – they would not give up or run away and became a menace by sniping. One tank managed to get forward to the central cross-roads of the town, but was bazookered from a doorway. A factory which had fallen to D Company became a bastion from which to operate.

To review the picture at last light: A Company were on the right flank, B Company at the edge of the wood, and C and D Companies in the northern part of the town. By now there was no fight left in the enemy, and late that night he pulled out what he had left.

Our losses in officers consisted of Major D.W. Smith MC, Lieut. G.A. Smith MM, Lieut. N. Rowe, Lieut. T.M. Rourke MC, Lieut. L. Dawson, killed; Capt. R.C. Wilson MC, Lieut. L.N. Sabel, Lieut. R.J. Lincoln, Lieut. G.D.H. Dicks, Lieut. W. Lewis, wounded. Our losses in other ranks were 37 killed and 115 wounded, 4 missing. Success had been achieved but at a heavy cost.

At the time of the attack on Kervenheim, R.W. Thompson, War Correspondent of the *Sunday Times*, was at Battalion HQ and his account of the battle appeared in that paper and was subsequently published in his book, *Men under Fire*. For the first time, in his experience in the campaign, the Chief Censor allowed the use of the name of the regiment. He describes the action at Kervenheim as 'typical of the worst battles in the Reichswald Forest. From the moment of crossing the Maas the infantry had a gruelling slog in appalling weather conditions. It was as hard as anything in the war.' Excerpts from this book, written under fire, paint vivid pictures, which faithfully capture both the horror and the heroism of war:

In the battle of Kervenheim. Thursday 1 March
It's two in the afternoon. Masses of blue smoke veil the burning mass of Kervenheim from which the black silhouette of the church steeple stands out solid against the grey driving mist of rain. That steeple has been the cause of a great deal of our trouble. So has that house five hundred yards away to the right flank. It still is. All day the spandaus have crackled to strew this unavoidable piece of open ground with the bodies and blood of Englishmen. The Nazis are still there holding out fanatically and some of these heroes lying now on the fringe of the woodland belt will die before that house is in our hands. The Colonel has come up. He speaks to each man as he walks along the positions: 'Going better now, going along

much better now. D company are well in. You've done fine. Good boys. It's been tough.'

The faces look up to him from the wet earth of the woodland fringe, red boyish faces under the netted tin hats. The whites of their eyes are very white and their eyes shine. They smile at the Colonel. They are glad of his words. They call him 'Two-gun Pete'. He may or may not know that. Peter Barclay is a man they have faith in. Some of them answer:

'Thanks, sir,' and say, half to themselves, an echo of the Colonel's words – 'Tough, yes sir.'

The account then details the events of two days culminating in the attack on Kervenheim:

Thursday 1 March

. . . The barrage was still terrific, and the fires still blazed unabated, seeming to have closed in upon us. . . . I stood by the side of the second in command, the Major with the large wide grin.

At this point I made an entry in my diary: 'The silent procession of human pack animals. It is the infantry, the men who fight.'

So they filed past, their faces framed in their scarves under their tin hats, like visors. On their backs their packs and short spade or pick, their rifles slung. Steadily they trudged along in single file. As each Platoon Commander led his platoon the officer by my side would say: ''Lo, Harry (or John or Norman). Morning.' And the answer: ''Lo, Charles [sic]. Morning.'

. . . Presently we pause by the burning shell of a farmhouse. Patrols have gone forward to make a recce. A company is strung out close in to the hedge ahead of us. Another company is behind us. I can make out the figures dimly along the line of the trees about fifty yards from the road. I walk along a line of men, and there is a kind of wonder in me, and a sense of despair to make you know about them. Here is one with the heavy cases of mortar bombs. Another with the heavy mortar tube on his shoulder. Another with a Bren over his shoulder. They pause and wait, and plod on, ready to fight, ready to charge with bayonets fixed, ready to die. I just want you to know about it.

0710 hours

The sunrise is beautiful, the eastern sky full of feathery clouds stained scarlet, and now the heavier cloudy sky to the west behind us is the dusky colour of ripe peaches. A young officer has just come in from a patrol. He's been right into Kervenheim. His face is broad with smiles and excitement. He is panting slightly, keyed up, keen. His report is clear and valuable. The CO stands with his head slightly lowered listening intently. The young officer has located a platoon of enemy in a house, and several spandau nests. He has also chased some Boche. Suddenly the CO seems to wake up from his intense concentration on the story.

'Well done, Norman. Absolutely first class. Grand work.'

The boy is thrilled. He salutes and runs out of the shell of the building in which we are standing.

'He's a good officer,' says the Colonel. 'He loves it. Always out on these patrols.'

Note: I've had to cross his name out from this part of my diary because he was killed two hours afterwards [Lt. N.W. Rowe].

1200 hours

. . . But the infantry of the Royal Norfolks have gone in again for about the third time, and they are staying in. It's been inferno this last two hours. It has been impossible to write more than an odd note. I have never seen such heroism as that of these R.A.M.C. men. Every few minutes they come in slowly under terrific fire, sometimes with walking wounded, an R.A.M.C. man in the middle with the arms of two Tommies round his neck. Sometimes coming slowly and carefully with their stretchers, and then on the armoured carriers rushing back over a few hundred yards of heavily shelled road with their bodies protecting the wounded and their arms holding them steady.

It began to rain an hour ago. Another hour of this and tanks will be quite useless. . . .

I have found myself flat on the ground or crouching behind a tank, or a scout car, and twice right out in the open with the air full of vicious flying metal, and always looking into somebody's face. Curious. You don't believe in your own immunity any more. It just disappears in some conditions. Faces are always flaming red bronze, very dark, and the whites of the eyes shine. Perhaps that order about wait till you see the whites of their eyes was because of this. . . .

The faces of some of the boys coming in are indelible on my mind. A boy, red face wide-eyed with wonder under his tin hat, a kind of reproach. Poor kid. His legs are all shot up, but he's dragging along with one of these R.A.M.C. heroes. The other boy on the other side is pale, white, ginger-haired. His arm is in a mess. A young officer comes in half-hopping: 'It's going O.K. now.'

'Are you hit?'

'Only a bit of stuff in the thigh.'

From the forward edge of the wood I look over the smoke and flame veiling Kervenheim. The tower of Kervenheim church stands out from rich billowing clouds of blue smoke shot with flame.

A Tommy on a Bren says: 'B Company lost all its officers. . . . How many came back, d'you know?'

'I counted twenty,' I said.

The shell-bursts are shattering the trees worse than ever. There were six wounded in that last burst. Right in the midst of it the R.A.M.C. men work calmly, and the armoured carriers swoop and swerve back towards safety.

1430 hours.

The CO had a word for everyone.

'Well done . . . well done,' to a kid bringing back two prisoners. 'First class,' to the remnants of one company momentarily in reserve. 'Thanks . . . thanks.'

It's still damned dangerous here, but the Norfolks have won Kervenheim. 'We'll sit on the river line all night,' says the CO. 'Another rotten night.'

. . . An officer, weary-eyed, shook hands just as I left. 'We won,' he said. 'We always do.'

To which I would like to say: 'Amen. Thank God and the Infantry.'

It should be noted, in these extracts, that where comment is made about RAMC men, the writer is no doubt referring to the battalion stretcher-bearers, infantrymen, members of the regiment, trained to deal with casualties and part of each company. They wore armbands bearing a red cross but carried no weapons although sharing all and possibly more of the dangers. They performed their task with the utmost dedication and fully deserve the praise given to them. Many soldiers owe their well-being, indeed their lives, to the stretcher-bearers. Proof of their bravery, if proof was needed, is evident in the list of Honours and Awards and in the record of citations of Individual Acts of Gallantry and Fine Service available, on request, at the Royal Norfolk Regimental Museum.

CHAPTER ELEVEN

Model Battle

The weather was cold on 2 March, slight snow showers were recorded. The companies in Kervenheim had spent a quiet night and in the morning found that the enemy had withdrawn under cover of darkness. By midday the battalion was on the move again, and found billets in Winnekendonk.

The next objective for 185 Brigade was the village of Kapellen, to the south-east, surrounded by a natural water obstacle on almost all sides. To capture Kapellen it was necessary to first occupy a large wood with a big country house called Haus Winkel, the battalion's target. The CO decided, in view of the losses at Kervenheim, to infiltrate by night with the whole battalion. Any daylight advance over the open stretch of ground leading to the forest which encompassed Haus Winkel would be very costly, for not only was the intervening ground bare and featureless but in addition the outer belt of the Siegfried Line, with its attendant wire defences and anti-tank obstacles, passed across it.

Lt. J.A. Laurie (Canada) leading Pte. Scott, Cpl. Lubbock and men of 18 Platoon, D Company, out of Kervenheim.

Haus Winkel was some 4 miles east of Winnekendonk and a mile south of Sonsbeek. The battalion moved forward at 2000 hours on the 3rd in preparation for the infiltration which commenced in the early hours of 4 March. *Battalion History*:

Silently the whole battalion crept up to and into the big wood without incident. This was largely due to very skilful piloting and route-marking by Major J.B. Dye, commanding the leading company, C. The first the enemy knew about this was when one sentry nearly walked into the CO, who fortunately saw him first and quickly and quietly disarmed him. The advance then proceeded through the dense dark forest. The whole battalion worked its way through in single file. The eeriness was intensified by sounds of Germans in the woods close to the route taken as the battalion passed through. However, so skilfully was this move carried out that each company passed through to its objective without opposition; without, in fact, arousing the slightest suspicion. Several prisoners caught completely unawares were then quietly sent back, and each company consolidated firmly on its objective. . . .

The tracked and wheeled column, meanwhile, had not had an easy job. Everywhere roads were cratered and bridges blown. Eventually, after a lot of trial and diversions, and by making a bridge with its own Class 9 bridging, carried by the carrier platoon, the column came on to the last bit of the route, which had also been used by the marching personnel. By this time it was light, and at the last farm, before joining up with the battalion, three prisoners were taken. Just beyond this farm the leading carrier blew up on an R mine. Every inch of the way up to here had been checked for mines by our own pioneers, but over this particular bit the whole battalion had marched about two hours earlier and it was considered free of mines for this reason.

The CO, Lieutenant-Colonel F.P. Barclay DSO, MC, distressed by the losses at Kervenheim, describes in his memoirs the battle and the action which followed thus:

A series of sticky and not so sticky battles followed until Kervenheim, which was a sod. The tenacious defence, because it was a German pivot position held by grounded parachutists, took us a whole day to overcome. The following day my Brigadier sent for me to go back to his HQ. My remonstration that I could not leave my forward position was dismissed. 'I want you to capture the next village, tomorrow morning after breakfast will do.' I explained that were he to come forward and look for himself he would see that it was as flat as a pancake and bare as a baby's bottom, but that instead I would get round it and cut it off that night. In my hearing he then got on to the blower to the Divisional Commander. 'I've got a marvellous idea General, I'm sending Peter Barclay round to our next objective to cut it off tonight!'

Carriers continuing the advance after the capture of Kervenheim.

The plan, aided by marvellous aerial photos, was amazing. A silent night infiltration in single file for a distance of about three miles through the Siegfried Line – or what there was of it in that area – across two awkward streams, through two minefields and finally a forest: beyond this was the schloss Haus Winkel, our objective, that commanded the road that would cut off the enemy. 'I shall need two prams', I said to the Regimental Sergeant Major. 'Very good, Sir', as though this was a perfectly normal request. In ten minutes they were there. Absolute silence was essential. We could take no motor driven vehicles with us: the vital wireless sets for the gunners could not be manhandled; stretchers were impractical so prams seemed the only answer; and so it proved.

This manoeuvre was so exciting – a challenge fraught with hazards – that I still retain a vivid recollection of the entire episode. Off we went in single file, led by Major Jack Dye and his company marking the route where necessary, some six hundred of us, over the streams OK, through the barbed wire OK, past the line of infantry positions OK, past houses with Germans talking inside OK, through the tank lines with the tank crews brewing up under their lean-to tarpaulins, then through two minefields to the edge of the forest. The minefields presented a problem; if they were only anti-tank mines, fine, we could just walk over them; if they were anti-personnel or mixed we would have to detect and remove them, marking the cleared path; a tedious business. By good fortune they were all anti-tank mines, so over we went. As the forest was reached I halted the column and went forward to check we had hit it in the right place. I had just crossed an intersecting cross-ride which I was hoping for and continued on a short distance to confirm, when suddenly I heard, then saw, a German soldier approaching, his Schmeiser rifle slung over his shoulder, muzzle pointing forward in a menacing position. I just had time to side-step into the adjoining rhododendrons, but not to whip out my revolver. As he passed me I prodded my finger into his ribs and whipped the rifle from him. Off came his helmet and for the second time in the war I saw a man's hair stand up on end in fright.

This occurrence was particularly timely. As my soldiers were so tickled pink at having got so far without all hell being let loose, they were not being quite so quiet. This prisoner being marched back down the line had the required salutary effect, for the forest, I could hear, was full of Germans. . . .

Major H.M. Wilson MC, responsible for the vehicle column which had to make a long detour to get to the battalion objective, here provides more detail of the problems to be overcome:

At about 1.30 a.m. a long column headed by Jack Dye, armed with reels of 4x2 flannelette to blaze a trail, set out. This route marking was very useful if a bit unorthodox as it was a black night till a waning moon got up about 4 a.m. We had not gone more than half a mile when we came to a blown bridge over a small river. It effectively prevented any vehicles from going any further on that particular route so Peter told me and Robin Dunn, our Gunner, to go off and find a way round for our fighting vehicles and join up again as and when we could. Robin and I had all sorts of adventures that night and as dawn was breaking we caught up again with Jack's 4x2 so now it was a straight run in, or so we thought. We were just going through a farm yard in our carriers when out of the corner of my eye I saw two German soldiers standing in a barn doorway. I immediately stopped the column and put these two prisoners into the leading carrier and jumped into the third one myself. Robin was in the second carrier with his Gunner wireless communications.

I noticed that these two Germans were wildly gesticulating as I shouted to get going again and follow the 4x2. Off went the column but we had scarcely gone 400 yards than the leading carrier blew up killing the two Germans and blowing our poor driver about 50 feet into the air. We were well in the middle of a minefield of 'R' mines, nasty powerful ones. We stopped in our tracks to find a mine immmediately between the tracks of Robin's carrier, an inch either side and that would have been the end of him. Our mine drill was good by now and the Regimental Pioneers soon pulled out sufficient mines to allow us to pass through.

There was a counter-attack when the enemy discovered the battalion in possession of the position and concentrations of mortar and shell fire plastered the area but the attack was held off.

D Company jeep crosses the Siegfried Line, where, as the popular song of the time said, 'We're going to hang out the washing on the Siegfried Line'.

After five days in this area the battalion was ordered to move north-east and take over a stretch of the west bank of the Rhine. Advance parties left and on 12 March the battalion moved to take over from the Recce Regiment of 43 Division, to occupy positions stretching over some 2,000 yd of river frontage near the village of Till, overlooked by enemy OPs on the far bank in Emmerich and Dornich. To screen the move-in, smoke was laid down by corps troops until after the Rhine crossing.

With 11 Platoon in B Company, Lieutenant Balsom remembers the period prior to the Rhine crossing, in which the battalion should have taken part had it not sustained so many casualties at Kervenheim and was instead allotted a stretch of the Rhine bank.

We had particularly to guard against German patrols infiltrating across the river, as they were eager to learn of the preparations for the crossing. Vigilance was most important. After France and Holland the men were well experienced – well organised with Sgt. Flint as Platoon Sergeant, (he had replaced Sgt. Smith who had left us to gain his commission and was sadly killed with A Company at Kervenheim) Section commanders like Cpl. Hartley and those who had joined us as young soldiers at Tinchebray, such as George Hardy and Cliff Human, were now seasoned veterans. The first time we moved up to spend a period of guard in a farm near the river we arrived soon after dark and organised positions and periods of watch and patrol for the night. When not on watch we were all able to take our rest. Early next morning I moved round all our positions to see that all were lively and 'standing-to'. I saw what I thought were two of the lads having a little extra 'kip' under the hay and gave the protruding boots a kick in the half light. Two figures leapt out of the hay with their hands up. We took the two prisoners to the rear as soon as possible.

During this period some raids were made by the enemy across the Rhine but without success, while a massive build-up of armour, guns, munitions and bridging for the Rhine crossing was taking place behind the battalion. The consequences of a kindly act are related here by Sergeant Ted Carr:

I was still acting CSM when civilians asked for the smoke screen to be lifted so that they could get their cattle in. This was granted. The German spotter planes were soon out. In the afternoon of March 13 I was talking to the cook outside our billet which was a farm house. Suddenly we heard a shell. It hit the house. I had run in one direction, the cook in the other. He was killed and I was hit in the back with a piece of the driving band of a 60mm shell. At midnight of the same day I was operated on and the next day moved to hospital in 's-Hertogenbosch for five days, then for five weeks in Brussels Hospital. After this I went to De Haan (just outside Ostend) for rehabilitation. I was there on VE-Day.

Alan Solomon, C Company, remembers this period well:

Advanced one day along a country lane and dug in late afternoon in a small hedge enclosed field not far from a crossroads. Just beyond the field on the right was a farmhouse. Rifle fire was heard from the farmhouse and eventually the lads brought out a German soldier, who sat on a fallen tree trunk about 10 to 12 feet from my trench, and I was detailed to keep an eye on him until he was sent back with the ration truck later. I sat on the end of the trench with my rifle pointed in his direction when suddenly (I swear by accident) it went off and a bullet ploughed between his feet. God, he flew up in the air. The CO and CSM were not amused! Personally I thought I had done very well. It was much harder to miss a bl—— great target than hit it!

About 6 am the next morning up came a tank to help us clear a way into a village on the right. Got as far as the crossroads and had his track blown off by a mine. Some of our lads who went with the tank were killed and injured. Once again that horrible task of collecting identity tags.

When we moved to the River Rhine we again took a farmhouse as Coy HQ. This was a lovely house with a large hall with stairs leading up to a balcony, and this was stacked with crates which were full of silverware, all sorts of booty that had been taken from Holland and Belgium. Beautiful things. [These were returned to Holland shortly after VE-Day by Harrie de Rooij.]

7 March. American troops reached the Rhine at Remagen and captured the railway bridge intact. Heavy fighting took place to retain it but, after the damage it had suffered, it collapsed ten days later, although not before temporary bridges had been built alongside. Bonn was entered on 9 March, and by 10 March the Allies were in possession of the west bank of the Rhine from some 40 miles upstream from Bonn down to Nijmegen.

22 March. American forces secured two further bridgeheads over the Rhine, at Nierstein and Oppenheim. In preparation for the crossing of the Rhine in the area of Wesel, more than 250,000 tons of ammunition, stores and equipment had been carried to dumps behind the front line. On the night of 23 March a bombardment commenced on a 25 mile front together with heavy bombing on Wesel, timed to coincide with an attack by a commando brigade which, as a result, was able to occupy most of the town before dawn, by which time three bridgeheads had been established and the only major resistance left was in the vicinity of Rees. Two airborne divisions, the British 6th and the American 17th, landing during the morning further enlarged the bridgehead and by that evening Allied forces had driven 6 miles beyond the Rhine.

Within three days of the crossing twelve bridges had been constructed over the Rhine and the Allies had penetrated 20 miles beyond.

On 25 March Winston Churchill visited the Rhine front and crossed the river where, it is alleged, he expressed his feelings for the enemy most forcibly by relieving himself on the east bank.

At 0400 hours on 29 March the battalion set out to march to the bridge opposite Rees [London Bridge], crossing the Rhine in late morning and marching through the utterly destroyed town of Rees to farm buildings to the south-east where the men settled down for two days.

At 1900 hours on 1 April the battalion moved forward again and by midnight was established in Lichtenvoorde in Holland. They left at 18.00 hours the next day and duly arrived at Enschede. The following day a recce party led by the CO went forward to plan the attack on Lingen, a small German town standing on the east bank of the Ems Canal, of both strategic and tactical value to the enemy, defended by a variety of German forces, Para., SS, Wehrmacht and 'Home Guard'.

Battalion History:

At 1600 hours, 3 April, the battalion left Enschede and were soon across the frontier back into Germany. After about twenty miles the column had to wait for several hours whilst a bridge which kept slipping was fixed by the sappers. Eventually the whole battalion got across, but it was not till dawn that we arrived at our destination. . . . The KSLI were to force an immediate bridgehead. The Warwicks were then to pass through to the

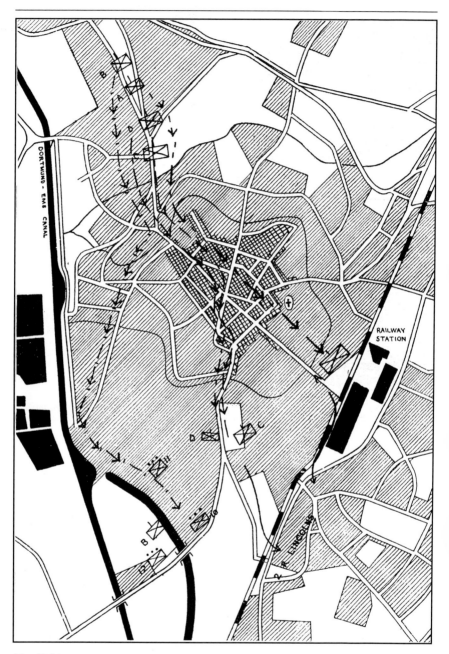

Map X: Lingen.

Sgt. Langford DCM with his 'Wasp'.

north-east quarter of the town, and we were then to pass through and clear the town proper.

By midday (4th) the battalion was well in contact; there was sniping from many houses, and little strong-points had to be dealt with. B Company got on very well with their right on the canal and made its objective, but soon it looked as though they would be cut off, as infiltration was taking place between them and the remainder of the battalion. C and D Companies now filled the gap between A and B Companies, and the whole battalion was fully extended. It was a real soldier's street-fighting battle, but we would have given anything for a squadron of Crocodiles. Unfortunately we only had one Wasp that was working, and this, under Sgt. Langford, did extremely well and saved many nasty situations. . . . [Sgt., later CSM, E.J.L. Langford was subsequently awarded the Distinguished Conduct Medal for his action in this battle.]

After the main square of the town had been passed, the stiffest opposition was met. Major J.B. Dye, commanding C Company, got hit, and it was only after a frantic effort with the one and only Wasp that he was extricated from where he had fallen directly under the nose of a spandau. . . . By 1800 hours, things were fairly well under control and a number of houses were burning nicely, but the battalion was just about exhausted. There had been no sleep for the majority for two nights past, and it is a very tiring job to keep searching houses with Boche almost everywhere and the type that is not prepared to give in.

In one of the two leading companies, B, Lieutenant Balsom recalls:

It was after midday the next day, 4 April, when at last it was our turn to attack – B Company right again and A Company left. Clearing houses on our way, we pressed on and soon seized our objectives – 11 Platoon's was a magnificent grain silo near the canal on the far side of town. There we stopped and made our dispositions ready for any counter-attack. It was as well that we did, as we had outstripped the rest. The war at this time was so fluid that there were still groups of Germans behind us that were encountered by the other companies as they came to link up with us. Groups went from strongpoint to strongpoint as they could.

Ernie Seaman, still with B Company in this battle, was reminded of it in latter years:

What about Lingen, another lively spot but I couldn't remember much about it until I met Maj.-Gen. Jack Dye not many years ago and he reminded me that I was the stretcher-bearer who picked him up in the middle of the street amongst all the bullets flying about.

But my luck held right through to the end, one of just three stretcher-bearers left who landed on D-Day, the others were L/Cpl. Shingfield and Sgt. 'Trunky' Allen.

Major H.M. Wilson MC describes crossing a Class 9 Bailey bridge at first light into the town of Lingen. The Warwicks had a finger-tip hold on the bridgehead but no more. The CO and his IO crept forward with the leading company into the town square. So far they had been unopposed because the Warwicks had hit the enemy hard in the initial phase and at the river crossing. He continues:

I crept along just behind ready to call up another company according to how things went. Suddenly it started and the enemy seemed to come alive all round us and a great deal of shooting went on. We sent for our flame-throwing carriers, a new toy which we were longing to use and here was the golden opportunity. It was not an easy battle as the enemy would keep popping out of cellars or suddenly appearing at upper windows and shoot at you; one needed eyes all round to catch them before they had a go at you. One company got cut off and we had a job to open up a way to it but by the evening things were more or less under control and our casualties were not very serious which was pure luck considering the amount of sniping to which we had all been subjected.

Ken Wilby, 18 Platoon, D Company, has poignant and painful memories of Lingen:

As we advanced into Lingen we went house-to-house fighting again and the first house we went into I found was a doctor's house – the doctor was in it and his daughter, about nineteen years old, in the cellar, hiding. The daughter ran out as soon as she found that we were English, she ran forward, put her arms around me, kissed me and bade me welcome. The reason was, they were more frightened of their own troops than us, apparently their own troops had been treating them roughly.

Then we continued to carry out the house-to-house search and after finishing this particular street came back – when we got round the corner the Germans, whom we had not seen, opened fire but we soon found where they were, in a cellar, firing through a little gap about a foot high between the footpath and the cellar. We fired back and shouted to them to give in because it was hopeless for them, but they would not so we sent for the flamethrower which came up and fired on the Germans in the

The battle for Lingen.

Three enemy officer cadet prisoners with (left to right) Pte. Wilby, Pte. Phillipson, L/Cpl. Gould.

cellar – then they came out, they all surrendered, and they were pitiful sights, all their faces were black, skin peeling off, I felt a bit sorry for them, for a moment.

Something that's always been on my mind – I can't remember where it was, but I know it was in a bake-house. There was a young German in the bakery and he kept throwing grenades through a hole in the wall, like a ventilator. I looked around and I could only see one position where he could escape and that was through a narrow road on the left hand side. Once again I trained my Bren gun on the position I thought he would come out and truly enough he did exactly the thing I predicted, anyhow I shot him, he was only a few yards away and I could tell he was only a young boy, about fifteen. . . . I put another burst into him. The point I'm trying to get at is if I hadn't put that second burst into him, would he still be alive today?

That's the reason that sometimes I think about it, would he still be alive today if I hadn't fired a second time? He was only a young lad of fifteen. I have that on my mind still.

Private E.E. 'Chalky' White had served in other regiments and joined 1st Royal Norfolks some three weeks before D-Day, landing on D+1 in a reinforcement platoon, joining the Anti-tank Platoon in the early hours of D+2 as a member of 'Tubby' Pratt's gun team.

We were engaged in the attack on Lingen, there were several buildings alight, including a block of flats said to hold some 300 fanatical SS troops; we never found out for sure, because they did not surrender – or come out alive. We occupied a fairly large house consisting of three floors, all beautifully furnished, our section leader, a regular soldier (Lance/Sergeant Ernie Newman) who had the most dazzling white teeth in the battalion (and proud of them), got organised and we 'established' ourselves.

After having fought our way through France, Belgium and Holland we were now battle-seasoned veterans and had everything 'worked out to three decimal places'; the procedure was at the first opportunity (we took turns) someone made a cup of tea. The great moment arrived and we sat down to enjoy it – Cor! it tasted awful. Somebody enquired of the tea-maker (Joe Ely), 'Where did you get the water from?' his answer was, 'The bath upstairs was full of water, it should be alright, it's been boiled'. Thereupon our sergeant with the brilliant choppers said, 'Oh I cleaned my teeth in that!' . . . it was the last of our tea ration.

My 'awareness' has helped me many times, for example, at Lingen, I was advancing down the street (the houses had no front gardens) when I came to a house with the front door blown in, I stood on the stone step and had a quick 'peek' to make sure Jerry was not waiting for me. I heard a shell coming and threw myself into the hall, as I did so the shell landed on the step where I had been standing, the blast knocked me over and a tiny piece of shrapnel hit me under my right eyebrow (I picked it out afterwards) and although it bled I still got a black eye. I carried on and put it down to another 'near one' – and later found an old German in the cellar armed with a Luger.

The muzzle velocity of the SP gun, almost certainly an 88 mm, was so high that a shell from the gun exploded on target 900 yd away within the same second it was fired! Thirty years later it dawned on me that you cannot hear those shells coming – I heard it *before* it was fired!

On the journey into Germany Lieutenant-Colonel Barclay had seen a litter of dachshund puppies and determined that he would have one. However, he was told to go forward 30 miles to prepare for the battle of Lingen which he describes as '. . . a very nasty one . . . Our adversaries were again grounded parachutists and fought tooth and nail; it took us many hours to dislodge them during which Major Humphrey Wilson, my second-in-command, displayed conspicuous gallantry, which won him the MC' Battalion HQ was established in a draper's shop. Just prior to the battle Lieutenant-Colonel Barclay remembered the puppies and decided to send his driver back to get one of them:

How to get Digby back through this lot to get a puppy? I had noticed one particularly bobbery one – that was the one I wanted. Sudden brainwave;

when my General wanted to get somewhere in a hurry he mounted a large black and white check flag – as in motor racing – on his car and everyone had to get out of the way. This shop conveniently stocked white and dark blue handkerchiefs. In no time we had a superb flag pinned together and off went Digby on his long journey – puppy collecting. Of course he had a ball. Everything had to get off the road, tanks, guns, lorries, the lot, while he sailed majestically on his way.

So hot was the battle that my thoughts were at once elsewhere. After some hours of intense fighting we had captured the place and I got into my jeep for the pursuit. Suddenly a cardboard box descended on my head from behind; in it were silk stockings galore. 'What the devil are you doing with these Digby?' 'Well if your wife doesn't want them my girl will.' Then I was conscious that he appeared to be in the family way. 'And what on earth have you got in there?' 'I was wondering when you were going to ask me that.' In went his hand out came the puppy. 'Are you sure it's the right one?' 'No doubt about it sir, they were in a loose box in the stables and this little chap kept chewing at the straps of my leggings and we had a lovely drive back and all.'

'Bremen', a rough haired black and tan was with me for a long time to come and became an important part of the establishment.

In April, as Allied troops advanced further into Germany, they came upon evidence of concentration camps and saw the shocking conditions and wholesale death which the depravity of their captors had forced on the prisoners, sights for which no previous experience could have prepared them.

On 10 April Churchill announced, in the Commons, the total number of fatal British casualties as a result of war since September 1939 – 216,287 members of the Forces, 59,793 civilians and 30,179 merchant seamen.

12 April. President Roosevelt died.

15 April. British troops entered Belsen which held thirty thousand prisoners, comprising Jews, German anti-Nazis, members of all European countries but principally Russians and Poles. The camp contained ten thousand unburied bodies, dead of starvation, and in all thirty-five thousand bodies were found. With the approach of the Allies the inmates of many other concentration camps had been force-marched into Germany or put to death.

On that day Canadian forces captured Arnhem.

Allied forces were now spreading east against crumbling resistance. Movement was constant, and available routes forward were congested with all manner of traffic. On 7 April the battalion moved out of Lingen to a wooded area some 4 miles beyond. The next day a further journey of about 80 miles was made to a position south of Bramsche. This required that the troops march out and cross the only available bridge before starting the journey proper in TCVs. The vast majority of the battalion vehicles became

Ready for the next stage, after Lingen.

bogged down on tracks leading from the woods and it was not until 04.30 hours the following morning that the battalion was able to start the main part of the journey, arriving at Wallenhorst about midday.

They now came under command of XII Corps, their area of responsibility covering about 4 miles along the line of a canal in very lovely country. There was little contact with the enemy although a patrol led by Lieutenant K. Wilson (Canada) was fired on by a party of enemy in the vicinity of the only bridge not blown – after artillery fire and further offensive patrols from the battalion the enemy fled.

Almost immediately they were ordered to rejoin XXX Corps to take part in the capture of Bremen and accordingly, two days later, 11 April, the battalion motored another 80 miles to Barrien.

Over the next few days just two incidents are on record. The first was an operation successfully carried out by C Company under Major V. Evans MC to clear a small wood and thus secure a start line for the operation against Leeste. The second was the aerial bombing of Battalion HQ by a flight of ME109s which showered the building with small HE bombs.

Early on the morning of 15 April the Warwicks started their attack on Leeste. A platoon under Lieutenant G.G. Loynes from B Company was sent to cover the left flank of their start line necessitating the clearance of an enemy platoon from the vicinity – successfully accomplished, though not without cost.

B Company and their tank
officers being briefed on the
model for the battle of
Brinkum.

The brigade plan was that the Warwicks should push on beyond Leeste to
the outskirts of Brinkum then 1 Norfolk would pass through and capture
Brinkum. By midday it had become apparent that opposition was stronger
than anticipated but the Warwicks successfully cleared Leeste and the
battalion started moving through at about 1600 hours.

Brinkum was a compact town, covering an area roughly 1,000 by 800 yd.
The far side of the town ended abruptly against low-lying ground flooded
by the enemy. It was situated at an important road junction where the road
from Leeste joined the main road from Barrien to the south and that from
Delmenhorst to the west. The attack commenced in the early evening from
Leeste along an open stretch of road before the built-up area was reached.
Battalion History:

After clearing a bridge of two enormous bombs the battalion, with under
command a squadron of 4/7 Dragoon Guards, a troop of Crocodiles
from 4 Royal Tank Regiment, and in support a platoon of MMG, a
platoon of 4.2 inch mortars of the Middlesex Regiment, and a troop of
Valentine SP 17-pdrs, advanced on Brinkum.

All went well in the opening stage. D Company led, with C and
A Companies echeloned back on the right and left respectively.
D Company, under Major J.P. Searight, reached the first buildings on the
outskirts of the town without incident, but both C and A Companies
came in for a bit of sniping, and Lieut. J. Laurie was killed by an unlucky
bullet. Lieut. K. Wilson was wounded later in the battle. These two
Canadian officers had landed with us on D-Day together with Lieut.

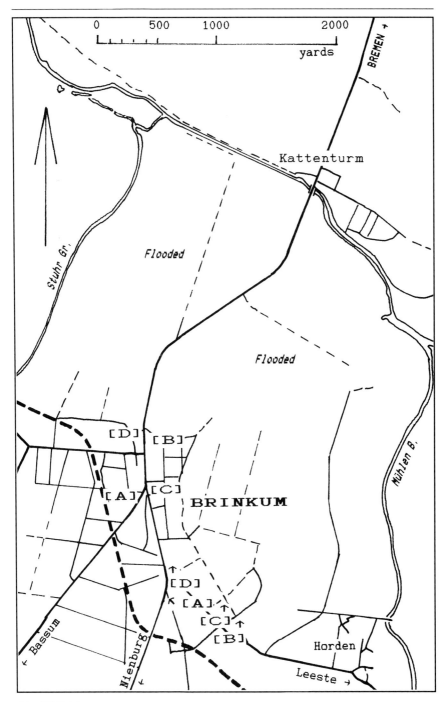

Map XI: Brinkum.

R. Vezina, who was also wounded in this battle. They had all been wounded previously and had given the battalion most outstanding service. They are a big loss to us.

By 2000 hours D Company was about three hundred yards into the built-up area, with C Company still fighting in the area of their right rear; here the tanks were giving valuable support, and already several houses and two farms were blazing nicely. A company was now close up behind D Company, and a few shots were fired at them from the south-west. At this stage it became necessary to clamp down for the night. . . .

By 0400 hours next morning D Company advanced without incident to the road junction. A company was on its left so as to come up on the west side of the main road and drive up to a main lateral half-way through the town proper. As far as possible A was to keep level with C Company, which was doing the same on the right of the axis. D Company was to remain firm at the road junction, giving what fire support it could until A and C Companies had reached their objectives, and then B and D Companies were to finish the operation on the right and left respectively. The tanks and Crocodiles went with the leading companies and were taken on by B and D companies for the last phase.

By first light on 16th April the stage was set for the advance to begin. The Crocodiles with A Company under Major Atkinson went really well, the tanks also co-operated in text-book style. The enemy, although they knew their number was up, fought fanatically. By 1400 hours A and C Companies had reached their objectives, and prisoners were beginning to come in nicely. The artillery now softened up the last bit of the town before B and D Companies went through. By 1700 hours all that then remained was a small housing estate to the north-west of the town. By this time all companies were fully extended and pretty exhausted, so a company of Warwicks came under command and helped us finish the job. In all we counted some 60 dead, and took 5 officers and 203 other ranks prisoners. Our own losses were 3 killed and 12 wounded.

Brinkum had been a model battle for co-operation of all arms.

CSM T.G. Catlin MM:

. . . our next main operation was the town of Brinkum. Major Atkinson moved the company before first light across open country to the edge of the town, this proved to be to our advantage. Our task was to clear the left hand side of the main street; our leading sections moved forward but soon came under heavy machine gun fire. A Crocodile tank moved up to support us – with its help we soon moved forward and within a short time the Germans came out, clothing alight, only too eager to surrender. It was noticeable how young they were.

The company reached the town centre but snipers were causing casualties – one of the leading section commanders, Cpl. Alger, was hit in the head; with the help of our stretcher bearers we got him out but, alas, he did not survive, he proved to be A Company's last casualty of the war.

Major H.M. Wilson MC:

Our Battalion group was by this time formidable. We had a squadron of 4/7 Dragoon Guards, a troop of Crocodiles (tank flame throwers), some SP guns for good measure and the call on the complete Corps artillery – a Victor target in fact – should it be needed.

Peter divided up Brinkum into convenient report lines for a three phase set-piece attack. We had all day to do the task and we were going to do it thoroughly with the least number of casualties to ourselves and the maximum to the enemy. The only exit out of Brinkum towards Bremen itself was via one road which was on an embankment or causeway surrounded by flood water. If the enemy decided to use this in daylight he would be a sitting target to the massed artillery who had the range all nicely worked out.

By 10 o'clock we had the first part completed. By 1 o'clock the rather tougher middle piece, which needed lots of flame from the Crocodiles and finally the last bit fell by 6 p.m. We had killed or captured the entire enemy in Brinkum for a loss of about 15 casualties very few of which were fatal.

On 21 April the battalion moved out of Brinkum to Leeste, relieved by the Suffolks, to prepare for an assault on the village of Kattenturm which, in

After the capture of Brinkum. (Left to right: Maj. F.C. Atkinson, OC A Coy, Lt.-Col. F.P. Barclay DSO, MC, Maj. J.D.W. Millar, OC B Coy.

the event, was carried out by 8 Brigade. On the 24th the battalion moved to a concentration area to the east of Leeste in preparation for an attack on Habenhausen. At midnight on 24/5 April 8 Brigade started their attack on Kattenturm and 2 Warwicks shortly after commenced their operation to capture the village of Arsten by using 'Buffaloes' across the flooded areas. The 1 Norfolks followed through after some initial delay due to the fact that only one road was available for movement forward and this had first to be cleared. Floods prevented the use of any other route.

At 1300 hours on the 25th B Company led off under Major J.D.W. Millar meeting very little resistance. The *Battalion History* relates what happened that evening:

At 1900 hours the pioneer officer, Lieut. A.R. Gill, went out with two NCOs to prove the route we were to take in the morning for our final advance into Bremen. He caused great anxiety at Bn HQ, as there was still no sign of him by 2300 hours. A patrol from A company was just setting out to look for The Body when sounds of an approaching column was heard. Shortly, Lieut. Gill, heading a hundred odd prisoners, appeared out of the night. What had happened was that he met a Boche officer and corporal, who had explained that if the party proceeded to a brickworks about a hundred men were waiting to give up but were too frightened to come out unless escorted by a British soldier. Lieut. Gill had been about three miles beyond where he had been sent and received the wrath of the CO on return – this was turned to admonishment with a twinkle! That day the battalion had taken 3 officers and 163 other ranks prisoners with no loss of any kind to the battalion.

25 April. Americans met Red Army forces on the River Elbe, some 75 miles south of Berlin. Berlin itself was almost completely surrounded.

28 April. Partisans killed Mussolini and others of his government.

29 April. German forces in Italy surrendered.

CHAPTER TWELVE

Keynote of all our Successes

Early the next morning (26 April) the battalion set out to march into Bremen. Few shots were fired and by degrees the civilian population came out of their cellars and other hiding-places while the liberated Poles, French, Czechs, and Russian slave-workers made merry.

In late afternoon D Company were well ensconced in Beck's Brewery, the only building not a mere shell, but the enemy must have realized this for it was shelled quite heavily. By the evening Bremen had become the scene of much activity: staff cars, military police, route-marking parties, American task force representatives, naval types and engineers.

The CO's memories of Bremen, as do those of most of the men of the battalion, centre on Beck's Brewery:

We approached Bremen – on the River Weser – which happily proved a walk-over. A large number of demoralised soldiers were captured, one of my officers, on a solo reconnaissance, bringing in a hundred or two! Beck's Brewery, in the centre of the city, was given as the focal objective

Men of the battalion in Bremen (IWM BU 4482).

and little time was taken in getting there! In the Beck complex was a fantastic gift department, the size of a small hangar, with every imaginable 'Beck' labelled gift, from wrist watches to grandfather clocks: we had a good picking. The sharks from our own rear lines of communication were quick to hear of this treasure trove and amazingly quick on the scene, complete with two ten-ton trucks but an accurate enemy artillery stonk, to our satisfaction, blew the vehicles to bits. Bremen boasts, or did, the biggest wine cellars in the world. I went to visit one such. A vast number of barrels had been punctured, just for the hell of it; the floor was covered with about two feet of wine in which floated several corpses: worse ways to die than that, one felt.

Again the feeling, confirmed here by Major Wilson, that the troops at the sharp end were pushed aside while others came forward to occupy the prime positions:

The advance on Bremen was merely a question of motoring up to its outskirts and walking into the middle of the city unopposed. In the middle of the city we occupied Beck's brewery and filled up all available transport with a free issue of beer. We were forced out of the brewery that evening by REME workshops and other back area units, such was the speed of advance and honest front-line troops like ourselves had to go and live in the country outside.

Alan Solomon tells of the havoc caused by bombing:

We were dug in a mile or two from Bremen before the push on the city. There were 1,000 bomber raids on Bremen then. It was an awesome as well as wonderful sight to see them going over, but they made the ground shake so much that our trench, which was in rather sandy soil, nearly caved in and we had to move out and dig another. We advanced through the outskirts of the city all one day and holed up at night in some of the houses. Then the CO had me and a runner taking leaflets round the houses telling them what they could and couldn't do etc. It was pretty scary going round to houses and trying to get them up from the cellars. But we did find one woman who was a teacher and could speak English so that helped a bit, but when she asked if we could spare some men to help bury two Germans laid out in her outhouse we had to gently refuse with a 'Sorry, not to-night', or words to that effect.

On into the city and we were amazed at the size of the bomb craters. Some looked big enough to lose 3 or 4 double-decker buses in.

Prisoners were surrendering constantly and included men from all countries subjugated by the Germans. Ken Wilby mentions two he met.

We were the first section to enter Bremen and the only building we could find that was more or less standing was Beck's Brewery and we had a right good session. Outside I met two Russians who had been prisoners of war and they brought this bucket out and said 'Do you want a drink?' Wanting to be friendly with them I said 'Yes'. They gave me a cup of drink out of this bucket and, when I tasted it, it was a bucket full of gin so we had a really good time, me and my two Russian friends!

Lance-Corporal Vic Everitt, D Company, tells a story which illustrates the differing attitudes between fighting troops and 'Base Wallahs'. Certain it is that the battalion CO backed his men to the hilt:

We took off from Habenhausen and advanced along the main road into Bremen without any problems whatsoever, all we saw were hordes of German civilians watching us, wondering perhaps where we all came from.

We were almost up to the bridge over the River Weser when we were first fired upon by what we thought to be a self-propelled gun operating from the other side of the river, but there were no casualties at that time.

Just as we got to the brewery my section commander, Corporal Smurthwaite, was hit and wounded and in due course carried off back to first aid. That left me in charge of the section and we carried on,

17 Platoon, D Company in Bremen. Left to right: Pte. Johnson, Pte. Freeman, Pte. Foley, Pte. Crowther, Pte. Denmark, Sgt. Rust, L/Cpl. Gould.

cleared the brewery and after it was cleared, consolidated, had a meal and a brief rest.

I was then instructed to take my section down to the rear of the brewery, where there were gates across a large yard which was obviously the loading bay for brewers' drays etc, close the gates and stay there. When we got there it was chaos, there were vehicles from every formation in 21st Army Group even including the Navy, Royal Air Force, Marines, you name it they were there, all clamouring to get more beer and they were loading their trucks as hard as they could go.

We tried to shut the gates but we were beaten, it was an impossibility. Col. Barclay turned up at about this time and asked the problems and I told him – with his help and, of course, with his authority, we managed to clear the yard. We then shut the gates; Col. Barclay said to me, 'Nobody will get beer from you or from here unless they have a chit signed by me', and away he went.

About an hour later a small truck pulled up and a Major got out, came across, said 'Who are you?' and I told him.

He said 'I want some beer.'

I said 'Sorry sir, I can't give you beer without a chit from Col. Barclay.'

He said, 'Do you know who I am?'

I said, 'I'm afraid I don't, sir.'

He said, 'I am the prospective Town Major for Bremen and in due course I shall be in command round here.'

I said, 'I'm still sorry sir, you can't get any beer.'

He said, 'Who are you?' and again I told him, so he said, 'Right, I shall have you court-martialed for insolence and who is this Col. Barclay and where will I find him?'

I said, 'He is the Colonel commanding the 1st Royal Norfolks and you will find him at Battalion Headquarters wherever that happens to be at this particular moment.'

He said, 'Right, by the time I've finished with him he won't have a platoon, let alone a battalion', and away he went.

We stayed on duty all night until the battalion moved out about 7 or 8 the next morning to Oldenburg and in that period of time neither the Major nor any representative of his came back to collect beer. I rather think he obviously did meet Col. Barclay.

On 27 April the battalion moved out of Bremen and headed back to Kattenturm for a promised three days' rest and reorganization. That evening, however, orders were received to move on again the next day to relieve a Canadian brigade. The new location was about 4 miles west of Delmenhorst, on a ridge from which could be seen all the low-lying country up to the River Weser. By 1 May positions well forward had been established and few enemy were seen. Everybody knew the end of hostilities was very near.

Captain R.C. Wilson MC, recovered from a second wound, describes his final return to the battalion in the last days of the war in Europe:

My final memory is a happy one. I had to miss the Rhine crossing, Lingen and Brinkum, but was rapidly getting fit again, and was determined to be back with the Battalion before the final whistle blew. I contrived a posting but also received a message that there was no chance of transport – I must make my own way. I got across the Channel, and then had a glorious hitch-hike from Ostend to near Bremen. Everyone knew the campaign was near its end, and a sense of euphoria reigned. One just hailed the nearest military vehicle, asked where it was going and begged a lift for so long as the direction was right. It always seemed easy to cadge a meal somewhere, and a place for a few hours sleep. In this way I got back to the Battalion near Delmenhorst after three days of hectic but enjoyable travelling. I took over one of the forward companies near a Nazi open-air theatre. I remember the 'Cease Fire at 0800 hours' message coming in, and it was all over.

The *Battalion War Diary*, filled with brief, factual, often laconic comments, seldom mentioned names but with the euphoria of success and the imminent end of hostilities, recorded on 4 May 1945:

The last patrol into enemy teritory was carried out today by Lt. R.J. Lincoln with 18 Pln, D Coy.

This is the story of that patrol:

On the night of 3 May I received orders to take my platoon forward on a fighting patrol the next day. The map showed that the ground was absolutely flat, interlaced with drainage ditches and tracks running roughly north and south – one transverse road served a number of small hamlets in the centre of the valley, the other followed the near bank of the river. Beyond the river the ground was higher and overlooked the valley, the defence overprint on the map showed numerous gun positions and an airfield to the right.

After an early breakfast we set off with little sign of enemy activity. We all knew that the war was very close to its end but we had no idea what enemy, if any, might be this side of the river or if they would fight more strongly, in desperation, or give up. I had been away from the fighting for two months, after being wounded, this was to be my re-introduction to the hard facts of infantry war.

We left the cover of lanes and hedges and commenced our crossing of marshland which offered no shelter whatever from enemy eyes. We moved along a farm track, after a few hundred yards we crossed a bridge over a dyke and suddenly, without warning, a salvo of air-burst shells exploded directly above us.

I dropped to one knee; for what seemed an age I froze there, not knowing what to do, my mind a blank from the sudden shock of the shelling, worsened by previous experiences and enforced absence from action. There was no place to take shelter, no place to go. What felt like an eternity was almost certainly no more than two or three seconds – the shelling did not continue and there was only one decision that could be made – to go on.

We had suffered no casualties and reached the hamlet on the first transverse road without further problem, painfully conscious that we were observed, exposed to an enemy we could not see and totally uncertain of what lay ahead. Leaving the cover of the hamlet we moved again northwards along a straight stretch of perfectly flat road towards the military camp a mile ahead. We approached the camp cautiously – it consisted of about a half dozen wooden huts in a wired compound – but we saw no sign of movement and, on investigation, found it deserted.

After the first sudden shock of air-burst shells at the beginning of the day we encountered no further enemy activity at all yet, all the time, we remained very much aware of being watched.

Alf Tredgold who had been batman to Jack Laurie, took me under his wing on my return to D Company and was with me on this patrol. He has reminded me that, across the river, we heard the enemy singing, probably drowning their sorrows for they, like us, knew the end was near.

Shortly after I arrived back at Company HQ a message was received over the field telephone, it read:

'Cancel all offensive ops forthwith and CEASE FIRE
0800 hrs 5 May 45. Further details later.'

Can you imagine what that message meant to a group of poor bloody infantrymen who knew the war was nearly over and who had just spent a day in full sight of the enemy?

Our relief was intense – we all agreed that, as the Company was billeted in a building which, by good luck, possessed a large hall with a stage, we should immediately arrange a celebration that very evening to mark the end of war in Europe. The Company had acquired certain liquid comforts in Bremen, a piano was found, candles were begged from anyone who had them and, with a limited supply of hurricane lamps, stuck along the front of the stage as footlights – we had no power supply. After the evening meal the whole Company, which had only once before, at New Year, found itself in one single building, celebrated with songs and stories and conversation long into the night. 'Wilkie', the CSM, shone as a raconteur of Norfolk dialect stories and everyone who could entertain in any way played their part.

One of my most vivid memories is of that particular evening – after the concert the Company officers sat together in the small room we used as a mess and talked and laughed together – the comradeship of friends with whom you've fought in war, on whom you've depended for your life and who have placed their lives in your hands, is of the greatest value – we talked not of the future or of world events but of friends, past and present, of experiences shared, secure in the knowledge that tomorrow our war would end – we were happy.

Lance-Corporal Jack F. 'Tubby' Pratt had joined the Royal Norfolk Regiment in 1939 and in spring 1940 was sent to the BEF in France as a reinforcement for the 2nd Battalion just before the Germans broke through the Low Countries. Ordered to retreat, his unit force-marched to Cherbourg and returned to this country on an old boat, some of the last troops of the BEF out of France, very lucky to get home. He joined the 1st Battalion The Royal Norfolk Regiment in Surrey in July 1940, in 17 Platoon, D Company, subsequently transferring to the Anti-tank Platoon when it was first formed. He recorded this memory on tape and it was a very moving experience to hear this story, told in the accents of my native county, in the words of a true Norfolk man:

Of thousands of experiences one in particular stands out in my memory, one I would call 'The Last Shells to Drop on the Norfolk Regiment'.

We were engaged in street fighting in Bremen. . . . After a day or so I was ordered to an 'O' group and was told that we would be moving from Bremen to Delmenhorst in the Canadian sector the following day. On the 4th of May, I think it was, we moved in convoy to Delmenhorst. When we arrived I was guided by a DR to a forward position in an old small-holding – a house, other premises and a big orchard and garden – in support of B Company. I had no sooner got there and settled into the position – we took over some trenches, German trenches I think – than I was called to an 'O' group again. It was late in the evening, my orders were that we weren't going to advance any further and could make ourselves comfortable in the houses around us. I was told that an attack was not expected, that we might have prisoners give themselves up through the lines and that the Armistice should be signed in a day or two.

This was good news. Just before Bremen we had been made up to strength with reinforcements and I had a full gun-team. Bill Holden was my carrier driver, L/Cpl. Plunkett my second-in-command and, in addition to the gun-team, I also had a DR attached to me, about 7 men in all.

I went back and told the lads: 'Well, lads, the war's expected to finish any time and we can make ourselves comfortable in the houses around us; in this house,' I said, 'which is just behind us here.' It wasn't a very smart house but it was shelter and that was the one thing we wanted.

We went into the house; some of the lads said, 'I'm going to sleep in this room, I'm going to sleep in that room.' I said 'No you're not, you're all going to sleep in one room', because I knew very well once I'd got them spread around the house I'd never find them when I wanted them to go on sentry-go. They did a bit of moaning, mumbling that 'the war was nearly over' and 'he's going to make us all sleep in this one room'.

I made my guard roster out and posted my first two sentries, came back again into the house and said, 'What we'll do, we'll use this left-hand room.' The house was only small, only two downstair rooms and an old kitchen at the back with bedrooms over the top so I said that we'd use the room on the left.

That's what happened, they all bedded down in the left-hand room. I said, 'Well, I'm going out now to contact the company positions on my right and left,' and I went out first to the right and found two sentries in the garden of a house. While I was there some shells came over so I jumped into the trench with the two sentries. I should think there must have been seven or eight shells dropped all in the vicinity of the small-holding and orchard where my chaps were. The shell-fire eased up and I said to the sentries, 'I think that's all over now, I'll get back to my section.'

I walked through the orchard, through the smoke from the shells, the majority of which had dropped in the orchard and garden. When I got near the house the lads were all running around like wild men. I said 'What's gone wrong with you lot?' They said 'We're pleased to see you, we thought you'd had it.'

A shell had hit the house and completely wrecked one of the two ground floor rooms, the room on the right not the one on the left I had insisted the section sleep in. The shell had made a direct hit on that room – I didn't have any casualties but if they'd been in that other room they would have all been casualties.

This made me think. I'm not a very religious man but I ask myself, what influenced me to take the left-hand room instead of the right? It's always remained a puzzle to me – was it good luck? was it a decision made for me? – I know that someone was looking over us anyhow. I will never forget that, I think that those shells were the last to fall on the battalion, fired by a German gun using its last few rounds of ammunition.

I don't know if it was the will of God – I've thought about it thousands of times since – it was a very lucky experience. I often see some of the lads, one or two of them are still alive, and I jokingly remind them about it. I say 'You've got me to thank that you're where you are now.'

That's the way things turn out – I think we were all very lucky.

29 April. American forces entered the concentration camp at Dachau where they found thirty-three thousand inmates, starving, emaciated, the same horrific conditions discovered previously at Belsen. The guards were killed.

British bombers parachuted 6,000 tons of supplies into Holland behind the German lines in the area of Rotterdam and Den Haag.

30 April. Americans in Munich and in Turin. With Russian troops less than a mile away Hitler killed himself.

1 May. Hitler's close associates committed suicide.

2 May. Berlin surrendered.

3 May. Emissaries arrived at Field Marshal Montgomery's HQ to offer surrender. He would only accept complete surrender of all German forces in Holland, north-west Germany and Denmark, other German forces must surrender to the opposing Allied armies. His terms were accepted the following day.

5 May. German forces in southern Germany surrendered unconditionally. The concentration camp at Mauthausen was entered where a hundred and ten thousand prisoners were found.

6 May. General Jodl sought to surrender those forces facing the Western Allies – General Eisenhower would not accept this. Finally Admiral Dönitz authorized surrender of all forces one hour before midnight on 8 May.

8 May. Victory in Europe Day.

The *Battalion War Diary*, normally a very impersonal document, on 5 May 1945 reflects the universal optimism brought about by knowledge of the end of the war. It states:

5776281 L/Cpl. Banks H. takes the message from higher formation over the phone to tell us to cease fire. Message is passed to the CO who tells companies they can have reveille and breakfast when they please and that there would be no parades during the morning.

Major H.M. Wilson MC remembers a stirring moment:

At Reveille, Drum Major Jessop sounded the 'Cease Fire' on a bugle kept just for that purpose – 'There's no parade today' sang out the bugle.

The following day the *Battalion War Diary* records:

It is raining heavily this morning and so the inspection by the CO and the march past have to be cancelled. Instead the Battalion is marched to D Company area for a church service conducted by a visiting padre from Div HQ.

Our own padre, Rev. J.F. Green, who has been with us since before D-Day, has left us for the Far East. The Battalion has suffered a great loss for Padre Green was one of the most popular and well-liked officers in the Battalion and contributed to a very high degree to the high morale and smiling faces which are always seen amongst the men of the 1st Battalion The Royal Norfolk Regiment.

A final, brief postscript is recorded in the *Battalion History*:

Advance parties had already left to reconnoitre our peace-time home on 1st May, and after several changes we were allotted a good camp situated at the edge of a poison gas factory about ten miles from Minden. On VE-Day the battalion arrived at this our first peace-time station. . . .

And so ended the campaign. Perhaps the most brilliant ever fought, certainly the most successful. Many great men have already stated their reasons for this success – co-operation, good training, air superiority, etc. Within a front line unit one gets a slightly more intimate view, and there is no doubt that our success has been due to good leadership, regimental tradition, and conscientious loyalty. Out of these things is born high morale, and this has been the keynote of all our successes.

The battalion Padre, Revd F.J. Green, with Lt. R.S. Hilton.

Epilogue

On VE-Day, 8 May 1945, the battalion moved south to barrack accommodation in a wooded area containing buildings previously used to manufacture poison-gas at Espelkamp, some 10 miles from Minden. Good living quarters, washing facilities, a theatre, a static water tank doubling as a swimming pool, a playing field, electric light and time to relax – at least for a short while, for war still continued in the Far East.

The battalion received a singular honour; it was asked by the Supreme Commander, General Eisenhower, to send a company to Supreme Headquarters Allied Expeditionary Force. B Company under Major J.D.W. Millar was chosen.

On 5 June 1945 a message was published to all ranks in the battalion as ordered by the Army Council which, after making reference to the long struggle and to the constant efforts of all soldiers, stated:

> In victory we remember those who, by death, wounds or sickness, have paid its price; our sympathy goes out to the kin of those who have lost their lives and to the wounded and disabled.

For a few days after VE-Day fighting continued in some areas of the Russian front. On 11 May three hundred and seventy-four thousand German troops surrendered in Czechoslovakia and it was not until the 15th that all German resistance ended when enemy troops in Yugoslavia surrendered.

In America great debate raged over the two major choices open to the Allies – to drop an atomic bomb on Japan or to invade Kyushu in the autumn and Honshu in the spring. Estimates of casualties to Allied forces, mostly American, during assault landings on the Japanese main islands varied between 1 and 2 million; this high cost was considered excessive and the choice was made to drop the bomb.

Apart from a limited bombing raid in April 1942 it was June 1944 before major strikes had been made from the air on Japanese cities during daylight hours. In March 1945 night bombing raids commenced. On 9/10 March an estimated one hundred and thirty thousand people were killed as the result of a firestorm raid on Tokyo. Subsequently other Japanese cities were attacked in the same way with around two hundred and fifty thousand fatal civilian casualties.

16 July. First atomic bomb tested in New Mexico.

6 August. Atomic bomb dropped on Hiroshima, eighty thousand killed; total number of victims of that blast estimated at one hundred and thirty-nine thousand.

202 THANK GOD AND THE INFANTRY

8 August. Russia declared war on Japan.

9 August. Second atomic bomb dropped on Nagasaki; ultimate deaths from this bomb estimated at forty-nine thousand.

15 August. The Japanese Emperor announced by radio that he had ordered the Japanese government to accept the terms for surrender proposed by the Allies but it was not until 28 August that the first American troops arrived in Japan and two more days before British forces entered Singapore and Hong Kong.

2 September. Formal acceptance of Japanese surrender signed aboard American battleship *Missouri* in Tokyo Bay.

12 September. Lord Louis Mountbatten, in Singapore, accepted the formal surrender of all Japanese forces within South East Asia Command. Isolated pockets of Japanese troops continued to surrender until spring 1946.

Shortly after the cessation of war in Europe the British 3rd Division was selected to form part of a representative Commonwealth Corps, together with a Canadian Division and an Anzac Division, to assault Japan in company with American forces, planned for 1 November 1945. The division prepared for a brief leave in the UK to be followed by a short period of training and re-equipping in the United States. If the decision to drop the atomic bombs had not achieved its purpose this history of the 1st Battalion would, without any doubt, have continued with further accounts of very considerable loss of life.

Following the surrender of Japan 1 Norfolk was withdrawn from 3 Division. Many younger members of the battalion were transferred to other units within 3 Division before the Division went to Egypt. The battalion moved to Solingen and remained in Germany as part of the Army of Occupation until February 1951, returning to Great Britain for reinforcement and training until mobilized for service in Korea at the end of August 1951.

The Royal Norfolk Regiment was honoured by the City of Norwich. On 6 March 1945 the Norwich City Council resolved, in appreciation of the services of the County Regiment, to confer upon the regiment the privilege, honour and distinction of marching through the city on all ceremonial occasions with bayonets fixed, colours flying and bands playing.

The Illuminated Copy of this Resolution was presented to the Colonel of the Regiment, General Sir Peter Strickland, by the Lord Mayor, Councillor E.F. Williamson JP, at a ceremony held in front of the City Hall in Norwich on 3 October 1945. The Guard of Honour was commanded by Major David Jamieson VC, the four parties comprising the Guard of Honour, representing the various battalions within the regiment, were commanded by Major J.B. Dye MC, Captain R.F. Howard MBE, Major B. Savory and Captain E.T. Gibbons. The King's Colour was carried by Captain E.H.T. Ridger, the Regimental Colour by Lieutenant R.J. Lincoln.

The memorial to those men of the battalion who were killed at Kervenheim, erected by the battalion in March 1946.

The men of the 1st Battalion The Royal Norfolk Regiment still living will never forget those whose names are recorded in the Roll of Honour, will never forget the heavy toll of human life. In eleven months 20 Officers and 260 Other Ranks lost their lives, well over a thousand others were wounded, missing or suffered battle exhaustion. When these casualties are measured against the total strength of the battalion, 36 Officers and 809 Other Ranks, the severity of the fighting in which the battalion was, at times, engaged can be more clearly judged. It is on record that 111 Officers served in the battalion during the campaign, of whom at least fourteen returned after recovering from wounds (some of them twice). The battalion will therefore have received the equivalent of more than 89 officer reinforcements, making a total of 125, to fill 36 positions. It has been stated that, 'Contrary to public opinion, the chances of survival of a British regimental infantry officer in the 1939–45 War were less than in the 1914–18 War'. Precise records relating to other ranks are not available but they shared equally all dangers, many also returning to the battalion after recovering from wounds. Front-line troops in the campaign comprised less than 10 per cent of total Army strength – figures quoted above give some indication not only of the rigour of infantry battle but also of the odds of survival.

The bond which still unites the men of the 1st Battalion is a tribute to the spirit which existed at that time and the support which each man gave to and received from his friends. The force of will and strength of purpose inherent in an infantry soldier made it possible for him to overcome the cold, the wet, the loss of sleep, uncertain and irregular meals, shelling, mortaring, machine-gun fire and much more, and still get up and move forward into even greater danger when required to do so.

It has been the greatest privilege to read and to listen to the memories of the men of the battalion. The feelings aroused by those memories were never stronger than when, recently, on the anniversary of the cessation of hostilities in north-west Europe, to the day, I visited the Royal Norfolk Regimental Chapel in Norwich Cathedral erected in 1931 as a memorial to all the men and women of Norfolk who lost their lives in the First World War.

I sat in the chapel, quite alone, enveloped in history. I could sense all about me the presence of so many people: the early Saxon builders of the first chapel; the artisans who raised the mighty cathedral; the countless thousands who had worshipped there; the many, many unknown and unsung soldiers in red and in khaki who had fought and fallen in military service in the regiment since 1685. Above my head were the old Colours, worn and threadbare, all proudly borne in the past by generations of soldiers. In one of the stained glass windows I could see the badge of Britannia as it was before 1935, before the regiment was honoured by the name of 'The Royal Norfolk Regiment'. On the walls of the chapel wooden panels commemorate many campaigns, all of them bearing the names of past members of the regiment save one, the first, dated 1702, FLANDERS, which bears the inscription:

REMEMBER ALL WHO, AT ANY TIME, HAVE SERVED IN THE REGIMENT.

To sit in the chapel, alone, surrounded by a silence, a stillness far removed from war, was a very moving, emotional experience for an old soldier. I remembered, above all, the men, the individual personalities with whom it was my privilege to serve. In that quiet place I reflected on two recurrent impressions gained from the numerous accounts in this book. First, the narrow, near-miraculous escapes from instant death experienced by so many and secondly, the care and compassion of a man for his fellow soldier.

Memories can be disturbing; some men exclude all thought of those times from their minds to shut out grief and hurt, and all of us have particular recollections which we carry with us but about which we seldom speak. I have remembered, over the years, the pale, frightened young face of a

A view of the War Graves Commission Cemetery in the Reichswald.

German soldier peering out of a dug-out in Holland. He saw me and quickly withdrew into the dug-out. I threw a grenade into that dug-out and could not wait to see the result.

After more than forty-five years, I met Peter Gould, who had been a member of my platoon in Holland. We talked of people and places, we spoke of good times and bad. I mentioned this incident and he remembered it, and from him I learned that he had later gone into that dug-out and seen the effect of that grenade on the sheltering German soldiers. And what he told me he saw does not make it any easier for me to forget that frightened face or to come to terms with what I, as a soldier, had to do.

Closely coupled with that memory is another. At that same time a young soldier, who had joined my platoon only the evening before, was killed as he lay waiting to advance. The image of his body, face down on the ground, will be with me always because he had no time to make friends, no time to get to know his mates, no time to enjoy the comradeship of his section – just a few, very brief hours of unsettled rest in a waterlogged slit trench, a move forward in the dark of night and sudden death.

The loss of so many young men, the sadness, the futility and waste of war is clearly apparent from the Roll of Honour. And in their memory we must do all we can to ensure that such a conflict never happens again.

One contributor ended his memories with the following comment which for many of us clearly and concisely states why those days remain always in our minds:

I shall always remember Normandy as a place of death, destruction and lasting sadness, which started for me at 7.30 a.m. 6th June 1944, and which is now slowly fading from vivid memory into another generation's history. As my generation becomes thinner on the ground the fears and the heroism are fading away but the sadness will last forever.

. . . I believe I have no business to forget my fallen comrades. I would be ashamed to forget them. Perhaps only in war do we achieve an exalted state of existence. For me that was Normandy. The rest of life is a daily sequence of small insignificant things followed by others. Now as old men we return to the silent fields and the poignancy of abundant cemeteries where a name is instantly remembered.

Memories of those who died are brought clearly and intensely to mind by visits to war cemeteries, such as the Reichswald War Cemetery in Germany just over the border from Holland, east of Nijmegen. A perfect autumn morning, with a clear blue sky – the cemetery, with its immaculate turf and line upon impeccable line of white headstones, lies surrounded on all sides by forest and by a peace so profound, so stirring, so fitting for those who lost their lives so violently. It is the most peaceful, superb setting that anyone could wish for their lost loved ones.

Memories of quiet conversations with old soldiers make one conscious that for them the war provided the most extreme range of feelings, of emotions, of experiences that any man is ever likely to face; a time of intense excitement, of acute sensations, of harsh ordeals, a time of which they are justly proud, even if they will never admit it.

The bond which links men who have fought side by side in battle is very strong; the deep-rooted feelings generated by the sharing of hardship, of danger, of trust remain with them always.

> He that outlives this day and comes safe home,
> Will stand a tip-toe when this day is nam'd, . . .
> This story shall the good man teach his son; . . .
> But we in it shall be remembered;
> We few, we happy few, we band of brothers;
> For he to-day that sheds his blood with me
> Shall be my brother;

King Henry V
William Shakespeare

Honours and Awards

VICTORIA CROSS
Cpl. S. Bates   (Died of Wounds)

DISTINGUISHED SERVICE ORDER
Lt.-Col. F.P. Barclay MC   Lt.-Col. R.H. Bellamy

DISTINGUISHED CONDUCT MEDAL
Sgt. C. Hopkins   CSM E.J.L. Langford

MEMBER OF THE BRITISH EMPIRE
Capt. (QM) R.F. Howard

MILITARY CROSS

Major W.E.G. Bagwell   Lieut. R.J. Lincoln
Major E.A. Cooper-Key   Major I.A. MacGillivray
Lieut. G.D.H. Dicks   Lieut. T.M. Rourke ★
Major J.B. Dye   Major D.W. Smith ★
Major H.R. Holden   Major H.M. Wilson
Lieut. J.A. Laurie ★   Capt. R.C. Wilson
[Awarded in 7th Battalion]
Major F.H.Crocker

MILITARY MEDAL

Lieut. G.A. Smith ★   Pte. J. Parsonage
Sgt. S. Allen   L-Cpl. E. Seaman
CSM T. Catlin   L-Sgt. J. Shepherd
Sgt. C. Hansen   L-Cpl. C. Shingfield
Sgt. C. Parker   Cpl. W. Simpkiss
Cpl. C. Thirtle
[Awarded in 7th Battalion]
Sgt. E. Barleycorn   Pte. G. Pennington
Sgt. E. Kay   Pte. H. Wright

Croix de Guerre with Gilt Star
Capt. H.J.H. Beeson

Croix de Guerre with Bronze Star
Sgt. C. Savidge

Mentions in Dispatches

Lt.-Col. F.P. Barclay DSO, MC	RQMS E. Jolley
Major E.A. Cooper-Key MC	L-Cpl. C. Marshall
Revd F.J. Green	Sgt. W.F. Nelson
Capt. R.W. Hodd	Pte. H. Roberts
Major W.J. Smart	L-Cpl. J. Scothern
L-Cpl. E. Ballard *	L-Cpl. E. Seaman MM
Pte. R.G. Burgess *	L-Sgt. J. Shepherd MM
Cpl. A. Chambers	Sgt. A. Smith
Sgt. D.E. Chandler	CSM C. Wilkinson

Commander-in-Chief's Certificates

Capt. H.J.H. Beeson	Pte. A. Hart
Capt. M.R. Fearon†	Pte. F. Houghton
Capt.(QM) R.F. Howard MBE	Cpl. L. Kemp
Major J.D.W. Millar	CSM A. Lemon
Capt. M.C. Wiggins	L-Cpl. H.J. Manning
Major H.M. Wilson MC	Pte. H.J. Marshall
C-Sgt. H. Amis	Sgt. W. Nelson
L-Cpl. W. Boggan *	Sgt. W. Paskell
CSM J. Brown	Cpl. C. Raven (ACC)
Sgt. L. Franks	Pte. D. Shrimpton
Pte. A. Frost	Sgt. T. Stimpson *
Sgt. H. Graves	C-Sgt. N. Thorne

Divisional Commander's Certificates

Major F.C. Atkinson	Capt. R.S. Hilton
Major W.E.G. Bagwell	Major H.R. Holden MC
Capt. D.B. Balsom	Capt.(QM) R.F. Howard MBE
Lieut. C. Barnby	Lieut. J.A. Laurie MC*
Capt. H.J.H. Beeson	Lieut. W. Lewis
Lt.-Col. R.H. Bellamy DSO	Major I.A. MacGillivray MC
Lieut. G.D.H. Dicks MC	Capt. C.W. Morgan
Major J.B. Dye MC (2)	Lieut. E.H.G. Olley
Capt. M.R. Fearon†	Major D.W. Smith MC*
Capt. D.W. Glass	Lieut. R. Vezina

Major H.M. Wilson MC

CSM T. Adams MM	Sgt. K. Larkins
L-Sgt. L. Addison	Sgt. G. Legg
Sgt. S. Allen, MM	L-Cpl. E. Long
Sgt. E. Barleycorn, MM	Pte. W. McNamara
Sgt. S. Bennett	Cpl. J. Marcroft
L-Cpl. A. Blood	L-Sgt. T. Marshall
RSM W. Brown	L-Cpl. C. Matthes
Pte. R. Bryant	Sgt. J. Ming
Pte. A. Burr	Pte. W. Mitchell
Pte. A. Capes	L-Cpl. B. Moloney
L-Cpl. L. Cartwright	Sgt. J. Moore

CSM T. Catlin MM
Pte. W. Chamberlain
Sgt. D.E. Chandler
Pte. R. Churchill
Pte. A. Codling
L-Sgt. D. Cole ⋆
Sgt. A. Collings
Pte. H. Cotterill
L-Sgt. J. Covill
Pte. H. Cushway
Cpl. D. Davies
Sgt. H. deRooij (Interpreter)
Cpl. J. Dunnington
Cpl. L. Dykes
C-Sgt. J. Ellis
Cpl. R. Fairhurst
Cpl. J. Farmer
Pte. A. Fisher
Pte. H. Flatt
CSM S. Flint
L-Cpl. A. Frost
CSM R. Fuller
Cpl. L. Gay
Pte. W. Green
L-Cpl. N. Griffin
Sgt. C. Hansen MM (2)
Cpl. T. Hartley
Cpl. F. Hawkins (2)
Cpl. J. Hazard
Sgt. C. Hopkins DCM
Sgt. C. Huffee (2)
C-Sgt. T. Jackson
Cpl. A. Johnson
Sgt. E. Kay MM
Sgt. W. Kett
C-Sgt. A. Lacey
CSM E.J.L. Langford DCM

Cpl. V. Mortara
Sgt. W. Nelson (2)
L-Cpl. T. Newcombe
Pte. W. Nicholls
Pte. R. Nichols
Pte. N. Orange
Pte. J. Parsonage MM
Cpl. T. Patterson (ACC)
L-Cpl. S. Raine
Pte. W. Rudd
Pte. R. Sansom
Sgt. C. Savidge
L-Cpl. E. Seaman MM
Pte. L. Sewell
Pte. D. Shepherd
L-Cpl. C. Shingfield MM
Cpl. W. Simpkiss MM
L-Cpl. E. Sizer
Sgt. R. Smart
Sgt. A. Smith
Sgt. G. Smith
L-Cpl. L. Southgate
Pte. F. Stansfield
Sgt. H. Stephenson
L-Cpl. D. Suffolk
Cpl. C. Thirtle MM
Sgt. R. Thomas
L-Cpl. A. Thompson
C-Sgt. N. Thorne
Pte. W. Townsend
Pte. J. Vincent
Pte. D. Westropp
Pte. J. Whiteside
Pte. K. Wilby
C.S.M. C. Wilkinson
Cpl. J. Woodward
L-Cpl. P. Wrigley

⋆ Killed in Action
† Died Prisoner of War

Reprinted from *The History of The 1st Battalion The Royal Norfolk Regiment.*

Citations relating to most of these Honours and Awards, also reprinted from the *Battalion History*, are available to be seen, on request, at the Royal Norfolk Regimental Museum in Norwich, listed in alphabetical order.

Roll of Honour

'To live in hearts we leave behind is not to die.'
Thomas Campbell, 'Hallowed Ground'

6 June 1944

5783204 Pte. R.G. Attew
7953941 Pte. G.C. Baldwin
3602771 Pte. A. Barker
5772226 Pte. W.T. Canham
5778737 Cpl. J. Cobon
14413180 Pte. R.R. Cook
5771384 Bandsman H.A .Dinwoodie
5782358 Pte. D. Forbes
5777744 Pte. R.F. Gillingwater
6457757 L-Sgt. G.A. Hollox

5962158 Pte J. Hudson
5777781 Pte. H.A. Hurrell
5956830 Pte. A.M. Lambert
14418034 Pte. R.K.G. Leah
14646610 Pte. R.J. Leeder
14331016 Pte. H. Longdon
5775929 Pte. B. Ringham
5771706 L-Cpl. W. Thompson
5772422 Pte. E.J. Warden
5772625 Pte. A. Woolf

7 June 1944

5772388 Drummer J.W. Allen
5778640 Cpl. R.C. Amond
5780086 Pte. C. Asseter
14437080 Pte. F.O. Brogan
251603 Lt. J.F. Campbell
6206710 Pte. J.F. Caudwell
5775927 Pte. W.A. Farrance
14618257 Cpl. D. George
5783324 Pte. G. Hales
5775911 Pte. W.J. Hills

6105132 Pte. W.H. Horsman
5775524 Pte. A. Kearton
14410308 Pte. J.R. Mussett
5888703 Pte. R. Noble
186438 Lt. W.M. Sharp
14417105 Pte. H. Swayne
5772011 Pte. S. Symonds
5784240 Pte. H. Taylor
271324 Lt. G.M.C. Toft
5780614 L-Cpl. L. Tovell

8 June 1944

5771870 L-Sgt. F. Clark

14409748 Pte. H.D. Jarvis

11 June 1944

5777527 Sgt. J.E. Purling

273652 Lt. J.F.J. Williams

13 June 1944

5783848 L-Sgt. J.O. Walter

14 June 1944

5772390 Pte. D. Anderson

4805950 Pte. R.W. Hill

19 June 1944

62355 Major F. Fitch MC

6008890 Pte. J.E. Parker

24 June 1944
91828 Capt. M.R. Fearon [2]
*The Royal East Kent Regiment.**

27 June 1944
5775884 Pte. C.H. Scott

4 July 1944
5771799 CSM R.M. Bell
Attached: Brigade HQ

402003 Pte. T. Glen

8 July 1944

5773552 Cpl. S.F. Bird	14631813 L-Cpl. R.R. Johnson
5779534 Cpl. J.B. Bowman	14414297 Pte. E.G. Laker
5773518 Pte. C.J. Bradshaw	5771650 Pte. S.G. Last
14631614 Pte. D.W. Brown	5783355 Pte. R. Lincoln
14407623 Pte. J.L. Coyte	14404510 L-Cpl. A. Manlow
14674589 Pte. G. Davis	5776503 Pte. E. Morton
14421971 Pte. D.R. Entwistle	14528954 Pte. J. Ormston
14402887 L-Cpl. J.E. Fisher	14414305 Pte. J.T. Stolworthy
5778769 Pte. L.G. Fox	5890650 Pte. P.R. Toseland
5769968 CSM J.B. Gainsbury	5777035 Pte. A.T. Wallis
5773076 Pte. D.A. Hall	5775833 Cpl. J.A. Wood
5771832 Drummer L. Holroyd	5771993 Cpl. W.S. Wright
5772125 Pte. E.H. Jermany	

9 July 1944

14643370 Pte. J.A. Allen	14643305 Pte. B.H. Haste
14408104 Pte. L.H. Frankland	14414921 Pte. R.P. Townend

10 July 1944
6021075 Pte. J. Weston

18 July 1944

14407766 Pte. D.W. Francis	1567875 Pte. J. Mason

20 July 1944

821979 Pte. J.R. Banwell	311373 Lt. R.H. Williams

21 July 1944

5778672 Cpl. F.H. Barham	5778748 Pte. S.H. Dunham
5784270 Cpl. A.L. Bruce	6151074 Pte. E.C. Jones
14406646 Pte. R. Coe	5783410 Pte. A. Thrower

23 July 1944

5679620 Pte. F.W. Budd	6149807 Pte. J.W. Fuller

25 July 1944
5770769 Pte. E.G. Ballard

27 July 1944
307592 2/Lt. J.E. Treherne [1]
*The Oxfordshire and Buckinghamshire Light Infantry.**

30 July 1944
307863 Lt. G.C. Higginson

4 August 1944
14413259 Pte. C.R. Hunt
5771704 L-Cpl. A.R. Jones
5772279 Cpl. H.H. Mortimer

5784588 Pte. A.W. Tibbs
5771679 L-Sgt. A.H. Wilson

5 August 1944
5116132 Pte. G. Bakewell
5779760 Pte. P.S. Carroll
5116236 Pte. D.E. Evans

5784403 Cpl. R.W. Farthing
14329172 Pte. G. Waters

6 August 1944
5112085 Pte. J.F. Barnett
5772242 Pte. G.E. Bircham
5673005 L-Cpl. J.O. Board
5932595 Sgt. R.O. Bruce
5773460 Pte. A.J. Bryant
5116206 Pte. C.E. Carter
5769927 L-Cpl. F.J. Chambers
14552816 Pte. R.S. Harris
14643412 Pte. H.W. Howling
14657095 Pte. H.A. Humphries
14404339 Pte. E. Insley
14701631 Pte. W.H. Jackson

14214867 Pte. D.H. Jenner
5770778 C-Sgt. H.T. Kennet
14408216 Pte. H. Makin
14416483 Pte. J.F. Moles
5776762 Pte. A.G. Nichols
5776555 Sgt. C.A. Rehbein
5781525 L-Cpl. E.J. Shawl
14626579 Pte. J.C. Tomlin
5771629 Pte. W.J. Welch
5771770 Cpl. R.A. Wilson
5771955 Pte. R.V. Woolnough

7 August 1944
14674764 L-Cpl. H. Bond
5771053 L-Sgt. H.W. Burling
3455953 Pte. F. Chapman
14295516 L-Cpl. D.C. Hammond
5769530 Pte. J. McGrath

14404530 Pte. K.B. Metcalfe
14423790 Pte. B.M. Roberts
5779734 Cpl. A.P. Whitton
14568779 L-Cpl. E.G. Wright

8 August 1944
5779898 Cpl. S. Bates VC
1139478 Pte. J.R. Fuller

6289203 L-Sgt. H.G. Hills
14669766 Pte. J.A. Walker

9 August 1944
253653 Lt. J.D. Drew
*The South Wales Borderers.**

14425942 Pte. H.J. Unwin
6016653 Pte. A.H. Wood

20 August 1944
5122102 Pte. F. Conlon

24 September 1944
5384521 Sgt. W. Parry

25 September 1944
6479255 Pte. J. Taylor

28 September 1944
5783307 L-Cpl. L. Day

4 October 1944
3866087 Pte. J.K. Mansley   1114489 Pte. A.T. Wallis

5 October 1944
4865417 Pte. S. Bennett   5783960 Pte. D.W. Crowson

6 October 1944
6895703 Pte. J. Morley

12 October 1944
5780214 Pte. C. McEvoy

13 October 1944
5961339 Pte. H. Ormand

14 October 1944
14426657 Pte. B.C. Anger   14714650 Pte. A.W. Halls
5773761 L-Sgt. S.W. Cook   14425068 Pte. E.C. Hort
14416057 Pte. W.W. Crofton   3865475 Pte. C. Kenyon
5776530 L-Cpl. G.H.D. Earl   5772292 Pte. W.J.J. Rowland
14712419 Pte. H. Gorbell   14285239 L-Cpl. W.C. Stork
3861331 Pte. G. Grundy

15 October 1944
10527522 Pte. P.G. Cromack   5777273 Cpl. L.J.L. Reynolds
14611137 Pte. A.L. Jordan   14601169 Pte. R.E.A. Tull
5783628 L-Cpl. V.J. Longthorne

16 October 1944
4427755 Pte. R.F. Barritt   14568802 Pte. J.T. Hensby
5776013 CSM L.W. Brown   14669135 Pte. E.B. Johnson
5733686 Cpl. J.B. Cahill   5771243 Pte. E.G. Johnson
1830152 Pte. J. Cleary   5784253 Pte. G.C. Mann
5118748 L-Cpl. A.W.J. Drake   6476782 Pte. W. Miller
52520 Capt. R.S. Elford   5774429 L-Cpl. W.H. Moore
The West Yorkshire Regiment.★   14543121 Pte. K. Seymour
822395 Cpl. G. Emmerson   6412505 Pte. W.G. Sommerford
14283861 Pte. E.G. Gower   14428239 Pte. R.S. Wilkinson

17 October 1944

5683066 Pte. L.C. Bindon

6028978 Pte. A.H. Blowing

14643234 Pte. F.A.G. Chaplin

5680480 Pte. J. Cox

14624713 L-Cpl. C.L.D. Moore

14413483 Cpl. F.C. Parkinson

18 October 1944

5784370 Pte. L.D. Aldridge

5780730 Pte. G.W. Bailey

14418029 Cpl. C.D.F. Smith

21 October 1944

4805993 Cpl. W.O. Nangle

23 October 1944

14331063 Pte. R.H. Rumbles

3 November 1944

14404949 Pte. D.S. Goodwin

5 November 1944

5771996 Sgt. E.C. Ringer

10 November 1944

5771938 Pte. D. Ewbank

18 November 1944

3857873 Cpl. T. Fawcett

11001893 Pte. W.H.J. Webster

20 November 1944

1495977 L-Cpl. J.W. Pegg

22 November 1944

5772907 Pte. E. Murphy [3]

23 November 1944

5784290 Pte. R.G. Thompson

28 November 1944

11406491 Pte. P.H. Hall

3 February 1945

14730538 Pte. R.G. Burgess [3]

27 February 1945

327313 Lt. J.R. Williams

1 March 1945

14675687 Pte. G.D. Addy
14709999 Pte. R.J. Andrews
14413256 Pte. D.A. Barrett
5784268 L-Cpl. E. Basey
5105461 Pte. B. Beech
5882368 Cpl. F. Biggs
14766138 Pte. G. Bowden
5116194 Pte. R.T. Brayne
6024265 Pte. P.P. Cariello
5771763 Pte. J.L. Cator
5776000 Sgt. D.L. Cole
5778948 Cpl. E.G. Cubitt
228159 Lt. L. Dawson
    The Duke of Wellington's Regt.★
5784180 Pte. J.R. Ditton
5783677 Cpl. J.W. Duffy
6085959 Cpl. F. Ferminger
1692344 Pte. J. Gable
1151069 Pte. M. Garvey
14580975 Pte. H.B. Howman
14626128 Pte. C.R. Ladd
14411423 Pte. W.A. Lennard-French

989686 Pte. J.S. Lincoln
14722537 Pte. E. McCormack
14722067 Pte. H. Miles
14230886 Cpl. H. Morris
14660311 Pte. H.A.C. Onion
14418839 Pte. K.A. Parker
6783500 Pte. F. Parry
14422868 Pte. L.E. Pottle
14559796 Pte. A.E. Raison
14494154 Pte. H.J. Rant
5955820 Pte. G.S. Ratcliffe
14316826 Pte. K. Robinson
315734 Lt. T.M. Rourke MC
323418 Lt. N.W. Rowe
    The Royal Warwickshire Regiment.★
109406 Major D.W. Smith MC
336804 Lt. G.A. Smith MM
5436178 Pte. W.H. Sowle
5768460 Sgt. T.W. Stimpson
14520010 Pte. A.W. Warren
3392914 Pte. D.A. Williams
6481728 Pte. E. Young

4 March 1945

5780184 Pte. A.C. Cason

10 March 1945

331194 Lt. H.M. Fisher [3]
    The Hampshire Regiment.★

13 March 1945

859413 L-Cpl. E. Dugdale
The Army Catering Corps.★

22 March 1945

1799277 Pte. J. Connolly

4 April 1945

1625632 Pte. W.F. Akeroyd
2141429 Cpl. W. Boggan
14416010 Pte. W.F. Cosham

5772760 Pte. A.E. Rowland
14572787 Pte. E.J. Snook

5 April 1945

14828045 Pte. K. Crossley

5773861 Pte. A.J. Wrayburn

6 April 1945

6024082 Pte. A.F. Massey

9 April 1945
285368 Lt. F.J. Groom

14 April 1945
14825557 Pte. R.H. Scofield

15 April 1945
14817379 Pte. G.J. Barrow   14250093 Pte. H.J.W. Chapman
5775073 L-Cpl. G.A.J. Barwick   14819501 Pte. C.W. Netherclift

16 April 1945
14536255 Cpl. H.L. Alger   14821845 Pte. R. Plummer
CDN/171 Lt. J.A. Laurie MC
   The Royal Canadian Infantry Corps.*

17 April 1945
5622906 Pte. F. Bock

18 April 1945
1568917 Pte. C. Smith

1 May 1945
14820844 Pte. C.J.A. Chaney [3]

13 August 1945
5439056 Pte. G.N. Hampton [3]

NOTES
* Attached to the 1st Battalion The Royal Norfolk Regiment.
[1] Died of wounds.
[2] Died as prisoner of war.
[3] Accidental death.

The Roll of Honour has been copied from the *Battalion History* and amended from lists prepared by W.H. Holden who has photographed the headstone of every known grave or memorial panel of those men of the regiment who served in the 1st Battalion and lost their lives during the campaign. The album containing those photographs, which also includes those relating to men of the 7th Battalion, and gives the location of each grave, can be seen, on request, at the Royal Norfolk Regimental Museum, Norwich.

Appendix 1

ORGANIZATION

Division

The 3rd British Infantry Division was composed of three Infantry Brigades:

HQ Division

8 Brigade   9 Brigade   185 Brigade

In close support were:
2nd Middlesex Regiment and 3rd Reconnaissance Regiment
Together with the Divisional Artillery:

7th Field Regiment	20th Anti-tank Regiment
33rd Field Regiment	92nd Light Anti-Aircraft Regiment
76th Field Regiment	

And specialist units:

Royal Engineers	Royal Corps of Signals
Royal Army Service Corps	Royal Army Medical Corps
Royal Army Ordnance Corps	Corps of Military Police
Royal Electrical and Mechanical Engineers	

The units comprising the three Infantry Brigades were:

8 British Infantry Brigade	*9 British Infantry Brigade*
1st Bn Suffolk Regiment	2nd Bn Lincolnshire Regiment
2nd Bn East Yorkshire Regiment	1st Bn King's Own Scottish Borderers
1st Bn South Lancashire Regiment	2nd Bn Royal Ulster Rifles

185 British Infantry Brigade

2nd Bn Royal Warwickshire Regiment	Serial No. 67
1st Bn Royal Norfolk Regiment	68
2nd Bn King's Shropshire Light Infantry	69

Under command on D-Day:

27th Armoured Brigade	*1st Special Service Brigade*
comprising	comprising
13/18th Royal Hussars (QMO)	Nos. 3, 4 and 6 Commando
The East Riding Yeomanry	Nos. 41 and 45 Commando
The Staffordshire Yeomanry	

Battalion

Each infantry battalion consisted of Headquarters and six companies:

HQ Battalion

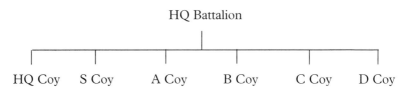

HQ Coy   S Coy   A Coy   B Coy   C Coy   D Coy

Headquarter Company (HQ Coy) Admin and Signals platoons – dealing with Intelligence, administration, personnel, discipline, medical, welfare, ordnance, supplies and signals.

Support Company (S Coy) the specialist platoons – the Carrier Platoon (four sections each of three Bren carriers), the Mortar Platoon (six 3 inch mortars in Bren carriers), the Anti-tank Platoon (three sections each of two carriers and two 6 pdr anti-tank guns) and the Pioneer Platoon of four sections.

Four Rifle Companies (normally lettered A to D).

Sergeants, June 1945. Back row: Sgts. Franks, Reeve, Thomas, Savidge, Smart, Webb, Rust, Shaw, Slapp, Toll. Fourth row: Sgts. Staind, Boyles, Collins, Bennett, Stocker, Addison, Nelson, Roff, Newman, Johnson. Third row: Sgts. Loades, Percival, Ming, Marshall, Kerrison, Smith, Weldon, Kay MM, Paskell, Hilling. Second row: CQMSs Howard, Ellis, Sgts. Allen, Heathcote, Pegg, Barleycorn MM, Bambridge, Graveg, Brown, Williams, CQMS Lacey. Front row: CSMs Langford DCM, Flint, Wilkinson, RSM Brown, Lt.-Col. F.P. Barclay DSO, MC, Capt. R.C. Wilson MC, CSMs Brown, Catlin MM, Fuller.

Company

Company HQ

Platoon   Platoon   Platoon

Each platoon in the battalion was numbered serially, i.e. HQ and S Companies comprised platoons numbered 1 to 6, A Company 7 to 9, B Company 10 to 12, C Company 13 to 15 and D Company 16 to 18.

Each Rifle Company HQ consisted of the Company Commander and his Second-in-Command; the CSM, CQMS, company clerk, stretcher-bearers, signallers, cooks, batmen/runners, snipers, drivers. Company transport was a jeep, a carrier and two or three 15cwt trucks.

The three Rifle Platoons in a Rifle Company each comprised a small HQ and three sections. The Platoon was commanded by a Lieutenant with a Sergeant as his Second-in-Command; each section was commanded by a Lance-Sergeant or Corporal with a Lance-Corporal in charge of the Bren LMG team which formed part of each section. In many instances, as a result of casualties, a Platoon could be commanded by a Sergeant and sections by a Lance-Corporal or senior soldier, or the Sergeant's duties taken over by a senior corporal. Sections were numbered serially through the Company, i.e. 16 Platoon, D Company would have sections 1 to 3, 17 Platoon sections 4 to 6 and 18 Platoon sections 7 to 9.

Numbers varied, due principally to casualties or, to a much lesser extent, sickness but at full strength a Rifle Company numbered 5 Officers and approximately 120 men. Battalion HQ, HQ Coy and S Coy together numbered 16 Officers and rather more than 300 ORs making a total for the battalion of 36 Officers and around 800 ORs.

Appendix 2

ORIGINS

The D-V Club

Formed in 1945 of officers who had served in the 1st Battalion The Royal Norfolk Regiment between D-Day and VE-Day. Has met every year since, without fail; more than two-thirds of the remaining thirty members gather annually in Norwich.

The 1st Battalion The Royal Norfolk Regiment D-Day Veterans

At the 1978 Regimental Association Dinner, about half-a-dozen men indicated that they would like to return to the Continent; Bill Holden offered to make enquiries and, in May 1979, organized a weekend trip to Normandy during which the group visited the assault beach, Manneville Wood, Arromanches, and several cemeteries.

All thoroughly enjoyed the brief trip and determined that a group should be formed to meet regularly, their first proposal being that a visit should be made to Helmond in Holland and a larger party numbering forty-five went to Helmond in September 1979. The visit proved most successful – so the Association was formed.

Meetings are held monthly from March to December in Norwich.

A memorial has been erected in France by this group, at Pavée (Sourdevalle) to the memory of Corporal Sidney Bates VC at which Revd F.J. Green conducted the dedication ceremony. A memorial was also raised near Grimbosq to mark the 7th Battalion's battle there in early August 1944 and the award of the Victoria Cross to Captain D. Jamieson.

The Association later erected a memorial at the Molen Beek, between Overloon and Venraij, which was dedicated at a ceremony in 1988, the materials for the memorial, which is in the form of a pyramid to represent the Divisional sign, include flints brought from Norfolk and was built by Bill Holden and a friend with help from local inhabitants.

A granite column, generously given by the French people, is to be erected at Pavée, near the memorial to Corporal S. Bates VC, and will be dedicated at a ceremony to be held on 5 June 1994. It will be inscribed in memory to all those men of the Monmouthshire Regiment, the Royal Norfolk Regiment and other supporting units who lost their lives in the bitter fighting at this spot. The Royal Norfolk Regimental Association has donated generously to this memorial, as have members of both regiments.

Vrienden Royal Norfolk Regiment

In 1980 Bill Holden, holidaying with his family in Helmond, met Jan van Erp, known to him in 1944 only as 'the boy on the bike'. Jan made contact with other individuals with the result that a group was formed in Helmond called 'The Friends of the Royal Norfolk Regiment' which from that time has made all necessary arrangements in Holland, planning journeys, meals and accommodation according to the requirements of the British group and raising funds for incidental costs.

They now comprise a very helpful, extremely friendly group with a sense of humour very like the British and have done a great deal to perpetuate the memory of 1st Norfolk's entry into Helmond – a memorial area in Helmond was created to commemorate the liberation of Helmond by the Royal Norfolk Regiment and, in 1984, at a moving ceremony, a Battalion plaque was unveiled by the veterans on the 40th anniversary of the liberation of the town. Nine English oak trees were planted nearby to symbolize the 9th of Foot and the square in which they stand was re-named 'Royal Norfolk-Plein'.

The Norwich based group retain the fondest memories of their Dutch friends and can quote innumerable instances of the warm welcome they always receive and the exceptional, sometimes embarrassing, generosity of their hosts, offered so very freely as a mark of their heartfelt thanks for the liberation of their country from the oppressor.

Members volunteered to renovate the memorial at Kervenheim, cleared the area, repainted the names, and re-gilded the Britannia plaque. It must be acknowledged that a great debt is owed to the officers and members of the 'Vrienden Royal Norfolk Regiment' for their considerable hospitality, ever-present good humour and constant efforts on behalf of the men of the Royal Norfolk Regiment and their wives.

The undoubted success of both the Veterans and the Vrienden is due in large part to the untiring activities and good nature of Bill Holden who has given unstintingly of his time, effort and more – supported unfailingly by his wife, Doreen. He has also prepared an album containing photographs of the headstone or memorial panel marking the grave of every man serving in the 1st and 7th Battalions who lost his life during the campaign – this involved visits to thirty-four war cemeteries on the Continent and three in England, and required lengthy research and checking. He has presented the album to the Regimental Museum in Norwich where it is now available, on request, to those seeking information about relatives.

Glossary

2 ic	Second-in-Command.
25 pdr	British Field Artillery, towed or mounted on a tank chassis, used for close support. 3.45 in calibre, max. range 13,400 yd, rate of fire – 3 shells per minute.
36 grenade	More commonly called the Mills bomb in the First World War, a cast-iron fragmentation grenade with either a 4 or a 7 second fuse.
68	The Battalion serial number within the Division.
88s	German 88 mm high velocity gun developed for a variety of uses, including anti-aircraft defence, and superior to British 75 mm. Fired 23 lb shell to a max. range of 17,500 yd.
ADS	Advanced Dressing Station.
'A' Echelon	Troops and vehicles responsible for maintaining contact between Battalion and 'B' Echelon.
AP	Armour Piercing or Anti-Personnel.
A/Tk	Anti-tank.
Artificial Moonlight	Searchlights behind the front line, unfocused and directed forward at a low angle.
ATS	Auxiliary Territorial Service, subsequently titled the Women's Royal Army Corps (WRAC).
AVRE	Assault Vehicles (Royal Engineers) – also called 'Funnies' – specialized armoured vehicles based on tank chassis which included DD or swimming tanks, 'Flail' or 'Crab' tanks, bridging and track-laying tanks.
'B' Echelon	Troops, vehicles and equipment held in reserve from Battalion.
BEF	British Expeditionary Force 1939/40.
Besa	Slang corruption of BSA denoting tank mounted machine-gun.
BLA	British Liberation Army
'Blighty'	First World War expression to indicate a wound severe enough to warrant being returned home to 'Blighty'.
Bren	The standard Light Machine-Gun issued to British infantry firing .303 ammunition.
Buffalo	Tracked, armoured, amphibious vehicle designed to carry troops.
Carrier	A lightly armoured tracked vehicle carrying a Bren as its principal armament.

CCS	Casualty Clearing Station.
Chindits	British, Indian and Australian troops operating as a guerilla force behind Japanese lines.
Churchill	The largest British tank in use in British Armoured Divisions, weighing 37/41 tons, speed from 12 to 15 mph, armed with a 17 pdr gun and also providing the chassis for numerous AVREs (see above).
CO	Commanding Officer.
Compo rations	Composite ration packs containing all requirements for fourteen men for 24 hours.
CQMS	Company Quartermaster Sergeant.
C-Sgt	Colour Sergeant – CQMS as above.
Crab	See Flail tank below.
Cromwell	British tank armed with either a 75 mm or a 17 pdr gun.
Crocodile	Flamethrower tank based on Churchill chassis.
CSM	Company Sergeant-Major. Warrant Officer Class 2.
DD tank	A 'swimming' tank converted from a Sherman fitted with twin propellers (Duplex drive) attached to the tracks and a high canvas skirt for buoyancy.
D-Day	Codename for day on which operation commences.
Doodlebug	See V1 below.
DR	motor cycle despatch rider ('Don.R.').
FDL	Forward Defended Location.
'F' Echelon	Fighting vehicles and attendant troops with forward elements of Battalion.
Flail tank	A Sherman tank fitted with a rotating drum carrying heavy chains to beat the ground in front of it to explode mines (also called a 'Crab').
FOO	Forward Observation Officer (RA).
Funnies	See AVRE above.
FUP	Forming Up Point (place).
Gas Cape	Oilskin cape originally provided for protection from poison gas sprays – used as a waterproof.
Gunner	Royal Artillery.
HE	High Explosive.
H-Hour	Time at which an operation commences.
'I'	Intelligence.
IO	Intelligence Officer.
Kapok bridging	A portable foot-bridge formed by a boarded walkway supported on floating pontoons of kapok.
LCA	Landing Craft, Assault – small craft to carry the first wave of troops.
LCI	Landing Craft Infantry.
LCT	Landing Craft Tank.
LMG	Light Machine-Gun. See Bren above.

LSI	Landing Ship Infantry (carried LCAs).
MG	Machine-gun.
MMG	Medium Machine-gun.
MO	Medical Officer (RAMC).
Moaning Minnie	A German weapon, the *Nebelwerfer*, a cluster of metal tubes, mounted on wheels, firing a salvo of short-range rocket bombs which made a peculiar and distinctive shrieking noise when fired.
Mulberry	Codename given to prefabricated harbour.
NAAFI	Navy, Army and Air Force Institute, providing canteen facilities and supplies not issued by the Services.
NCO	Non-commissioned Officer.
Nebelwerfer.	See Moaning Minnie above.
'O' Group	Any occasion at which the senior commander gives orders.
OP	Observation Post.
OR(s)	Other Rank(s).
Panzer	German armoured fighting formation.
PIAT	Projector Infantry Anti-tank. A portable weapon, fired from the shoulder, projecting a specially shaped, finned bomb.
QM	Quartermaster, responsible for all supplies.
RA	Royal Artillery.
RAMC	Royal Army Medical Corps.
RAP	Regimental Aid Post.
RASC	Royal Army Service Corps.
RE	Royal Engineers.
Recce	Abbreviation for reconnaissance or reconnoitre.
RHU	Reinforcement Holding Unit.
RSM	Regimental Sergeant Major. Warrant Officer Class 1.
RT	Radio Telephony – term used for all types of radio sets.
RV	Rendezvous – meeting place.
Sapper	Royal Engineer.
Schmeisser	Standard German sub-machine-gun.
Schu(h)mine	Anti-personnel mine in wooden case not revealed by mine detectors.
SHAEF	Supreme Headquarters Allied Expeditionary Force.
Sherman	33 ton American tank, capable of 24 mph, armed with a 75 mm gun firing a 13 lb shell – range 10,000 yd; 1 in 4 British Shermans, named 'Firefly', were armed with the 17 pdr gun which had a range of 17,000 yd.
Siegfried Line	Fortifications to defend Germany.
S-mine	Shrapnel mine – a German anti-personnel mine buried in the ground with only three wire prongs protruding – pressure on the prongs caused the mine to be fired to waist height, there to explode spraying shrapnel in the close

	vicinity.
SP	Self-propelled.
Spandau	Standard German infantry/tank machine-gun capable of a superior rate of fire to the Bren.
Stand-to	100 per cent alertness for all troops.
Sten	Mass produced, simple sub-machine-gun firing 9 mm ammunition.
Stonk (Stonking)	Heavy artillery or mortar concentration.
TCV	Troop carrying vehicle.
Teller mine	German anti-tank mine, about the size of a large dinner plate, 4 in thick.
Thunderbolt	Allied fighter/bomber.
Tiger	54 ton German tank capable of 23 mph, armed with 88 mm high velocity gun. The 'King' Tiger, weighing 68 tons, mounted the 88 mm 43, superior to any similar Allied gun.
Typhoon	Rocket-carrying fighter aircraft.
'Uncle' target	All Divisional artillery.
V1	*Vergeltungswaffe Eins.* Very basic pilotless winged bomb with 150 mile range, carrying 1,870 lb of HE.
V2	*Vergeltungswaffe Zwei.* Rocket with range of about 200 miles containing 2,000 lb of explosive and ascending 60 to 70 miles in flight.
Wasp	Flame-thrower based on standard carrier.

Index

Page numbers in italic type refer to individual accounts.
Awards and Roll of Honour are not indexed.

Extracts quoted from Publications